SEXUAL PREDATORS AMONGST US

SEXUAL PREDATORS AMONGST US

RONALD A. RUFO, EdD

CRC Press
Taylor & Francis Group
Boca Raton London New York

CRC Press is an imprint of the
Taylor & Francis Group, an **informa** business

CRC Press
Taylor & Francis Group
6000 Broken Sound Parkway NW, Suite 300
Boca Raton, FL 33487-2742

© 2012 by Taylor & Francis Group, LLC
CRC Press is an imprint of Taylor & Francis Group, an Informa business

No claim to original U.S. Government works

Printed in the United States of America on acid-free paper
Version Date: 20110617

International Standard Book Number: 978-1-4398-5447-1 (Hardback)

This book contains information obtained from authentic and highly regarded sources. Reasonable efforts have been made to publish reliable data and information, but the author and publisher cannot assume responsibility for the validity of all materials or the consequences of their use. The authors and publishers have attempted to trace the copyright holders of all material reproduced in this publication and apologize to copyright holders if permission to publish in this form has not been obtained. If any copyright material has not been acknowledged please write and let us know so we may rectify in any future reprint.

Except as permitted under U.S. Copyright Law, no part of this book may be reprinted, reproduced, transmitted, or utilized in any form by any electronic, mechanical, or other means, now known or hereafter invented, including photocopying, microfilming, and recording, or in any information storage or retrieval system, without written permission from the publishers.

For permission to photocopy or use material electronically from this work, please access www.copyright.com (http://www.copyright.com/) or contact the Copyright Clearance Center, Inc. (CCC), 222 Rosewood Drive, Danvers, MA 01923, 978-750-8400. CCC is a not-for-profit organization that provides licenses and registration for a variety of users. For organizations that have been granted a photocopy license by the CCC, a separate system of payment has been arranged.

Trademark Notice: Product or corporate names may be trademarks or registered trademarks, and are used only for identification and explanation without intent to infringe.

Library of Congress Cataloging-in-Publication Data

Rufo, Ronald A.
  Sexual predators amongst us / Ronald A. Rufo.
    p. cm.
  Includes bibliographical references and index.
  ISBN 978-1-4398-5447-1 (alk. paper)
  1. Sex crimes. 2. Female sex offenders. 3. Child sex offenders. 4. Online sexual predators. 5. Sex offenders--Psychology. 6. Criminal behavior, Prediction of. I. Title.

HV6556.R84 2012
364.15'3--dc23   2011025185

Visit the Taylor & Francis Web site at
http://www.taylorandfrancis.com

and the CRC Press Web site at
http://www.crcpress.com

I would like to dedicate this book to my beautiful wife, Debbie, who has always been my inspiration to reach for the stars and never look back.

I would also like to dedicate this book to my three wonderful daughters—each special in her own way.

Table of Contents

Foreword	xvii
Preface	xix
Acknowledgments	xxi
About the Author	xxiii
Introduction	xxv

1 Characteristics of a Sexual Predator 1

Sexual Predators—What Are We Dealing With?	1
Causes of Sexual Violence	2
Characteristics and Patterns	3
Cognitive Behavioral Theories	4
The Social Bond Theory	6
Profile of a Female Sexual Offender	6
Profile of a Male Sexual Offender	7
In My Opinion	8
DR. LAURA BARROW	
Definitions of Chapter Key Terms	10
References	11

2 Grooming the Victim 13

Grooming	13
Progression of Behavior for Grooming a Victim	15
Secrecy and Living a Double Life	15
Fantasies and Masturbation	16
Motivation, Desire, and Fascination	17
Manipulation	18
Seduction	18
Isolation Strategies	19
Persuasion	20
Deception	20
Children Not Coming Forward	21
Parental/Predator Abuse and Emotional Blackmail and Guilt	22
Profile of a Female Sex Offender	24
Profile of a Male Sex Offender	26

	In My Opinion MS. MARYANNE LEACH	27
	Definitions of Chapter Key Terms	28
	References	30
3	**Child Abuse and Incest**	**31**
	Child Abuse	31
	Sexual Abuse of a Child	31
	A Female Victim's Perspective on Sexual Abuse	32
	Traits of Female Victims of Sexual Abuse	35
	A Male Victim's Perspective on Sexual Abuse	35
	Traits of Male Victims of Sexual Abuse	38
	Terms Related to Sexual Abuse	38
	Incest	38
	Sexual Violence	43
	Stockholm Syndrome	44
	Profile of a Female Sex Offender	44
	Profile of a Male Sex Offender	45
	In My Opinion DR. ELENA AZAOLA	46
	Definitions of Chapter Key Terms	47
	References	49
4	**Pedophilia and Sex Offenses**	**51**
	Pedophilia and Pedophiles	51
	Paraphilia	51
	Paraphilia and Victims with Disabilities	52
	Sexual Perversion	52
	Infantophilia	55
	Hebephilia	55
	Ephebophilia	56
	Teleiophilia	56
	Exhibitionism	56
	Martymaculia	57
	Frotteurism	57
	Fetishes	57
	Voyeurism	58
	Clergy, Pedophilia, and Sexual Abuse in the Catholic Church	59
	The Survivors Network of Those Abused by Priests	61
	The Geoghan Case	61
	The Birmingham Case	61

Table of Contents ix

        The Shanley Case   62
        The Paquin Case   62
    Sexual Addiction   63
    Behaviors Associated with Sexual Addiction   64
    Sex Rings   65
        Solo Sex Rings   66
        Transition Sex Rings   66
        Syndicated Sex Rings   66
    Prostituted Children   67
    Interstate Sex Trafficking   67
    Child-Sex Tourism   67
    Profile of a Female Sex Offender   69
    Profile of a Male Sex Offender   70
    In My Opinion   71
    MRS. BARBARA DORRIS

    Definitions of Chapter Key Terms   72
    References   74

5 Female Sexual Offenders   75

    Introduction   75
    Characteristics of Female Sex Offenders   76
    Mothers Who Abuse Their Children   77
    A Female Abuser Dominated by a Male Partner   78
    A Female Abuser Who Holds a Position of Authority   78
    A Female Abuser Who Is Curious and a Risk Taker   80
    Females Who Abuse Family Members and Relatives   81
    Female Sex Offenders and Major Components in Their Abuse   81
    Key Examples of Risk Factors for Women   82
    Key Examples of Risk Factors for Adolescent Girls   82
    Recidivism   83
    Treatment for Female Sex Offenders   84
    Profile of a Female Sex Offender   85
    Profile of a Male Sex Offender   85
    In My Opinion   86
    DR. ERIN BASALAY

    Definitions of Chapter Key Terms   87
    References   87

6 Child Pornography   89

    Introduction   89
    Child Erotica   90

Child Pornography and Victimization	91
Law Enforcement and Child Pornography	91
Child Pornography Laws	95
Seven Laws Regarding Child Pornography	95
Stanley v. Georgia (1969)	95
Miller v. California	96
Sexual Exploitation of Children Act of 1977	96
Ferber v. New York	96
Child Protection Act of 1984	97
The Child Sexual Abuse Act of 1986	98
Child Protection and Obscenity Enforcement Act 1988	98
Osborne v. Ohio (1990)	98
Communications Decency Act 1996	98
The Child Pornography and Protection Act of 1996 and Virtual Child Pornography	98
Profile of a Female Sex Offender	101
Profile of a Male Sex Offender	103
In My Opinion	103
MR. DANIEL T. COYNE	
The Floyd Durr Case	106
The Brad Lieberman Case	106
Definitions of Chapter Key Terms	107
References	108

7 The Internet and Sexual Predators 109

Display of an Internet Chat Room Conversation	109
The Internet and Sexual Predators	110
Online Child Enticement	111
Online Behavior	111
Risks of the Internet	112
Perceptions of Internet Safety	112
Triple A Theory	114
Internet Addiction Symptoms	114
Internet Enabled and Sexual Behaviors (IESBs)	115
Chat Rooms and Instant Messaging	115
Media Information and Newsgroups	117
Popular Websites	117
Facebook	117
MySpace	118
Security on Social Websites	120
Webcams	120

Table of Contents   xi

Sexting	121
Cybersex	121
Cappers	122
The Internet and Schools	122
Profile of a Female Sex Offender	124
Profile of a Male Sex Offender	124
In My Opinion	125
MS. ANNE COLLIER	
Definitions of Chapter Key Terms	128
References	132

8   Law Enforcement on the Internet   133

Law Enforcement Involvement in Investigating Internet Crimes	133
Lieutenant Andrew Donofrio	135
Detective Alan Kruk	136
Commander Michael Anton	137
Detective Mark DiMeo	139
Detective Bob Collins	142
DNA Evidence	143
DNA Testing	143
CODIS	144
Police Reports	145
The Entrapment Defense	145
Computer Evidence and the Fourth Amendment	147
Dateline NBC	148
Perverted Justice	148
Wiretapping	149
The Legal Impossibility Defense	149
Profile of a Female Sex Offender	149
Profile of a Male Sex Offender	150
In My Opinion	150
DR. FRANK SCHMALLEGER	
Definitions of Chapter Key Terms	151
References	152

9   Incarceration, Recidivism, and Rehabilitation   153

Introduction	153
Incarceration	153
Recidivism	154

Castration	155
Chemical Castration	156
Depo-Provera	156
Depo-Leupron	157
Cyproterone	157
Triptorelin	158
Surgical Castration	158
Sex Offender Treatment Programs	160
Mental Health Treatment	161
Group Therapy	162
Profile of a Female Sex Offender	162
Profile of a Male Sex Offender	163
In My Opinion MR. MIKE SULLIVAN	163
Definitions of Chapter Key Terms	164
References	165

10 Tragic Stories That Resulted in Landmark Legislation — 167

The Jacob Wetterling Story	167
The Jacob Wetterling Act	167
The Jacob Wetterling Crimes against Children and Sexually Violent Offender Registration Act of 1994	169
The Jacob Wetterling Improvements Act 1997	169
The Jessica Lunsford Story	170
Jessica's Law	170
The Megan Kanka Story	171
Megan's Law	172
Megan's Law of 1996	173
The Adam Walsh Story	174
The Adam Walsh Child Protection Act	174
Adam Walsh Child Protection and Safety Act of 2006	175
Sex Offender Registration and Notification Act (SORNA) as Part of the Adam Walsh Child Protection and Safety Act of 2006	175
The Dru Sjodin Story	176
Dru's Law	177
Dru Sjodin National Sex Offender Public Website	178
The Pam Lychner Story	178
The Pam Lychner Sex Offender Tracking and Identification Act of 1996	178

Table of Contents   xiii

Chelsea King's Story	179
Chelsea's Law	179
Profile of a Female Sex Offender	179
Profile of a Male Sex Offender	180
In My Opinion	181
MS. KIMBERLY HART	
References	183

11   Sex Offender Registration and Notification Laws   185

Earlier Issues with Sex Offenders	185
Registered Sex Offenders	186
Civil Commitment	188
Notification Laws: Do They Protect the Public or Invade Privacy?	189
Opponents of Notification Laws	189
Sexual Registration and Notification Laws	190
Sex Offender Registration	191
Global Positioning System	192
Geographic Information System	192
e-Stop	192
Homeless Sex Offenders	194
Profile of a Female Sex Offender	194
Profile of a Male Sex Offender	195
In My Opinion	195
FATHER TONY PIZZO	
Definitions of Chapter Key Terms	197
References	197

12   Specific and Significant Laws Regarding Sex Offenders   199

Walter Mondale Child Abuse and Treatment Act	199
Protection of Children against Sexual Exploitation Act 1977	199
Child Abuse Victims Act of 1986	199
Victims of Child Abuse 1990	200
Child Online Protection Act and the Children's Internet Protection Act	200
Sex Crimes against Children Prevention Act of 1995	200
Communication Decency Act (CDA) of 1996	200
Telecommunications Act 1996	201
The Child Pornography Prevention Act (CPPA)	201

	The Child Online Protection Act (COPA) 1998	201
	Protection of Children from Sexual Predators Act of 1998	201
	The Campus Sex Crimes Prevention Act of 2000	202
	Prosecutorial Remedies and Other Tools to End the Exploitation of Children Today (PROTECT) Act of 2003	203
	Children Safety and Violent Crime Reduction Act of 2005	204
	PROTECT Our Children Act of 2008	205
	Keep the Internet Devoid of Sexual Predators Act of 2008 (KIDS)	205
	Children's Internet Protection Act (CIPA)	206
	Effective Child Pornography Prosecution Act of 2008	206
	First Amendment Rights	207
	Fourth Amendment Rights	207
	Eighth Amendment Rights	207
	Internet Dating Safety Act	208
	Profile of a Female Sex Offender	209
	Profile of a Male Sex Offender	209
	In My Opinion	209
	FROM AN ILLINOIS ASSISTANT STATE'S ATTORNEY	
	Definitions of Chapter Key Terms	211
	References	212
13	**Internet Safety and Education**	**213**
	Authoritative Parents	213
	Behavior	213
	Behavior outside the Home	213
	Computer in a Common Area	214
	Computer Lingo	214
	Educated and Computer-Savvy Parents	215
	Law Enforcement on Internet Safety	215
	Limit Time on the Computer	216
	Meeting a Predator in Real Life	216
	Open Communication	216
	Parents	217
	Predators on the Internet: Hiding Their Identity	217
	Sexual Predator as a Friend	218
	Safe Childhood Program	218
	Secrets and Secret Relationships	218
	A Child's Self-Confidence	219
	Sexual Advances on the Internet	219
	Sharing e-Mail Accounts	220
	Sharing Personal Information	220

Table of Contents   xv

    Strangers on the Internet   221
    Websites: Reporting   221
    What Kids Do Online   221
    Firewalls, Antivirus Software, and Privacy Filters   222
    Safe Internet Sites   222
        BeNetSafe.com   223
        GetNetWise.org   223
        i-SAFE   225
        NetSmartzKids.org   226
        NetSmartz.org   226
        SafeKids.com   227
        WiredSafety.org   227
    Conclusion   227
        My Thoughts on Sexual Predation   227
            The Internet   228
            Parent Awareness   229
            Computer Technology   229
            Law Enforcement   229
    Definitions of Chapter Key Terms   230
    References   232

Definitions of Terms   **233**

Contacts   **245**

Index   **247**

Foreword

Sexual Predators Amongst Us provides the reader with a complete background on the use of the Internet by sexual predators. Sexual predators have existed in society probably since the beginning of time, but never before have they had such a useful and powerful weapon as the Internet. As one will note after reading Dr. Rufo's book, it is almost as if the Internet had been designed especially for them. *Sexual Predators Amongst Us* is not a book written by an academic person trying to gain tenure, but rather a book developed by a police officer who is actively involved in preventing the sexual exploitation of children.

It is clear when one meets Dr. Rufo that he is first and foremost a dedicated police officer who is highly motivated in his crime prevention activities. Prior to meeting him several years ago, he and I had corresponded by e-mail and telephone. In each of the contacts, I was impressed by his dedication to crime prevention. When Dr. Rufo asked me to read his manuscript and write a foreword, I eagerly accepted because he is an interesting person to talk to and has provided me valuable insight into crime prevention activities. I discovered that his manuscript was not only interesting, but also a valuable resource for anyone interested in preventing sexual exploitation of children. His writing is clear and easy to understand. The book is not an academic discourse of sexual exploitation, but rather a guidebook to be used by individuals interested in preventing the exploitation.

The book starts with the characteristics of sexual predators. The second chapter provides an explanation of how the predator "grooms" his victims by gaining the victim's trust and then exploiting the victim. Dr. Rufo also explains why victims who are children accept the predators and therefore become their prey. There is a shift in the book in Chapter 3, which discusses child sexual abuse. This is a necessary chapter for those readers who are not knowledgeable about child sexual abuse issues and concepts. Chapters, 4, 5, and 6 discuss pedophilia, female sex predators, and child pornography; they provide background and information regarding these subjects. These chapters provide the reader with a basic knowledge of the issues and how certain activities are related to sexual exploitation of children.

The first five chapters provide readers with an understanding of the issues and problems involved in the sexual exploitation of children. The final seven chapters deal with how the Internet has contributed to sexual predation, law enforcement roles in combating this crime, incarceration, recidivism, sex offender registry laws, and tips in preventing child exploitation.

Sexual Predators Amongst Us is a welcome addition to the literature on sexual exploitation and should be a valuable tool in fighting this horrible crime. I recommend it as a book that should be read by all, not just those individuals involved in crime prevention.

Cliff Roberson, LLM, PhD
Academic chair, graduate program, School of Criminal Justice,
Kaplan University
Editor-in-Chief, Professional Issues in Criminal Justice Journal
Professor emeritus, Washburn University

Preface

This book is designed as a university textbook or supplementary text for courses regarding sexual predators and their traits and characteristics. It also focuses on Internet sexual crimes as they relate to online predation and will be a valuable part of the occupational library of a criminal justice professional. The text is valuable for courses such as criminology, crime in America, Internet crime, and behavioral studies. It is also suitable for police academies, parents, and schools for awareness training. Although the text is written as a college textbook, anyone with an interest in sexual predation and issues related to sexual predators will find it interesting and educational.

Students taking the previously mentioned courses may be working toward a bachelor's or master's degree, majoring in criminal justice, criminology, or sociology. A common prerequisite is a course in criminal justice, Internet crime, or behavioral studies. The book will be useful for any college-level course in the criminal justice field. What could be a teaching problem is the content of the book. As in any criminal justice class, there is exposure to sensitive materials.

Changes in this particular field are constantly occurring due to the advancement of technology. It is this author's goal to address these changes and enhance awareness. The primary purpose of the book is to serve as a comprehensive and readable textbook for a one-semester course that deals with sexual predation, deceptive characteristics of sexual predators, and the use of the Internet to exploit children. The book can become a permanent part of the vocational library of a criminal justice professional.

Approach

My goal is to open the eyes of criminal justice professionals, students, and the public to the fascinating concepts involving sexual predation and the Internet from an environmental awareness and technological standpoint. The material covered is organized and presented in a logical fashion, with each chapter building upon the previous chapters. In each of the chapters, my objective is to encourage the student to develop new insights into sexual predation concepts and characteristics. The book makes the subject interesting and offers thought-provoking and realistic examples and testimony. While each chapter builds upon the previous chapters, the text is written in a manner to reduce the necessity of memorization. Key words associated with the chapter material and their definitions are at the end of each chapter.

I sincerely hope this book will be an informative and helpful guide to understanding sexual predators' characteristics and traits, especially when these predators search the Internet to exploit a young victim. To all of the sexually abused children and teenagers who have become victims—my heart, thoughts, and prayers will always be with you.

Ron Rufo, Ed.D.

Acknowledgments

This book would not have been possible without the help of many dedicated and caring friends, who are special to me in so many ways. To Linda Dumke, the best editor in the world and a dear friend, thank you. Her suggestions have been excellent and improved my manuscript tremendously. Linda, I have said this all along, you are truly one of the finest.

To Drs. Cliff Roberson, Frank Schmalleger, and Jim Pastor, three well known authors and scholars in the criminal justice community, thank you for your guidance, friendship, and encouragement in helping me write my first book.

To Dr. Lauren Barrow, thank you for your direction and advice.

A special thank you to all the experts who gave their opinions concerning sexual predators: Dr. Cynthia Schumann, Ann Collier, Father Tony Pizzo, Commander Mike Anton, Mike Sullivan, Chicago Police Detectives Al Kruk and Mark Dimeo, and retired Chicago police detectives Robert Collins, Jeffrey Roberts, retired Lieutenant Andrew Donofrio, Dr. Basalay, Daniel Coyne, Mary Ann Leach, Barbara Dorris, and Kim Hart. Thank you too to Agnes Gal.

And finally I would like to acknowledge Carolyn Spence, Kathryn Younce, and Judith Simon of CRC Press and Taylor & Francis Group for their support and expertise.

About the Author

Ron Rufo has been a Chicago police officer for the past 17 years. He has spent most of his career as a crime prevention speaker with the Preventive Programs unit and has given hundreds of presentations in Internet safety, street safety, and workplace violence. Dr. Rufo has taught many classes in police procedures and policies and has been instrumental as a team leader in the Chicago Police Department Peer Support Group as a compassionate and caring person, especially in the tragic deaths of officers in the line of duty. Dr. Rufo has received numerous awards, commendations, honorable mentions, and letters of appreciation in serving the citizens of Chicago.

Dr. Rufo received his bachelor of arts degree in criminal social justice from Lewis University, Romeoville, Illinois; he graduated with highest honors and as a scholar of the university in 2000. He was awarded his master of arts degree in organizational leadership from Lewis University in 2002 and graduated with his doctoral degree in organizational leadership from Argosy University, Atlanta, Georgia, in 2007. His dissertation title was "An Investigation of Online Predation of Minors by Convicted Male Offenders." He has also contributed to the book *Terrorism and Property Management*.

Dr. Rufo is currently an adjunct professor at Kaplan University. Ron and his wife, Debra, reside in Chicago with their three beautiful daughters, Rita, Laura, and Cara.

Introduction

> The power of the Internet concerns me. It makes all of life's previously hidden vices more available and seductive, and it makes the most perverse, deviant behavior seem normal, thereby lowering even more the bar of human behavior.
>
> **Father Tom Nangle, Chicago Police chaplain**

> Sexual predators use a calculated dance of seduction.
>
> **Oprah Winfrey**

Watching television one cold night in December, I stumbled across the television series, *To Catch a Predator,* hosted by investigative reporter Chris Hansen. As a Chicago policeman, I have encountered many different criminals, but I have been fascinated by the determination, tenacity, and brazen attitude displayed by almost every sexual predator. I was amazed by the sheer number of men that came to the homes of what they thought were young innocent children, both boys and girls, to satisfy their own sexual desires. Truly, the intent was to take advantage of the situation when they walked into the decoy's home. Most of the unsuspecting predators lied about their true intentions and plans of their visit when confronted by Hansen. Many offered a litany of excuses why they were at the home of an adolescent. When questioned about why they there, most gave the excuse that they were there to comfort or just talk to the child.

At the time, I was working on my doctoral dissertation on a totally unrelated topic, but I decided that night to change the direction of my studies and research and focus on sexual predators. My dissertation title was "An Investigation of Online Sexual Predation of Minors by Convicted Male Offenders." The subject is still my passion and that is why I have decided to share my knowledge about and experience with sexual predators in this book. The book will mainly focus on male sexual predators because they account for 95%–99% of the offender population, though I will dedicate a chapter to female sexual offenders.

One of the largest societal transformations in the last three decades has been the rapid expansion and growth of computer technology, especially the easy access to communicating with anyone just by a click of a button. The tactics of and opportunities for sexual predators to attract young victims have changed as well. Sexual predators have greater opportunities to offend than ever before, and these have led to many legal and ethical challenges for society, law enforcement, and the criminal justice system to address. The National Crime Prevention Council has acknowledged that the Internet has brought new challenges in dealing with crime for lawmakers and law enforcement officials. The skyrocketing use of the Internet (it is estimated that 100 million Americans use it daily) and the rapid advancement of technology have caused lawmakers to adopt new policies and procedures to combat the additional problems associated with cybercrime—namely, child exploitation.

The 10-Ps of the Predation Process

I have found that most sexual predators integrate what I like to call the 10-Ps of the predation process when forming a relationship with a child. This is a 10-step progression in the sexual predator's quest to groom and maintain a connection with the child he intends to pursue and exploit:

1. *Proficiency.* Sexual predators are good at what they do.
2. *Prefer.* Sexual predators prefer a specific age group and rarely deviate from that preference. If a sexual offender was molested at a certain age, he is likely to target that same age group as an offender.
3. *Puberty.* Sexual predators will generally be interested in a child near the age of puberty or a child who is sexually inexperienced or curious.
4. *Plan.* The predator will cautiously and carefully scrutinize the child's behavior and activities and attempt to find out what the child is good at and what he or she enjoys doing. Active listening is a priority. The predator will plan each step to gratification. This could take a day to several months.
5. *Patience.* This is a skill that the sexual predator develops and acquires over time. He has the ability to persevere and be "laid back" in his approach. The sexual predator uses time to his advantage and is careful not to send up red flags in his strategy.
6. *Praise.* The sexual predator always finds the right words to say and will have little trouble building the child's self-esteem. This may be something the child is not used to, especially if he or she comes from a dysfunctional or abusive family.
7. *Persuasion.* A sexual predator has the uncanny ability to coax a child into doing what he wants the child to do.
8. *Privacy.* This is the ultimate goal for the sexual predator: encouraging a one-on-one meeting or to be alone with the child.
9. *Pleasure.* It is the sexual predator's intention to incorporate intimacy and any type of sexual contact while trying to make the child feel

special and that the gratification is consensual. Drugs and alcohol may sometimes be used in an attempt to make the victim more compliant.
10. *Power.* This is the power the sexual predator has over the child. The predator will intimidate the child to keep their secret and not reveal it to anyone. The predator might say, "We will get in trouble if you tell," which puts the blame on the child if the exploitation is revealed. Sexual predators use guilt, fear, and manipulation to keep the child quiet.

I have also coined a phrase that I share in my presentations with parents regarding Internet safety—the ABCs of Internet safety for parents:

A: Awareness of the problem of sexual predation on the Internet.
B: Be proactive in your approach to Internet safety.
C: Communication is key; tell the kids, "We can't keep it a secret; you can tell me."

Chapters in Review

Each chapter will

- Begin with a quote
- Provide key words associated with the chapter material and their definitions at the end of the chapter
- Address important topics related to sexual offenders and sexual predation
- Present a profile of a female sex offender
- Present a profile of a male sex offender
- End with an "In My Opinion" section in which experts in the health, psychology, law, government, criminal justice, academic and false allegation fields will voice their honest and objective opinions regarding sexual predators
- Provide references

Chapter 1 focuses on characteristics, traits, and patterns found in most sexual predators. This chapter will highlight causes of sexual violence, along with cognitive behavioral theory. The social bond theory will also be examined.

Chapter 2 emphasizes the grooming process that often involves young, innocent victims. Once the predator establishes a relationship, the grooming process begins with the ultimate goal to meet the child and fulfill the predator's sexual gratification desires. Sexual predators frequently live a double life. They will act one way in public and give the impression that they are a normal, trustworthy individuals within the community, but their underlying persona is revealed only when they are caught and arrested. Fantasies, masturbation, manipulation, seduction, and persuasion play a definitive role in a sexual predator's web of deception.

Chapter 3 highlights sexual abuse and incest in the family. This chapter tells the true story of a young woman who was sexually abused by her father during her childhood years. Another story is told of a young boy and how he was sexually abused by a family member and then again by a sexual predator in a juvenile home. This chapter specifically features the effects of incest and child abuse within the family environment and the differences of how male and female victims handle the abuse. Sexual violence and the Stockholm syndrome will also be discussed.

Chapter 4 addresses pedophiles, different paraphilias, and sexual perversion. Exhibitionism, frotteurism, fetishes, and voyeurism are also reviewed. Sex abuse by the clergy has been publicized in the news throughout the nation. This chapter spotlights a few newsworthy cases of priests that have been accused of sexual abuse. Sex addiction, sex rings, child prostitution, and sex trafficking are also discussed.

Chapter 5 gives the different perspectives associated with female sexual offenders and the factors most often associated with this group. The number of female sex offenders has been growing throughout the years, but many people often view this as a lesser problem compared to that of male sexual predators. This chapter features characteristics of, risk factors of, recidivism of, and treatment for female sex offenders.

Chapter 6 emphasizes and discusses details of child pornography and the stimulating effects that it has on sexual predators in child exploitation. It describes the sexual predator's fascination with fulfilling his fantasies through child pornography and masturbation to the final conquest of meeting, seducing, and exploiting a young victim. This chapter also concentrates on law enforcement's perspective on child pornography and the seven laws that pertain to the prevention of child pornography in the United States.

Chapter 7 discusses the Internet and how it has enhanced a new venue for sexually exploiting a child. The Internet always provides sexual offenders access to a myriad of innocent and unsuspecting children. According to Online Risks for Youth, of the 30 million children that use the Internet on a daily basis, 45% are under the age of 18. Unsuspecting teens establish online relationships and share intimate and personal information with strangers that may eventually cause them harm. The chapter encapsulates how the Internet is used to entice young victims through social networking sites and demonstrates the advancement of the distribution of sexual images using the webcam or sexting over the phone.

Chapter 8 involves law enforcement and its commitment to policing the Internet to capture sexual predators. This section highlights interviews with a few law enforcement officials regarding the behavior of sexual predators and

Introduction   xxix

their attempts to meet their intended victim. *Dateline NBC* and Perverted Justice (volunteers who pose as minors to try to capture pedophiles) spotlight how they have caught sexual predators trying to entice their victims through social networking sites and chat rooms. This chapter also discusses how DNA is used and focuses on an offender's First and Fourth Amendment rights and the entrapment defense.

Chapter 9 deals with incarceration, recidivism, and rehabilitation. Chemical and surgical castration has been considered a viable option to keep sexual predators from committing the same crime again. This chapter focuses on therapy, sex offender treatment programs, and their effectiveness.

Chapter 10 highlights laws specifically enacted for sexually horrific and gruesome crimes against children. The intent of these laws is to alert the public that sex offenders may live nearby and to promote awareness and public safety throughout communities. A few of the specific stories and resulting laws are as follow:

- The Jacob Wetterling story and the Jacob Wetterling Act
- The Jessica Lunsford story and Jessica's law
- The Megan Kanka story and Megan's law
- The Adam Walsh story and the Adam Walsh Protection Act
- The Dru Sjodin story and the Dru's law
- The Pam Lychner story and the Pam Lychner Tracking and Identification Act of 1996
- The Chelsea King story and Chelsea's law

Chapter 11 features sex offender registration and notification laws, which have been passed by all 50 states. This chapter highlights the sex offender registry and why sexual offender laws were implemented. Civil commitment, homeless sex offenders, geographic information systems (GIS), global positioning systems (GPS), and e-stop are also discussed.

Chapter 12 details many enacted laws and government policies. The laws that specifically target sex offenders were passed to assist in decreasing the recidivism rate of sexual predators and sexual violence in their communities. These laws focus on protecting society by being tough on sexual predators and their individual rights.

Chapter 13 discusses Internet safety and what parents can do to ensure that their children are safe on the Internet. Popular computer lingo, statistics, and safe Internet websites are emphasized. Sexual predators are astute in taking small amounts of information to find addresses, phone numbers, and any other contact information. Children should be educated about Internet safety, and their Internet activity should be monitored and questioned when a suspicious person or content is revealed. Parents must be vigilant in their efforts to protect against child victimization and understand the rationale and methodology of predators. The 10-Ps of the predatory process and the ABCs of Internet safety for parents are reiterated. A final summary of the author's thoughts is also included.

Characteristics of a Sexual Predator

1

I think some of the girls might have just been looking for a thrill. I took that thrill seeking and went beyond that thrill. In fact I did some damage.

Predator

With cell phones, your mom doesn't have to know everything about it. You would talk with him on the phone. The conversation would be normal, and then find some reason to get off [hang up]. The next time you spoke it would become more intimate; you would talk about things you would talk about online, and this often leads into phone sex.

Victim

Sexual Predators—What Are We Dealing With?

Male sexual predators are a distinct breed of individuals who usually prey on young victims and have no specific gender preference. Illinois Attorney General Lisa Madigan (2006) has stated that "sexual assault is a crime that does not discriminate; it knows no racial, economic, or age barriers." These sex offenders blend into a victim's environment just waiting to see how their intended target will react; they will seize the right moment to take advantage and control of the situation.

Predators perfect their skills and adeptness through building trust and confidence, while knowing their actions are wrong and despicable. Research indicates and statistics verify that 99% of sex offenders and sexual predators are male. The majority of victims are children and young women are more likely to become victims of this crime than men.

Gavin DeBecker, who wrote the book, *The Gift of Fear* (1997), acknowledged that one in three young females and one in six young males are apt to become a victim of inappropriate physical contact with an unsympathetic and unscrupulous individual. Dr. Anna Salter (2003), a noted psychologist on sexual offenders, acknowledged that there is a high probability that 9%–16% of boys in the United States will be molested before they reach adulthood.

Although the motivation of sex offenders may vary, most use some form of persuasion, manipulation, deception, and secrecy to get closer to their intended victim. Often, the sexual predators' motivation goes back to a past experience, possibly experiencing sexual abuse themselves. A sex offender takes on a manipulative role, often approaching a victim cautiously in the initial attempt to find a weakness.

A sexual predator may attempt to develop a friendship and become interested in the same activities as the young child or adolescent the predator intends to befriend. This may be the first approach or step toward manipulating the victim into having sex. Rufo (2007) found that most sexual predators have a distinct attraction for a specific age group. Dr. Salter conveyed that some offenders do engage the children emotionally as a way of manipulating them. Others think they are children and turn to the child to meet their emotional needs.

There are a number of reasons sexual predators go undetected while committing sexual crimes. Notably, with the small percentage of sex offenders arrested, it is apparent that predators are adept at what they do. Another significant reason is that children rarely come forward to implicate an offender; unfortunately, it is often someone that they trust and consequently adults tend not to take the child, or the accusation, seriously. Recent studies have shown that a few children actually do disclose abuse at the time it occurs. However, abused children that do come forward have a tendency to feel guilty and often blame themselves for the crime committed against them.

Most victims feel helpless when speaking out about their offender, or they may be frightened when revealing to their parents, relatives, or authorities the inappropriate act that has taken place. It is apparent that not everyone will report this horrific crime to the police. It is likely that the child may be threatened with physical harm or injury to a family member or a pet if he or she does not cooperate or defies the predator's advances.

Causes of Sexual Violence

What are the causes of sexual violence, and what are some of the factors that are involved? Sexual violence is seen as a complex area of human behavior because it incorporates the mind-set of criminal intent and human sexuality. According to Jeffery Roberts, a retired Chicago police detective in the sex and gang unit, sexual violence is a largely misunderstood area. Roberts further states that, to appreciate the complexity and fluidity of the topic, one only has to consider a few of the dimensions of human behavior intrinsic to sexual crimes, such as the following:

- Sexual crimes can be physically and nonphysically violent.
- Sexual crimes can be committed against a person, inanimate object, or animal.
- Sexual offenders may preferentially act out against children.

- There are offenders for whom paraphilia behavior is mandatory for their psychosexual pleasure and an integral part of their criminal behavior.
- There are offenders who experience remorse and guilt from the commission of their crimes and still others who experience no remorse at all.
- There are ritualistic offenders who develop complex fantasies to act out on their victim.
- Fantasizing about the child, sexual stimulation over the abuse the child endured, and masturbation reinforce the sexual arousal and gratification.
- There are offenders who act out impulsively with little or no premeditation, but rather only to satisfy their immediate gratification.
- Emotional needs, often from low self-esteem, are often satisfied after abusing a child.
- A sexual molester can take advantage of any situation.

Characteristics and Patterns

Every race, nationality, and religion has its share of sexual offenders and child sexual predators that often seem to act out solely based on achieving their own sexual gratification. Rufo (2007) confirmed that many sexual offenders and sexual predators come from dysfunctional families. Growing up in a dysfunctional family may be a precursor to a sexual predator's need to seek love, affection, and comfort from children. Sexual predators' feelings of inadequacy may cause them to use force or threatening behavior against their victims. The same inadequacies may often show themselves in a dominant position of control and power toward their victims.

There are many theories as to why sexual offenders approach their victims in a loving, affectionate, and gentle manner. DeBecker (1997) said that "there are two types of predators, the persuasion predator, who gains control over the victim through persuasion, and a power predator who gains control through force and strikes when he knows he can prevail." Sexual predators move methodically in their evaluation and approach toward their intended victim(s), often employing a cautious, low-risk strategy that they hope will keep them from getting caught. Rufo (2007) reiterated that there are two types of sexual offenders: one that likes to plan or groom his victim and the other, who acts on impulse. Both types of sexual offenders have little or no regard for the consequences of their actions or the effects on their victims and often rationalize their behavior and why the child resisted their advances.

Sex offenders feel safe and more comfortable with children because children are naïve, gullible, innocent, and trusting. They often lure or entice a child through affection, attention, gifts, or money and will use this strategy to exploit and demand gratification from the child. Such offenders view the child as a willing participant as they take advantage of their victim in a casual and comfortable environment with which the child is familiar.

Imagination and sexual fantasies about children and adolescents may feed the inner desire of the sexual predator. Certain patterns of behavior soon begin to develop. The involvement with the child and the family can be ongoing and consistent; the child may feel obligated or indebted to the sex offender by cooperating and consenting to the sexual relationship, and fulfilling their fantasies. The child may also exhibit curiosity about the situation, be seeking attention, be at a rebellious stage of his or her young life, or be influenced by adult dialogue and discussion. Oftentimes, because of trust, a younger child may not realize that a sexual act has already taken place. This will be further addressed in terms of the motivation that drives sexual offenders into this secretive and deceptive life and the grooming process of their victims.

DeBecker (1997) commented that when a sex offender chooses his victim, it is similar to a shark circling his impending prey. DeBecker also noted that a predatory criminal is always looking for his next vulnerable victim: someone that allows him to be in control. DeBecker indicated that everyone instinctively exhibits indicators of a person's true intentions. Relying on "gut feeling" is the first warning sign that something is wrong. Most people instinctively size up a person in the first 10 seconds after they meet. Many people doubt or do not trust what the gut feeling is telling them, frequently dismissing or making an excuse for the way they feel about a person. Predators can be very convincing in their approach of being sincere, trustworthy, and truthful. Many coworkers, immediate family, and friends of the sexual predator are amazed when they discover his secret life.

Cognitive Behavioral Theories

Many sociologists and psychologists have suggested that certain characteristics are responsible for the sexual behavioral characteristics of individuals. Research has shown that many different factors have a recognizable and clear correlation related to child abuse:

- *Children are seen as sex objects.* The sexual offender truly believes the child wants and is willing to engage in sexual activity. He visualizes the child experiencing pleasure from the sexual experience. The sexual offender credits the child with initiating the sexual behavior and

Characteristics of a Sexual Predator

interaction. The offender who thinks this way was possibly abused as a younger child.
- *Lack of control.* Sex offenders will often the blame the environment and the surroundings to which they are accustomed. This type of sex offender will be driven into having sex with children given the right opportunity. He will rationalize and justify his behavior and will quickly overcome any inhibitions about guilt and reoffending from any previous experience. Sex and children are all that the offender can think about. This type of sex offender can be categorized as sexually addicted.
- *Entitled to sex.* The sex offender is under the notion: "I deserve to have what I want, and I want sex now." There is a need and desire for sex and what is most important is attaining the sexual gratification that is craved—not caring who the victim is. The lack of empathy and compassion for the victim is apparent. The predator's actions are selfish and can be compared to the desires of a pedophile or rapist.
- *Behavior is normal and not harmful.* Many collectors and distributors of child pornography believe in this philosophy, which is often the monumental first step to sexual contact. They feel that the picture of a naked child being sexually abused is a harmless substitute for the real thing: no harm, no foul. The child is not recognized as a victim in the predator's eyes because he is not a participant in the abuse of the sexual satisfaction. The sex offender who employs this type of philosophy may experience interpersonal issues.

The following are excuses used by predators for why they did what they did. Their actions were reinforced by their fantasies or needs:

- He or she liked it.
- I knew deep down that he or she really enjoyed it.
- He or she came on to me.
- He or she has to learn about sex sometime.
- I was not doing anything wrong.
- He or she did not resist my advances.
- The timing was right.
- I could see it in the eyes that he or she wanted me.
- He or she got excited when I fondled him or her.
- He or she would hug me for a long time.
- He or she always jumped onto my lap.
- I want to teach the child about sex.
- He or she initiated it.

The Social Bond Theory

The social bond theory is another aspect associated with sex offenders and society. The cycle of sexual abuse, like any other addiction, continues to manifest itself from generation to generation. Many people who were once victims of sexual abuse have now become the abuser. Edwin Sutherland, a well-known criminologist, believed that criminal behavior was a learned trait, rather than an inherited trait. Schmallenger (2005) noted that Travis Hirschi is renowned for his thoughts on the social bond theory. Dr. Hirschi believes that a child who is abused or mistreated is more likely to commit an unlawful act and that individuals are less likely to commit crimes if they are able to connect with other people and have fulfilling relationships. He indicated that a person knows what he is doing when he disregards the rules and has no regard for them. Schmallenger mentioned Dr. Hirschi's four components of the social bond theory:

- Attachment: emotional attachments to significant others
- Commitment: to appropriate lifestyles
- Involvement: immersion in conventional values
- Belief: correctness of social obligations and rules of a larger society

Profile of a Female Sexual Offender

Nancy was 3 years old when her mom and dad divorced. She lived with her mom until she was 11 years old. Her mom was not able to take care of her financially, so Nancy went to live with her grandparents. Her grandmother was a wonderful woman who did her best to make Nancy happy. Her grandfather was an alcoholic who was verbally abusive and constantly badgered Nancy about her friends, school, and homework. Her grandfather first started fondling her when they were alone and always threatened her that she would have nowhere to live if she ever told anyone. His exploitation increased to sexual intercourse when she was just 14 years old. Nancy's schoolwork began to suffer and she began to become withdrawn and depressed. She was sexually abused on a daily basis. When her grandmother died, Nancy felt that she could not stay in the house with her grandfather any longer, so she ran away. Nancy went to live with one of her friends from high school. She found a job as a waitress and was soon living in an apartment on her own.

Nancy met a wonderful young man named Steve and they soon began dating. A few years later, Steve and Nancy married, bought a home, and began raising their two sons in a quiet town nearby. She never revealed the sexual abuse that she had suffered to anyone. One day at church, the couple saw an announcement about the need for foster homes for children from Southeast Asia. They became foster parents to a 14-year-old named Craig. At the time Steve volunteered with the National Guard. He was deployed for basic training for several months. During this time, Craig and Nancy became close. One night Craig asked if he could sleep in her bed, like her younger boys did. Nancy drew him close and began kissing and caressing him and was soon making love to him. This relationship spiraled out of control as they continued to have sex whenever they could.

Steve came home from basic training. Feeling emotionally torn, Nancy admitted her affair with Craig. Steve filed for divorce and was granted custody of their two young sons. Nancy was arrested and charged with felony sexual assault with a minor and was sentenced to 3 years in prison. Craig was placed into counseling and into a new foster home.

Profile of a Male Sexual Offender

Michael, a convicted sex offender who had been recently released from prison, had his parole revoked when he was caught with a 12-year-old boy with his pants down in his van. Michael was arrested again for sexually molesting a child. He had

  been banned from a book store for soliciting sex with young men;
  been caught and arrested for using a compact mirror to look at a young
     boy in the next stall in the bathroom of a department store;
  approached a boy from behind a urinal and molested him; and
  been arrested for grabbing a boy's genitals on a bus.

Michael's previous history of sexually molesting young boys began when he was in his early 20s. He had been abused by a 25-year-old camp counselor when he was 12 years old. When Mike was abused, he was scared that someone in camp might find out. He was embarrassed and ashamed that he was not able to fight back, often holding back the tears. He was sexually assaulted almost on a daily basis.

He had no one to tell; his mom and dad were divorced and he thought that no one would believe him because the camp counselor was a well-known and well-liked guy. Mike had nightmares about his abuse, but never revealed what had happened to him. It was only after a mandated counseling session after his first arrest that he admitted to being sexually abused at camp. Michael had always blamed his previous sexual abuse for his deviant behavior.

Michael admitted to the police officers that he felt that he was a danger to young boys. He felt that incarceration was the only way that he would stop sexually abusing boys when he had the chance. The camp counselor was eventually arrested after another young boy admitted the sexual exploitation to his parents. No one will ever know exactly how many boys this camp counselor abused, but 18 boys including Michael have admitted to being abused when questioned.

Michael admitted that counseling was helpful but that he always had these thoughts of young boys in his mind, especially when he masturbated. The judge gave him 5 years in prison and recommended that he continue to go to counseling. The judge set strict restrictions upon his eventual release from prison.

In My Opinion

Dr. Laura Barrow

Dr. Lauren M. Barrow of Kaplan University conducted her research focused on the criminal victimization of persons with disabilities—specifically, nonverbal persons. The anonymity of the Internet removes the stigma of a disability and offers the target population a unique environment for mainstream participation, so it became a valuable tool in her research efforts. Dr. Barrow's research since has involved the use of pop cultural websites as vehicles for criminal enterprise. More recently, she has worked to identify methods used by online sexual predators in order to proactively protect children and adults online.

Dr. Barrow (personal communication) observes that the Internet is an open community, where success has continued despite the dot-com bust of the past. She further claims that while it has attracted increased attention regarding the rise of criminal activity taking place on its sites, including commercial fraud, property crimes, and even violent assaults, little has been done to legislate or control its impact. Indeed, the reluctance on the part of the legislature to actively limit or control the content of the Internet effectively ties the hands of law enforcement when investigating crimes that take place online. Of particular interest to these researchers is the blatant use of the Internet as a sexual marketplace for predators of young children. While it is known that predators "troll" the Internet regularly seeking new victims, it is not always known how they find and later assault those victims. Adding to the complication of this issue is the fact that traditional meanings have become warped to fit within the virtual world. For example, "assault" represents an elusive concept, especially if physical contact does not take place.

According to Dr. Barrow, the occurrence of these crimes has become more commonplace, and specialized teams and agencies have emerged to combat them (cybertipline.com, ICAC investigative units, etc.); more information is gained and implemented in efforts to locate and arrest the offenders.

However, as with any new enterprise, there exists a hierarchy of ability and knowledge, and sexual predators are no different. Individuals just venturing into the arena of soliciting victims online are likely to "collect" their victims through triangulation. Her research has indicated that offenders identify and establish a relationship with one youngster and, from that connection, will link to other youngsters who are "friends with" or "subscribers to" their sites. How the first child is chosen can be as simple as searching for a particular year (2000 or "00") and then initiating a conversation with a child (age can be determined because a percentage of children use their birth year as part of their login).

It is important to note that just as deer hunters will find the best location, choose the right weather conditions, and willingly wait for days for the perfect shot, a sexual predator will employ the same tactics. In addition to searching the Internet for the right age group, they frequent sites that children often visit (nick.com, ClubPenguin.com, Webkinz.com), and they subscribe to video sites that children favor (Justin Beiber, Taylor Swift, etc.) in much the same way in which a pedophile frequents parks or schoolyards.

Once a child is identified, predators study the frequency of logins and the length of time spent online to identify children who might be home alone after school or who likely do not have many friends; the assumption is that if a child has 5+ hours a day to be online, little else occupies his or her time and there are few, if any, parental restrictions. They operate with the dual goal of obtaining the trust and confidence of their victims and evading detection.

To achieve that end, some specific elements are employed to groom victims. Grooming is a process wherein after a potential victim is identified, the offender begins the task of gaining that child's trust and allegiance. Predators often pose as children themselves and write of parental conflict or feelings of despair (family tragedy, poverty, bad grades, etc.); they report being victims of bullying or feeling all alone. The response is often positive within the offender's framework. The victim believes that he or she has found a friend: someone in his or her age group who understands and can relate to the situation.

New predators make mistakes in this phase. They move too quickly and attempt in relatively short order to have the child produce proof of loyalty (photo, video, phone call, etc.); more seasoned predators will linger in this phase. They will set up times to meet the victim online and they *will* be there. They will ask about the victim's day, who was mean to him or her, how he or she did on a test, etc. This can go on for weeks, but the predator knows that every day he is present and every question he asks brings him closer to the ultimate goal—sexual exploitation. This may not take place in person—indeed, few are, given the scope of the Internet—however, even a nude photo or video is a violation on some level, and a willingness of the child to produce that leads to an increased likelihood of more intrusive actions. While the public is frequently reminded that "digital is forever" and that choices have consequences, children do not make consequential analysis and therefore often choose to comply with the requests of their new "friend."

Enhancing the likelihood of success is the fact that offenders will "cluster" a victim. This means that when a potentially compliant victim is identified and a relationship established, offenders will establish multiple online identities and will have them all subscribe to the intended victim. The result is that the victim establishes a sense of popularity online that he or she could not achieve in person. The offender then uses those *identities* to gain more information using a "one against the other" approach (e.g., *you told Jonny something special that only he knows; what about telling me something?*). Eager to please and retain these new friends, the child shares something personal with each person. This method has two benefits: (1) In the event that a parent does intervene and block one of the "friend" identities, the others exist to continue the relationship, and (2) a lot of information is acquired in a short period of time.

Another victim characteristic that contributes to the rate of success is his or her age. Prepubescent children are naturally compliant and are used to adults instructing them as to what to do. They do not yet possess a sense of personal privacy since many life functions (bathing, eating, toileting) are still performed or monitored by adults, and their knowledge or understanding of sexual desires is nonexistent. As such, if an offender succeeds in gaining the trust and confidence of the child, he or she is likely to comply if asked to perform a sexual act on video. In the child's mind, it is little more than playing house or doctor with a friend.

While there is an increasing demand for legislation concerning online behavior, as of late, such efforts have not succeeded. In the meantime, the Internet provides virtual validation for this behavior, a forum to discuss "best practices" to contact and lure children online, and a virtual classroom to train and encourage one another to act out sexually with children (Hughes 2001). Concurrently, law enforcement has aggressively risen to the challenge of protecting children, and arrests and prosecutions of online predators have increased (http://www.unh.edu/ccrc/) in every jurisdiction across the country. Though, for every predator caught, many more either already exist or are emerging every day.

Definitions of Chapter Key Terms

Sex offender: Any person, more likely a male than female, who is convicted of a sex crime almost exclusively against a child. These crimes range from rape (sexual assault) to sexual harassment to child molestation to distributing and producing child pornography.

Sexual abuse: Unwanted sexual activity that is forced upon an individual or child through threats, intimidation, or coercion. This is another term for sexual assault.

Sexual abuse of a child: The mistreatment of children in a sexual manner, by sexually touching, fondling, or penetrating the child. Sexual assault or illegal sexual contact with a victim who is incapable of giving consent or by a person with authority.

Sexual predator: Often describes a person with an obsession and passion to target an innocent victim sexually to satisfy his or her needs for sexual gratification.

References

DeBecker, G. (1997). *The gift of fear, the survival signals that protect us from violence.* New York: Bantam Doubleday Dell Publishing Group.

Hughes, R. (2001). http://www.protectkids.com/dangers/onlinepred.htm.

Madigan, L. (2006, April 3). Madigan observes sexual assault awareness month: Releases quiz to increase public knowledge of sexually violent crimes. Illinois Attorney General's Office Press Release.

Roberts, J. (2001). *Violence against women: Adult criminal sexual assault offenders.*

Rufo, R. (2007). An investigation of online sexual predation of minors by convicted male offenders. Dissertation, Argosy University, Atlanta, GA.

Salter, A. C. (2003). *Predators, pedophiles, rapists and other sex offenders, who they are and how they operate.* New York: Basic Books.

Schmallenger, F. (2005). *Criminal law today,* 3rd ed., p. 99. Upper Saddle River: NJ: Prentice Hall.

Grooming the Victim   2

> Grooming is doing some step to bring a person certain acts. I break down her inhibitions. My goal is to meet a girl to have sexual intercourse.
>
> **Sexual predator**

> Grooming—it's weird; I really do not know how I started to lose myself. When I look back at my picture on the missing person's flyer, I look at my eyes; I can see that I am really not there.
>
> **Victim of a sexual predator**

Grooming

The art of sexual grooming is a common characteristic displayed by almost all sexual predators. Grooming can be compared to a master chess player waiting to make the ultimate move to take control: the sexual predator knows what the child needs and what he or she is missing in his or her life. Researchers are beginning to understand the communication process by which sexual predators lure their victims into a web of entrapment and how a child's innocence and vulnerability present an immense opportunity for abusive behavior by the sexual predator, who is very disciplined, calculating, and patient in attaining the ultimate goal of seducing a young child.

Access to the child is pivotal in the relationship in controlling the situation and focusing on the goal to sexually exploit their victim. Often the sexual predator seeks out the opportunity to sexually mistreat the child through continuous planning and manipulation. In his attempt to satisfy his sexual desires, the sexual predator will patiently draw upon a natural activity with which the child is familiar and that he or she understands. He may change his plan or course of action, depending on the situation. He will wait for the right moment to get the child alone, getting the victim to believe that he is harmless and poses no risk. Children invariably view adults as protectors, not offenders.

The sexual predator oftentimes could be a relative, family friend, member of the clergy, neighbor, caregiver, babysitter, coach, or mentor and uses the innocent fondness and affection of his prey to initiate his routine of control. Sexual predators do not want their actions to seem suspicious or out of the ordinary. They will attempt to use seemingly acceptable forms of touching, depending on whom they plan to seduce. If it is a girl, they may use playful tickling, bathing, back rubs, or made-up games. In an attempt to seduce a young boy, they may use wrestling, playful fighting, horsing around, or different physical sports activities to break down the barriers. Gifts, money, or favors are often used to quiet a victim about the sexual abuse that may take place or that has taken place already. This deliberate, scheming, and opportunistic approach will often test the child to see how far the offender can go before being stopped or caught or until the child complies with the sexual abuse. In an adult–child relationship, children are often too young to realize what is occurring and naïve to the fact that an adult would ever harm them. The sexual predator is considering the following:

- Is the intended victim a loner?
- Will adults believe that any abuse took place?
- What is the possibility of the victim being believed?

Grooming may include other activities, such as sitting on a child's bed and watching him or her get into bedclothes, accidentally touching, showing the child pornography, and making contact with implicit sexual suggestions. In a 2008 study, Loreen Olson, from the University of Missouri (MU researchers reveal communication tactics used by sexual predators to entrap children 2008), indicated that a common element that most sexual predators would like to attain is a "deceptive trust" with the child.

Berliner and Conte (1990) conducted a study that emphasized desensitization techniques. These techniques are a systematic progression of innocent verbal content and affectionate physical contact that create an illusion of caring that overcomes natural barriers to abuse. They further go on to say that sex offenders assess the risk of discovery and ultimately groom the victims into believing they have given permission for more intrusive sexual contact. The desensitization process fosters cooperation and reduces the possibility of disclosure. Both adolescent and adult sexual offenders frequently used threats or coercion as ways of securing and maintaining victim silence; threats of physical harm and/or the withdrawal of special privileges can be common. In general, adolescent sexual offenders used more modus operandi strategies than did their adult counterparts. Adolescent sexual offenders were more likely to threaten their victims directly with a weapon, give gifts, and expose them to pornography compared to adult sexual offenders, who are more likely to lure their victims with drugs and alcohol in order to better achieve compliance to a sexual act.

Berliner and Conte (1990) emphasize that family members are more likely to give gifts and use psychological tactics to promote victim helplessness. The complex grooming and silencing strategies that are exhibited by both adolescent and adult sexual offenders suggest that children may have limited success in preventing abuse. In fact, sexual offenders maintain that they have the ability to take advantage of a child's vulnerabilities in status conditions (child is living in a single-parent home), emotional characteristics (child is needy, unhappy, or shy), and situational factors (lack of effective supervision) to gain control.

Progression of Behavior for Grooming a Victim

A sexual predator uses the following tools to groom his intended victim:

- Secrecy and living a double life
- Fantasies and masturbation
- Motivation, desire, and fascination
- Manipulation
- Seduction
- Approach strategies
- Isolation strategies
- Persuasion
- Deception and entrapment
- Reasons for the victim to trust the offender

Secrecy and Living a Double Life

When one picks up a newspaper or watches the daily news reports on television, one is bound to see stories of a coach, priest, teacher, community leader, or average citizen getting arrested and being led away by police in handcuffs for getting caught with an abundance of child pornography or for sexually molesting a child. News reporters canvass the offender's neighborhood looking for neighbors, friends, and relatives to interview. A news camera focuses on individuals expressing disbelief over seeing their trusted neighbor going to jail. The person being interviewed often says that there was never any indication of any wrongdoing, especially the actions or behavior associated with a sexual predator. Neighbors or friends often say the offender was "a nice man," that they "trusted him," and that they "would have never expected this and it is shocking and hard to believe."

Most predators lead a dual life; they present themselves one way in public and another way in private as their sexual abuse and deviant behavior often thrives in secret and manipulative lifestyles. The secret life that most predators often conceal fools many people; therefore, the predator creates a facade that makes it seem as though any type of deviant behavior is completely out of character and never gives any indication that his conduct is that of a sexual predator. Their sex crimes often thrive in their secretive and manipulative lifestyles. Sexual predators are adept in planning their trysts with the sole intention of taking advantage and controlling their victims. They do the best that they can to keep their secret actions intact and will not confide in anyone, except maybe another sexual predator, about this sordid life.

The offender will attempt to keep his actions discreet and will often try to keep the child silent through several different strategies. Sexual predators learn and master the art of deception and will often become daring in their approaches and adaptation of the techniques that have been successful for them. They will continue to exploit the child, especially if the act is gentle and pleasurable and the child does not believe that what has occurred is wrong or bad.

One strategy is to involve the child in the dilemma or situation that if someone finds out, "we" will get in trouble. The predator has knowingly involved the child to take and accept the blame if someone finds out. Another strategy the sexual offender will often use is secrecy and he will try to make the child promise not to tell anyone. This is often accomplished by a threat that involves harming the child, a family member, a family pet, or a friend if any of the deviant actions are revealed. It is this fear that will enable the sexual predator to continue to persevere in his efforts to control the situation and his victim.

Fantasies and Masturbation

It is often a sex offender's goal to bring reality to his fantasies. Jeffery Roberts (2001) noted in his article, *Violence against Women:*

> Fantasy is the most important component of a sex crime [and] could be described as a mental rehearsal of a desired event. Fantasy provides the offender with an editing mechanism that allows him to focus on the reason for the crime, and most importantly it provides a template or map for the offender to follow as he commits his assault.

Sexual predators will often select their victims with the same preference of gender, age, race, or body shape about which they have fantasized. Imagination and sexual fantasies about children and adolescents may feed the inner desire of sexual predators. These internal reasons may stimulate their external cravings for young, innocent victims.

Rufo (2007) revealed a direct correlation between masturbation and sexual fantasies. A majority of sexual predators have indicated a dependency on fantasies and external stimuli to enhance their almost daily masturbation to fuel their desires, especially in their efforts to carry out their deviant acts. The act of masturbating and pleasuring themselves is a dominant trait of most sex offenders. A few studies have concluded that increased masturbation coupled with low self-esteem is a determinant factor in enhanced fantasies that reinforce deviant behavior. Erotic sexual fantasies and masturbation increase the elements of power and control. This type of behavior, along with sexual abuse within the family, may cause an individual to become more deviant in his thought patterns and sexual fantasies.

There are two types of sexual fantasies: those considered normal behavior and those considered deviant behavior. *Normal* fantasies can be thought as

- Nonconfrontational or nonthreatening acts (not necessarily sexual) on any person
- Thinking about nonrelated individuals in a positive manner
- Focusing on a person who is not a victim of any violent, deviant act that would harm someone
- In appropriate age range of the individual

Deviant fantasies can be thought as

- A noted variance in age of the individual fantasizing
- Thinking sexually about any family member or relative
- Coercing a victim into an abnormal or socially inappropriate activity
- Any sadistic act on any victim, regardless of age

Dandescu and Wolfe (2003) discovered that child molesters have a high incidence of deviant sexual fantasies. According to their study, a majority of sexual offenders often masturbated to deviant sexual fantasies before their first sexual offense and tended to masturbate more often to deviant sexual thoughts and fantasies following an offense. Erotic pictures, temptation, and addiction are factors that lead to acting out sexual fantasies. It is important to understand that pornography serves as psychological, as well as physical, stimulus to a sex offender.

Motivation, Desire, and Fascination

The enticing environment and the thrill of a possible interaction between the sexual predator and the child may spur the predator's motivation. In a 2004 study by Campagna and Martin, they relayed that sexual motivation is the driving force of the sexual predator. Often, a sexual predator shows that he is a "nice" person and can be trusted. In fact, a sexual offender often displays a facade to the community and outside world: He is a good person who would not be capable of performing a deviant sexual act on a child.

In her many and extensive counseling and therapy sessions with sex offenders, Dr. Anna Salter (2003) noted:

The offender uses the child as an object of sexual relief. He does not attempt to engage the child in any emotional way. Instead, he sees the child solely for self-gratification. The offender regards the child as a disposable object, to use and then discard. The sex act constitutes the extent and the duration of the relationship, and this usually is a temporary and unstable involvement.

Manipulation

Manipulation and power are major ingredients of what a sexual predator uses to trap his victim. A number of research studies have shown that the age of the victim may influence the predator's manipulation. There is no guarantee that an older child will notice the manipulation that is often disguised as affection. The sexual predator's opportunistic actions may fool parents, as well as other adults. Rufo (2007) disclosed that sexual offenders will often seek out someone that may be vulnerable, perhaps his own child or a friend of the family, often feeling entitlement because of the relationship with one another. The victim may not realize that the predator's affection is not genuine or sincere. Children and adolescents have limited life experience and are not able fully to recognize dangers that surround them. Children are taught at an early age to listen to and respect adults. Listening to an adult is often awarded by appreciation and approval.

Salter (2003) confirmed that "such offenders describe their victims as weak, defenseless, helpless, unable to resist, easily controlled and manipulated. This type of offender exhibits a lack of concern for the consequences or cost to others as a result of his sexual activity; he exhibits strong sexual needs that he is unable of delaying or redirecting." The sex offender may become frustrated with an uncooperative victim and may oftentimes have a difficult time keeping in disappointment and anger. Often, he will not take no for an answer and will threaten the victim with harm to the victim or his or her family. The victim may often have no one to turn to or not know of any viable way out of a threatening situation. Manipulation by the sexual predator can be emotional as well as physical as he relies on intimidation, coercion, and the use of secrecy to promote his sexually abusive behavior.

Seduction

Everyone enjoys being treated with respect and kindness and these are the same seductive tactics used by the sexual predator. The predator often relies on his victim to accept his reassuring and convincing confirmations. These tactics are similar to that of a con artist, waiting to engulf the "mark." This strategy can be compared to that of a patient fisherman, who throws out the line with a baited hook and then waits for the unsuspecting child to take the bait.

When a person seduces another person, it can be compared to courtship, or winning the person over, with sex as the primary goal. This way of thinking often encourages or begins the methodical process in which sexual predators think about seducing a child. The minds of sexual predators function in many devious ways; they often think, maneuver, and plan to attain the ultimate goal: having sex with a child.

Isolation Strategies

Perpetrators go to great lengths to isolate the child emotionally and physically from support and defense networks of friends and family. Isolation causes the victim to become more and more dependent on the predator. Being alone with the child is key to the sexual predator's success. A few isolation techniques include the following:

- Give the child a ride home or to school.
- Offer to accompany the child to the store, mall, park, or library.
- Use the child's friendship to spend more time together.
- Engage in accidental contact and sexual questions and discussions when alone.

Adams and Fay (2003) found that most sexual offenses toward children often follow a gradual pattern that could begin with common yet inappropriate behavior, such as tickling and touching in a sexual way during play. The touching is deliberate, but the child may feel awkward upon realizing that the sexual predator's action is inappropriate. As teens are naturally curious and with a little prompting may be rebellious, the sexual offender will use a deliberate approach to be a friend, confidante, and companion who is interested in his victim's activities. Do teens send out mixed messages when they are approached by this "fascinating" stranger? Children and teens are impressionable and curious, and often cannot tell what is reality and what is a dream world: Can this be my fairy tale or dream? Will this person sweep me off my feet?

Alicia, a young women who was a victim of a sexual predator, commented that "he would become your lover, your best friend, your confidante, and he would always be there for you. You would feel like you have an obligation to be there for him as well. I mean, he is always there for you." On occasion, the child or teen will initiate an intimate encounter, further giving the impression that he or she wants the relationship to start. Adolescents that are independent, rebellious, and curious will often flaunt that they are sexually promiscuous, prompting a stranger to be their willing participant by their open sexual display and conversation.

Persuasion

A sexual predator uses persuasion, which often involves a low-risk strategy that involves an act of kindness that lures the victim into the predator's world. This process may start out with thoughtfulness and compassion. The confidence level of the sexual predator often increases as the unsuspecting child is taken places and shown love and affection. A sexual predator will be content in asking provocative questions just to see how the child will react to his advances. The predator relies on his charm to break down the walls of trust of not only the child's family, but also the child's own defense mechanism. Children have a genuine trust of adults—especially those that show a genuine interest in their well-being and disguise their true intentions through a smile. A sexual offender will base his relationship with the child on this type of trusting behavior. The predator's ulterior motive is to break down the child's nervousness slowly and carefully as fondness and affection develop and sexual contact is ultimately realized.

Deception

A predator takes on the persona of an actor, playing a role for a child to see and believe. A predator may become so skilled at deception and lying that he may often mislead trained professionals in this field. Sex offenders often "convince" themselves of their lies and that what they are doing is not immoral: "Everyone else is doing it; why can't I?" It is not difficult for them to justify their deviant behavior and that they are not criminals. English (1997) noted that "sex offenders typically developed complicated and persistent psychological and social systems constructed to assist them in denying and minimizing the harm they inflict on others, and often they are very accomplished at presenting to others a facade designed to hide the truth about themselves."

A sexual predator may try to blame others, saying that *he* may be the victim. Sex offenders typically come up with an excuse that the child "came on" to them. Many sexual offenders will ultimately justify their actions by stating that the victim initiated the encounter or the victim actually wanted to have sex and they were only doing what the victim wanted. The physical pleasure overshadows the hurtful memories that the abuse has caused. Sexual offenders are in denial of the pain, heartache, and internal suffering the victim will eventually realize because of their selfish act.

In Salter's (2003) book, *Predators, Pedophiles Rapists and Other Sex Offenders: Who They Are and How They Operate,* she mentioned a client who was an admitted and convicted child molester, a musician who preyed on young children. His testimonial was very graphic as he described trying to mislead his next young victim:

When a person like me wants a child, you don't just go up, get the child, and sexually molest the child; there is a process of obtaining the child's friendship. When you get their trust, that is when the child becomes vulnerable, and you can molest the child. As far as the children go, they are easy. You befriend them. You take them places. You buy them gifts. Now in grooming the child, you win his trust and I mean, the child has a look in his eyes, it is hard to explain, and you just have to know the look. You know when you have that kid. You know when the kid trusts you. Sexual predators choose to follow this corridor of control, often displaying dual personalities in the process.

Children Not Coming Forward

A sexual offender who discourages other adults from monitoring a child's behavior or an offender who looks for a way to spend time alone with children frequently displays distinct and clear warning signs. Parents especially must be aware of the signs that something is wrong with their child. Sexual offenders are often hoping that parents, guardians, and their victims will not see their true intentions.

Parents, neighbors, relatives, and friends of a sexual predator may look the other way and deny that a problem exists when someone has sexually abused a child. Even though many youth are solicited online, they rarely ever report such occurrences. If these incidents are not reported, sexual predators go undetected and are free to prey on more victims. Children rarely disclose abuse at the time it occurred, and the offender's confidence increases when no one listens to the child's statements or explanations. Rufo (2007) indicated that a sex offender's confidence is reinforced when a child's outcries and revelations are ignored.

If a child molester knows that someone is watching, it may be difficult to find opportunities to abuse the victim without being caught. Recent studies have found that society has tolerated child abuse. There is gross underreporting of child abuse and the damage it causes. It is difficult to fathom how family members look the other way when they know that this abuse is occurring, normally to a young and innocent child. Sex offenders will often target children that display characteristics of low self-esteem. If a child has a tendency to be a habitual liar, a predator will use this to his advantage because most people may not or will not believe the child. This gives the predator additional confidence and power. Normally, a child will use silence to protect a friend, family member, parent, or loved one. The silence of not revealing the abuse is the pinnacle of helplessness that a child frequently endures for the rest of his or her life.

Monitoring and detecting a child's change of behavior may be a way of discovering that something is wrong or that possible child abuse has occurred. A few recent studies have revealed that a child may exhibit specific signs that often illustrate that a problem may exist. Parents and teachers are urged to be diligent and informed in their efforts in noticing these specific signs of trouble. Although there are a number of symptoms or indicators that a child has been sexually abused, a child may react to sexual abuse in many different ways. A few obvious signs are

- Unexplained, unexpected bed-wetting
- Taking an excessive number of baths
- No valid reason for not wanting to go with someone
- Staying inside the home, not wanting to go to a relative's or friend's home
- Experiencing nightmares or bad dreams
- Crying for no reason
- Not wanting to go to school; constant stomach pains
- Becoming withdrawn and reserved
- Bleeding rectally or vaginally (blood on a child's underwear, pajamas, clothes)
- Blood in stool or urine
- Trouble walking or a problem sitting
- Unusual infection, swollen tissue near the genital area
- Possible sexually transmitted diseases or unexplained rash
- Concealing feelings and keeping the abuse to themselves
- Accepting what has happened to them and not speaking about it to anyone
- Showing signs of anger or acting out

Parental/Predator Abuse and Emotional Blackmail and Guilt

The cycle of abuse continues:

- Parents that have abused their children have most likely been abused themselves. Is it genetic makeup or environmental predisposition? This is what the parent knew life to be. This is what the child will remember. Is there a possibility to break the chain or cycle of abuse?
- Most parents regret what they have done. This may be a combination of guilt for what they have done to the child and fear of the consequences if authorities find out.
- Some parents will seek out therapy or counseling for their inappropriate sexual behavior. A few parents offend again and continue the sexual abuse of their children or other family members.

- Children also deal with the guilt of keeping the abuse a secret or revealing what has happened and seeing the family break up or one or both parents being sent to jail. The parents will continue to remind the child what could happen if the family breaks up. The children will have the propensity of continuing the cycle again in the years to come.

The sexual predator is counting on the child not to reveal any abuse or sexual activity that might have occurred. Often, if a relationship develops, the child may feel a sense of loyalty to his or her attacker or fear that his or her parents may find out about the sexual touching or exploitation that has taken place. The sexual predator may entice the child using photographs or videos, thus exploiting the child's vulnerability by revealing the partially clad or nude bodies in a number of sexual poses. The predator may use this type of behavior for a number of reasons. One may be to enhance his fantasies and the second may be used as a possible tool to make the child feel guilty by threatening to reveal the pictures, videos, or past actions to others. The sexual predator is banking on the guilt the child may experience about being involved and the fear the child has about anyone finding out about the sexual details of what happened. These scare tactics are a strong factor in keeping the child from revealing any type of sexual abuse.

A parent could possibly prevent or stop the most aggressive sexual offender if the parent has open communication with his or her child and lets the child know that he or she can tell the parent anything. In addition, a parent or guardian must act on any suspicion—no matter how small—or run the risk of investigating after it is too late. Most experts agree that it is imperative for parents, family members, and health care professionals to trust their instincts and be aware of the obvious warning signs that something is wrong with a child.

In an article, "How to Recognize Grooming," Anne Collier (2009), cofounder of ConnectSafely.org and editor of *NetFamilyNews*, writes,

> Sometimes the very reason kids and teens spend time in social-networking sites to meet new friends. So it is not always easy for them to tell when new "friends" have bad intentions, and research shows that about 4% of online kids receive the kind of unwanted sexual solicitations that could lead to or be part of grooming. Grooming is the way sexual predators evolve from bad intentions to sexual exploitation. Basically, grooming is manipulation. It is the process pedophiles use to get children they target online to meet with them off-line with the simple goal being sex.

Collier goes on to say that "sometimes it involves flattery, sometimes sympathy, other times offers of gifts, money, or modeling jobs. It can also involve all of the above over extended periods of time." That is why it is called "grooming." Experts say the short-term goal of these manipulators is for the victim to feel loved or just comfortable enough to want to meet them in person, and these people know that "sometimes" takes time. That is OK, they would say, because groomers tend to have a lot of patience, and they also tend to "work" a number of targets at once, telling all of them that they are "the only one for me." You can imagine how well that can work with kids seeking sympathy, support, or validation online. Groomers design what they say as they go along, tailoring their flattery or offers as they learn about the victim.

Profile of a Female Sex Offender

Sylvia was a shy, quiet, 40-year-old teacher with lingering low self-esteem. She was a middle child of a verbally abusive, rejecting, alcoholic father and a passive mother. She was a shy, fearful, and lonely child who often felt different from and inferior to her brother and sister, who were both outgoing and popular. She coped with this by concentrating on her studies and trying to be perfect and do well in school.

Sylvia was sexually assaulted at the age of 12 by Nick, her next door neighbor, who was 10 years older than she. Nick went over to her house looking for her brother. Sylvia opened the door and said that her brother was not home and that no one would be home for a while. He turned to leave, but then asked for a glass of water. Nick was always in her home, so it seemed innocent enough to Sylvia. After he drank the water, Nick grabbed Sylvia and pushed her down on the living room couch. He tried taking off her pants and underwear as she frantically tried to push him off her. He tried kissing her and had his hands on her small breasts. His finger was able to penetrate her as she cried from the pain. Nick got off her and left quickly, warning her that she would be sorry if she ever told anyone. Sylvia was in a daze, not believing that her brother's friend had assaulted and sexually attacked her. She never revealed her secret to anyone.

Sylvia met her husband, Jack, in college and they married after they graduated. Sylvia and Jack struggled to find happiness in their marriage; Jack worked two jobs, and would often go drinking after work. They were never close and intimate and their sexual relationship had been nonexistent for several years. Sylvia had a difficult time getting sexually intimate because she did not trust anyone. Her greatest source of personal satisfaction came from her career rather than from her family. The couple had two daughters and an adopted son. Jack was offered a promotion at work, but that meant relocating to another state. The family moved to a new community where Sylvia had no family or friends and was "incredibly lonely." Sylvia's relationship with her husband became more troubled after the move because of disagreements over money and his drinking. Jack came home drunk every night and would often pass out on the couch.

Shortly after the move, Sylvia met Brett, a 12-year-old neighbor boy, through her daughter, Debbie. Brett was from a large family and was having behavior problems both at home and at school. The two children became close friends and spent a lot of time together. As Christmas approached, Brett was spending a great deal of time at their house and Sylvia looked forward to his visits. Brett began spending more time with Sylvia than with her daughter. He started spending the night and stayed in a spare bedroom. Sylvia and Brett grew close and shared personal things about their lives until, according to Sylvia, Brett became "the most significant person in my life."

Brett sometimes had trouble falling asleep, so Sylvia began cuddling with him in bed until he went to sleep. After a while they started kissing. Sylvia began to depend upon Brett for attention and affection. The physical involvement developed into episodes of mutual fondling, oral sex, and attempted intercourse over several months until Brett's sister became suspicious of the relationship and called a child protection agency. When first interviewed, Brett said that Sylvia was his "best friend." He described his sexual involvement with Sylvia but made no claim of coercion. However, after therapy, Brett began to perceive Sylvia as having taken advantage of him and became very angry with her.

When confronted, Sylvia admitted to being sexually involved with Brett, took full responsibility for the behavior, and voiced deep remorse and guilt for "betraying" him. She denied that she had ever been sexually involved with a juvenile before and she felt that the sexual activity had occurred because they each needed some love in their lives and the "chemistry" between them was just so strong. She said that at the time she had not felt she was engaging in the sexual behaviors alone because Brett was a very aggressive child whose responses encouraged her. She saw him as the dominant one in the relationship and reported becoming physically ill at the thought of losing him and his affection. She said that she cared for him more than she had cared for anyone in her life. Although she periodically felt guilty over the sexual relationship, she felt unable to stop it. After the abuse was disclosed, she reported feeling suicidal and despondent over her recent "loss" of Brett.

Sylvia's lifelong emotional isolation, low self-esteem, and lack of a satisfying relationship with her husband made her susceptible to reach out to Brett, with whom she felt safe and who reminded her of the one emotionally satisfying relationship in her life. Her involvement with Brett developed out of her need for emotional intimacy and gratification from a special person rather than from sexual desire or lust.

Profile of a Male Sex Offender

In the early 1960s, in a typical northside Chicago neighborhood, everyone knew each other. This true story is about a little girl named Ann and the sexual abuse that changed her life. She began her story by explaining the sad and traumatic incident when she was just a child. Ann remembers being 5 years old, a few months before she entered kindergarten.

Al lived with his family just two doors away from Ann. He was a child molester who went unnoticed because no one would have thought or believed that he was capable of being devious and manipulative because he was a happy, well respected, and likable guy under the guise of a Sunday school teacher and Boy Scout leader.

Ann remembers that, after church, her family and Al's family would spend time together in the backyard and often go on picnics. Her mom and dad were going through a divorce at the time. Her father was often not home during these Sunday get-togethers. Ann remembers that Al always had candy and small toys with him and always gave her something whenever he saw her. At one of these Sunday gatherings, Al called Ann downstairs into the basement of his home. He whispered to her, "Let's keep this our little secret," as he placed her hand on his genitals on the outside of his pants. He assured her, "I am your friend." Al would always orchestrate a way to get her alone and he did it in a way that would not raise any suspicion. He would always whisper, "Let's go play secret friends."

When Al did get her alone, he started by fondling and exploring her tiny body with his large hands. He would lift up her dress and take down her panties and penetrate her with his finger. He would often hug Ann long and inappropriately, holding her close to his body. He always said, "Don't tell anyone. Your mom and dad have enough problems going through their divorce."

Ann mentioned that, at such a young age, it was hard to fathom time frames. She believes the abuse happened more than 6 times but less than 20. She believes the secret meetings occurred over the course of from 6 months to a year. Ann said that she felt Al used this opportunity to take advantage of the situation because of the divorce.

The next scenario changed everything. On one occasion, Ann remembers Al leading her upstairs to a second-floor bedroom in his house. She remembers Al's brother-in-law waiting there in the bedroom. As soon as she walked in, Al's brother-in-law took out his penis from his pants. Ann could recall how scared she was. She started crying and ran from the house. This was the first time that she had seen a man's penis. Ann still did not tell anyone about this. She believes that she did not have the vocabulary. Soon after this happened, her parents were finally divorced. Ann, her mom, and her brother moved into an apartment in the same neighborhood, only a few blocks away. Al and his wife still came by for Sunday dinner after church services. Something in Ann's mind told her not to be alone with Al anymore. Al and his wife eventually stopped coming over to the apartment and the abuse stopped.

Ann's story represents a textbook case of grooming. She feels that she was chosen because her family's environment was in turmoil. Al operated on an element of trust with her family, friends, and other neighbors. Ann said, "He wasn't hurting me. I did not know what was going on." She remembers that Al was always around and playing with kids in the neighborhood and she always felt that he had abused other kids. Ann is now a grown woman living in Chicago.

In My Opinion

Ms. Maryanne Leach

Maryanne Leach, LCPC, is a therapist at a non-for-profit social service agency in Chicago that interacts with sex offenders who have mental health issues. She said that sexual offenders need help in more ways than just counseling (personal communication). She mentioned that when a sex offender is released from the Illinois Department of Corrections, most of the time he is released without any state identification. This, in itself, can cause problems in getting any type of service. This includes Medicare and Medicaid, medications, and linkage to the counseling services that are so desperately needed. Sexual predators' first hurdle in getting any kinds of services is showing proof that they are who they say they are.

Ms. Leach's first session with the sex offender involves an intake mental health assessment that lasts a minimum of 3 hours. She noted that often the sexual offender has a history of having been sexually abused. When the abuse occurs in the childhood years, the child often views this behavior as normal and does not recognize it as dysfunctional. Eventually, for the unaware child, the behavior may surface in terms of the child's sexually acting out, which comes to the attention of social services or others around him.

The abused child can develop physical and emotional difficulties. One's sense of self usually develops out of a healthy relationship bond with one's parent or caretaker. The child learns how to cope and emotionally self-regulate through this healthy relationship. For the child who is in the process of development, sexual abuse can affect the ability to attach and bond with caretakers. This results in relationship difficulties and a lack of trust, which extends from childhood all the way into adulthood. The sexual abuse affects the child's ability to develop a healthy internalized sense of self.

The abuse also affects the child's neurobiological development. The child can show emotional signs of depression, withdrawal, anxiety, and feelings of worthlessness. He or she may have great difficulty regulating emotions. As the child or victim matures into an adult, it is more likely that he or she will develop psychiatric problems and/or antisocial behavior. Some of these conditions may include depression, anxiety disorders, eating disorders, self-mutilation, compulsive disorders, or posttraumatic stress. The victim may also develop problems with drugs and alcohol in attempts to regulate emotions or block out flashbacks of the sexual abuse.

The act of sexual abuse has less to do with sex and more to do with aggression. It is a false perception of power. The sexual abuser may act out a reliving of his own abuse, only this time reversing the power roles. The abuser may perceive the act as a way of putting himself in control. Abusers can, at times, be loners. They are unable to develop healthy adult relationships. For all of these reasons, treatment is a necessary reality.

Ms. Leach articulated that sex offenders frequently minimize what they have done, and they are often not aware of how sexual exploitation has affected their victims. In her experience, the sex offenders rarely express any remorse and have a tendency to blame everyone but themselves. At times, they may even blame the child or victim stating that he or she was the promiscuous one. The biggest complaint that sex offenders have expressed is that they are angry because they are restricted in what they can do, where they can live, and to whom they must constantly be accountable (authorities).

In her present job, Ms. Leach considers herself more of a social worker assisting her clients in providing case management, housing, food, and assistance in getting proper medical attention. She does not follow their counseling long term but expressed that she does not think that they can be cured. In her opinion, because of all the factors leading up to and contributing to this behavior, the prognosis for a change of behavior for the sexual offender is not good.

Definitions of Chapter Key Terms

Adaptation: Adjusting to one's environment. Most sexual predators adapt to the environment of the victim they seek out.

Age of consent: This term varies depending on the state and the jurisdiction. The age of consent is often the age a person is considered or thought of as capable of consenting or acquiescing to sexual acts. Most states in the United States have their own age of consent, all agreeing that 16 years of age up to 18 years of age should be considered the age of consent.

Approach strategies: A calculated and systematic plan that sexual predators use to get to know and entice their victim.

Character: A person's moral and ethical actions. Sexual predators will often show this side of their personality when they are out in the public.

Deception: Misleading fabrication with the intention or act of deceiving someone. The act of being crafty, often giving the false impression of being a good person. Most, if not all, sexual predators have mastered the art of this behavior.

Denial: Denying that the accusations, allegations, or complaints against oneself are true. Most sexual offenders refuse to admit the truth or the reality of their actions taking place. They often deny or repudiate that a problem even exists.

Desire: An inclination or preference to covet things or a person. Sex offenders often have this feeling that accompanies an unsatisfied condition.

Emotional blackmail: The pressure of using penetrating threats by way of a victim's sensitive and delicate state of mind or circumstances.

Fantasies: Forming mental images, visions, or aspirations using imagination or conceptualization. This is most often associated with sexual predators, pedophiles, and sex offenders in their conquest of realizing what has replayed often in their mind.

Fascination: The capacity or influence of being passionately interested in someone or something. Most sexual predators have a fascination with sexually abusing their victim.

Grooming: The gradual erosion of sexual boundaries through plotting and calculated moves after gaining trust from the victim. This is the first step of the process that sexual predators use in their quest to sexually abuse their victims. This type of grooming often involves developing the child's sexual awareness and may take days, weeks, months, or, in some cases, years.

Guilt: Remorse caused by feeling responsible for, embarrassment about, regret for, shame about, and culpability for being the victim in a sexual crime.

Isolation strategies: A careful set of plans devised by the sexual offender or predator to get the victim alone in an attempt to have sex.

Manipulation: A sexual predator skillfully controls the situation with the intent of taking advantage of his or her intended victim.

Masturbation: Stimulation or manipulation of one's genitals.

Online grooming: Using the Internet to manipulate and develop trust of a minor as a first step in gaining information to use to meet the intended victim. The final triumph is to be able to sexually manipulate the victim when that meeting occurs.

Pattern of behavior: Routine or regular behavior. The sexual predator has two different and succinct patterns of behavior. One is how he acts during his daily routine or how the public perceives that person to be (e.g., caring dad, businessperson, friend). The other is how he acts in the surroundings of his victim (e.g., conniving, calculating, manipulating).

Persuasion: Coaxing interaction often used by the sexual offender through reasoning, rationalization, and assurance that the nature of the sexual encounter is normal, acceptable, and appropriate.

Secrecy: Custom or practice of keeping or maintaining privacy. A sexual predator depends on secrecy and concealment, especially if he is sexually involved with a young, innocent victim.

Seduction: Often associated with enticing a victim from veracious or virtuous behavior to commit a sexual act. Sex offenders will charm their victim for sexual favors or sexual intercourse.

Trust: Often associated with the victim believing in the honesty, righteousness, and sincerity of the sex offender.

References

Adams, C., and Fay, J. (2003). *Helping your child recover from sexual abuse*. Seattle, WA: University of Washington Press.

Berliner, L., and Conte, J. R. (1990). The process of victimization: The victim's perspective. *Child Abuse and Neglect* 14: 29–40.

Campagna, A. F., and Martin, A. (2004). Predators, pedophiles, rapists, and other sex offenders: Who they are, how they operate, and how we can protect ourselves and our children. *Journal of the American Academy of Child & Adolescent Psychiatry* 43 (11): 1449.

Collier, A. (2009). How to recognize grooming. SafeTeens.com.

Dandescu, A., and Wolfe, R. (2003). Considerations on fantasy used by child molesters and exhibitionists. *Sexual Abuse: A Journal of Research and Treatment* 15: 297–305.

English, K. (1997, January). Managing adult sex offenders in the community. *National Institute of Justice Research in Brief* (US Department of Justice), pp. 1–11.

MU researchers reveal communication tactics used by sexual predators to entrap children. *NewsRx Science*, 2008, p. 13.

Roberts, J. (2001). *Violence against women: Adult criminal sexual assault offenders*. Internal publication. Chicago Police Department.

Rufo, R. (2007). An investigation of online sexual predation of minors by convicted male offenders. Dissertation, Argosy University, Atlanta, GA.

Salter, A. C. (2003). *Predators, pedophiles, rapists and other sex offenders: Who they are and how they operate*. New York: Basic Books.

Child Abuse and Incest   3

It is empowering to have a secret.

Victim of a sexual predator

Thirteen-year-old girl[s are] child[ren]; whether they are starting to look a little older, they are pretending to be adults. They are not adults; they are just big children. Thirteen-year-old girls tend to run on attention, and pedophiles know this and they lavish them with attention.

Mom whose daughter was a victim of sexual assault

Child Abuse

Child abuse is the mistreatment and exploitation of a child, often by a family member who is most often male. Child abuse is also putting a child in imminent jeopardy that is most likely to cause the child severe harm. This chapter will focus on sexual abuse, physical abuse (nonaccidental, physical injury), emotional abuse (behavioral), and neglect (abandonment).

Sexual Abuse of a Child

The sexual abuse of a child encompasses any sexual activity with or sexual assault on a child by an adult or by an older sibling before the child has reached the age of legal consent. The most common type of sexual abuse is known as a dyadic relationship: one victim and one offender. Many states have made sexual assaults felonies that are punishable by lengthy prison terms. The length of the punishment is determined by the age difference between the offender and the victim. When the offender is an adult, the court system will often increase the minimum amount of the time to which he or she is sentenced. The adult sexual offender will often be required to meet strict conditions for release.

The perpetrator is frequently a male member of the family that is directly or indirectly related to the child. Most sexual abuse offenders have often been the victims of sexual abuse themselves. Sexual abuse includes sexual touching or fondling with hands, mouth, or objects, or copulation (penetration). Children can be coerced into disrobing and exposing themselves, viewing pornography and watching adults disrobe, or engaging in sexual activity.

Physical force is not often necessary since the perpetrator is apt to be someone with whom the child has a trusting relationship and is most likely in a position of authority over the child.

Perpetrators go to great lengths to conceal sexual abuse, oftentimes believing their sexual behavior is acceptable and not necessarily harmful to the child. Children who have been sexually abused may not report the behavior due to threats or a lack of understanding of what has happened. In addition, they may be confused by the simultaneous physical arousal they may feel and the clearly covert and possibly threatening nature of the event. Evidence of abuse may show in

- physical symptoms, such as rashes, redness, swelling, bruising, or injuries to the genital area and blood or discharge in bedding or underwear
- advanced sexual knowledge for the child's age
- provocative or seductive behavior toward others
- bed-wetting after the child has established the ability to stay dry through the night
- declining peer relationships
- fear of a person, place, or object associated with the abuse
- changes in school behavior or performance

In addition, older children or adolescents may begin to act out or to withdraw, use drugs or alcohol, begin to harm themselves, or become preoccupied with thoughts of death.

What is most disturbing in today's society is the sexual offender's willingness to commit a wanton and carnal offense against an innocent victim. Adults who sexually abuse children are considered to be among the most serious deviants in any society. Arcus (1998) articulated that children are said to be sexually abused when they experience sexual contact with an adult or older child through coercion and deceptive manipulation and they do not possess sufficient maturity to understand the nature of the acts or provide informed consent. Dr. David Finkelhor (2003), a leading authority in the field of child sexual abuse, explains the suffering a victim goes through, such as confusion about sexual identity, confusion about getting and giving care, low self-esteem, depression, and questioning the trustworthiness of others, along with guilt, shame, anxiety, and loss of respect for adult authority.

A Female Victim's Perspective on Sexual Abuse

I recently interviewed a woman, Lydia (not her real name), who was a victim, along with her siblings (two sisters and one brother), of sexual abuse by their father. Her father came from a large, poor family on the West Coast and eventually settled in the Midwest. Lydia's father, Don (not his real name), was the second oldest of four boys and three girls. Don came from a very abusive home. His father had a temper and was known to be physically abusive to all of his children. There were allegations of sexual abuse of his children, but only his youngest daughter ever spoke about it. It was apparent that the circle of sexual abuse eventually affected all of the children. This is where the story begins:

Lydia explained that her earliest recollection of abuse was at the age of 7; it continued until she was in her early teens. Her mom worked nights and this gave her dad, Don, ample time to be alone with the children at night. Don was active in his children's lives and professed to be a loving and devoted father. That loving image of a father was soon shattered. Lydia was the oldest girl and thus the first to be sexually abused. There were many instances where her father tried to manipulate and penetrate Lydia with his penis.

Lydia's father would take a seemingly playful and innocent encounter with his children and turn it into an activity of a sexual nature. He would hold their legs up when they did handstands and acrobatics poses and it would not take long for his hand to touch them inappropriately between their legs. These types of games were a daily activity and he even went so far as to masturbate in front of them. Her younger female siblings were also affected by the sexual advances of their father. The second oldest girl was molested in the family car.

Lydia often felt trapped; she said that her father tried to create opportunities to sexually abuse her, even when her mom was home. She tried to fight him off, but was not very successful. Despite her crying and tears and asking her father to please stop, her pleas fell on deaf ears. Her father would often pick Lydia up and take her into the basement so that her screams would not be heard. He would make sure the other children were not around. This occurred an average of three or four times a month and Lydia dreaded the nights that her mom went to work.

Lydia had enough of the abuse and even encouraged her dad to seek out other women. She told her mom about the constant sexual abuse. Her mom was in denial and did not immediately accept this account of her husband's behavior, often blaming Lydia for his actions. Her mom eventually asked her husband to leave. Two weeks passed before Lydia's father came back home. The abuse started up once again, but this time her father became mean in the process. Lydia just accepted his abusive behavior and hoped that one day the abuse would end. She began to catch her father watching her when she took a shower or when she was undressing in her room.

Lydia always had very good grades, but this soon changed. She could not take the emotional and physical pain of the sexual abuse any longer. After 3 years of fighting her father off; Lydia just accepted that this was how her life was going to be. She never told the police because she feared the repercussions from her mom and her already abusive father. Her grades soon plummeted as her interest in school waned. Lydia began acting out in school, frequently being suspended for cutting classes. She started hanging out with the wrong crowd, drinking, and experimenting with drugs. She was confused and worked several jobs just to stay away from home. Her self-esteem hit an all-time low; she felt worthless and soon became sexually promiscuous.

At this time, Lydia's father focused his attention on his youngest daughter, again inappropriately touching and fondling her every chance that he could get. At one point, Lydia's younger sister spoke to her school counselor about the sexual advances of her dad and their troubling family life. The school counselor began to investigate the situation and began asking questions about the family life, especially the relationship with her dad. The youngest daughter mentioned the counselor's inquiries to her mom, who threatened that if the police were called or if there were any outside interference, it would only break up the family. The younger girl knew speaking with her mom was fruitless and only confided her father's sexual misconduct to her immediate girlfriends. She ultimately lied to the school counselor, saying that her father's promiscuous behavior had stopped and that everything at home was fine. The school counselor believed her story. Soon after, she too became promiscuous and had little trust in men. The youngest daughter had mixed feelings of love and hate for her father, saying that he took away all of the trust that she had ever had.

At the age of 15, Lydia became pregnant by her boyfriend. Now she was forced to stay in a relationship; she moved out of her home and in with her boyfriend and his parents. She soon married, but knew early on that this marriage would not be the fairy tale life that she had often dreamt about. Their relationship was strained, and Lydia knew that she needed counseling. Her husband was very patient with her, even though their sex life was affected. He never really understood what she had gone through and how deeply she had been affected emotionally. In spite of counseling, the relationship continued to be affected by her past and their marriage ended after 17 years.

Counseling on a personal level seemed to help Lydia. She still went to visit her parents, reluctantly taking her daughters to see their grandparents. Lydia kept a watchful eye on her daughters, especially when they wanted to be with grandpa. Lydia noticed the same signs she had experienced with her father. She told her mom that she would not come over anymore because she would not allow her father accessibility to her daughters. Lydia even asked her dad, "Can I trust you with my kids, now that you are older?" His reply was "Don't trust me."

At the age of 40, Lydia remarried. Her father called and said that he had cancer and wanted to make amends with the entire family. He wanted to come clean. Lydia's husband noted that every time she was in her father's presence, she always acted differently and was not herself. Her father apologized for the pain that he had put her through. Lydia explained that her father never cried, but the day he called on the phone, he cried for over 10 minutes. She said that she felt that he truly was remorseful. Two years later, Lydia's father died of cancer.

After Lydia's father died she finally began healing. When she thinks back, she still feels angry and she always had that gut feeling that he did molest others. But in the end, she said that he was still her dad. She accepted her father's death and the day that he died her nightmares finally went away.

It was never known if he sexually abused his only son; but it is assumed that he was abused. His son refuses to talk to anyone about it, but has shown signs that he has been affected by his father's behavior. Currently, he is a heavy drug user; he has been arrested many times for DUI and trespassing. Lydia said that her brother's life is a mess and his situation is not very good. He often acts out and reacts to everything in a negative way.

Traits of Female Victims of Sexual Abuse

- Female child victims in incest cases are reluctant to report the offense for fear of upsetting the family structure.
- Some female victims will occupy a dominant role within the family system.
- Some female victims will present a passive affect.
- Female victims may attempt to nurture or parent their parents, repressing their own emotional pain.
- There may be an attempt to appear unkempt to ward off male attention because the victim may believe that she somehow is the cause of sexual interest.
- Some females will overcompensate by grooming themselves in a meticulous fashion because they believe that their bodies are unclean.
- A child female victim will often attempt to minimize her trauma to schoolteachers, police, or therapists.
- Guilt and shame occur if some pleasure was experienced during the sexual event.
- Acting out behavior can be displayed.
- Running away can be an alternative (Flora 2001).

A Male Victim's Perspective on Sexual Abuse

An interview that I conducted revealed a true story of a young man's dilemma; he was sexually assaulted by a female sexual predator and assaulted twice by two different male sexual predators, one of whom was a relative. Terry (not his real name) went into counseling when he was 24 years old. It was through this counseling and therapy that he was able to reveal the following exploitations in his life.

Terry remembers that, when he was 7 years old, he always accompanied his mom on visits to her neighbor's house. These visits happened two or three times a week. Terry recalls that these visits were not social in nature—his mom and her friend got high on cocaine every time. The neighbor had an older daughter who was forced to babysit him. These weekly meetings created a great opportunity for this 18-year-old heavyset girl to seduce him, making him touch and kiss her breasts as she fondled him. She would often pull his pants down and mount Terry, rubbing her genitals against his. He knew that what she was doing was not right, but she would threaten to hurt him if he said anything to anyone, especially his mother. Terry always gave an excuse why he did not want to go with his mom on these weekly visits, but she insisted because drugs were the only thing on her mind. This abuse took place until the neighbor moved away about a year later. To this day, Terry is bitter toward heavyset females and it takes him a very long time to trust any female.

Terry was 13 years old when he was abandoned by his mom and went to live with his aunt. He remembers his aunt as a caring person who took in other family members as well. His cousin Matthew, 26, who lived in Florida and had served time in prison for drugs, was also visiting his aunt for the weekend. One Saturday night, Terry and Matt were playing video games. Terry recalls Matt commenting about his basketball shorts and the way they fit his butt and asking whether he was a virgin or had ever had an orgasm. Terry told Matt that he was a virgin, and he did not know what an orgasm was; he said, "I guess I never had one." After about an hour, Terry went up to bed and fell asleep.

In the middle of the night, Matt came to Terry's room and asked him to come downstairs. Terry grudgingly went downstairs and noticed that everything was unusually dark; even the kitchen light, which was normally on, was turned off. Terry felt that something was wrong as Matt ordered him to come over to him. Matt grabbed him by the genitals and told him to be still. Terry was in shock and could only think, "Oh wow, I can't believe this is happening." He tried to pull away; this infuriated Matt, who held on more tightly and demanded that Terry do as he was told and be quiet.

Matt started to masturbate Terry, who knew that something was happening that should not be happening. He was in a total state of confusion. Matt took Terry's penis in his mouth, as Terry's heart began beating faster than ever. This was his favorite cousin; he trusted him and had never known him to act this way. Matt told Terry to lie down on his back as Terry ejaculated for the first time ever. Matt ejaculated as well and told Terry to clean up and that he could not tell anybody that this had happened. All that raced through Terry's mind was, "Why is this happening to me?"

Terry was 14 years old when he called the Department of Children and Family Services (DCFS) on his mom for her heavy drug use and being abusive and neglectful. He was very skinny and reserved when he was sent to a group home that housed young men who were wards of the state. This particular group home housed eight young men, ages 14 to 18, who were also abused and neglected. DJ was a 17-year-old juvenile sex offender who soon befriended Terry. Terry did not know that DJ was in this group home because of his past, which included many sexual abuse allegations. Terry was not comfortable in this environment and did not trust anyone. DJ had the room next door to Terry, and he would often try to talk to Terry about church and the teachings of the Bible.

One day, Terry was lying face down on his bed when DJ came into his room and began to speak about religious scripture and the Bible. Moments later, DJ jumped on Terry's back, pinning him down on the bed as he tried to pull down his basketball shorts and to penetrate him. DJ covered Terry's mouth and whispered, "You better not tell anyone and even if you do, no one will ever believe you. Everyone thinks you're gay anyway." Terry tightened up his entire body and would not allow DJ to violate him. After a few minutes, DJ got off him and masturbated in front of him. DJ left the room as Terry headed down the hall to the bathroom and showered for what felt like hours. Terry knew this was the only place in the group home where he felt safe. Only after the staff came looking for him did he go back to his room. After this incident, DJ would always try to get Terry alone and would either grab his own genitals or masturbate in front of him. Terry tried to avoid DJ at all costs.

On April 16, 1996, at 6 a.m., Terry woke up feeling pain in his rectum. Tears started running down his face as he noticed that his basketball shorts were pulled down to his ankles. He got up and ran to the kitchen to find the staff and cried uncontrollably, saying, "Don't ever leave me alone again please" as he ran out of the house. Terry went to church and asked God to give him the strength to say something to make this abuse stop. A short while later, Terry walked into the group home to speak to the director, a middle-aged woman who was always compassionate, but strict. The staff had earlier informed her that something was wrong and that Terry had left the building crying. The director was waiting for Terry when he walked in. She asked him what was wrong as she hugged him; Terry cried and told her everything.

The director summoned DJ to a meeting between the two boys and asked him if the allegations of sexual misconduct were true; DJ admitted that they were. The director stated that DJ had violated the agreement not to offend again. (DJ had previously molested two young men at the group home.) DJ was sent to another facility in Texas 2 days later. Terry stayed at the group home until his sophomore year of high school, when he found a new foster home to live in.

In Terry's short life he stayed in six foster homes and three shelters. He admitted that drugs were bad, but that they had a good use as well. He started doing drugs more and more. He said, "If it wasn't for the drugs, I would have cracked up a long time ago." He continually questioned himself, asking, "Am

I doing something wrong? Is my demeanor prompting this behavior?" Terry admits that counseling has taught him to cope with his past. He has stopped doing drugs, enrolled in college, and recently started a relationship with a young lady in his class.

Traits of Male Victims of Sexual Abuse

- A male victim fears being identified as unmanly and is ashamed because he was unable to protect himself.
- If molested by a male, he may fear others will believe he is a homosexual.
- If he was sexually abused by a female adult, he will be reluctant to report the offense and thus challenge society's standard of masculinity.
- Boys molested by their mothers assume responsibility for the action.
- Male victims fear that no one will believe their report of sexual assault.
- Male victims fear that nothing will be done if sexual abuse is committed by a woman.
- Boys fear that they may be harmed again if they report the sexual assault since the offender has threatened them and warned them not to tell (Flora 2001).

Terms Related to Sexual Abuse

- Sodomy (anal penetration)
- Sexual touching or fondling
- Objects that may penetrate any or all body orifices
- Removal of any clothing
- Sexual relations
- Sexually transmitted disease
- Urinary tract infections
- Lack of awareness and consent
- Coercion or manipulation by trust
- Sexual assault: conduct of a sexual nature, including indecent behavior toward someone; often associated with fear, anxiety, shame, humiliation, and mental suffering

Incest

Incest is defined as a sexual relationship that may also include sexual abuse of or sexual intimacy with a child by a family member or relative in a position of trust and authority. Incest can cause other problems for victims in many other ways. An incestuous relationship jeopardizes not only a child's physical safety but also his or her emotional and psychological well-being, sense of trust, and self-esteem. If the child cannot trust members of the family, how will he or she feel around others in society throughout life? Incest violates the laws of humanity, government, faith, and morality. Incest takes away the innocence of childhood.

Many studies have revealed that most sexual abuse of children is done by a family member and that this is the most underreported of all crimes. The most incestuous relationships occur between a male relative and younger female children. This crime often occurs with the incestuous relationship between a parent and a child (most often father–daughter and/or father–son), grandparent and a child (grandfather–grandson, grandfather–granddaughter), brother–sister, uncle–aunt, and niece–nephew.

The most commonly reported cases of incest involve father and daughter and stepfather and stepdaughter relationships, sometimes referred to as "intrafamilial child sex abuse." Oldest daughters are more likely to be victims of incest. A few reasons why incestuous fathers molest their daughters include the following:

- The father is dominant.
- The father thinks of the child as his possession, with which he can do as he chooses.
- There is discord with the mother of the child.
- The child has accepted the inherent responsible female role.

This type of crime is not acceptable, goes against social norms, and is considered taboo in most societies and cultures. Incest is often considered one of the most common forms of child abuse. Some of the deviant acts a predator may impose on a child include the following:

- Sexual penetration, including intercourse and sodomy
- Any sexual contact, including touching, kissing, or fondling
- Masturbation or manual stimulation of genitals
- Oral–genital contact
- Exhibitionism
- Exposure to pornography

A family member guilty of incest will use different methods of persuasion and often manipulate the victim. Valente (2005) noted that the child does not solicit these interactions but rather is manipulated by trust, coercion, or violence. Isolation and secrecy are part of the grooming process that often comes before the actual incestuous act. Like sexual partners, incest offenders will have a trusted relationship that uses intricate methods of persuasion to manipulate victims before the actual act of incest occurs.

Child abuse through sexual contact is almost always continuous in an incestuous relationship. The average age at which a child is victimized in an incestuous relationship is between 6 and 13 years old. Being trapped in an incestuous relationship is difficult to imagine—especially becoming accustomed to years of torment with little chance of it stopping. Being a victim of incest often lasts long after the abuse stops. These patterns of learned behavior and psychological power over victims will most likely produce the future sexual offender.

According to the National Children's Advocacy Centers (2010), between January and June of 2009, nearly 103,000 suspected offenders were investigated nationwide. This facility offers medical and emotional support to victims while investigating the allegations of child abuse. More than 32,320 of the suspected offenders were parents of the abused children, averaging about one-third of the cases reported; 21,710 were another relative, averaging about one-fifth of the cases reported, and 6,420 were stepparents, averaging about 1/16 of the cases reported.

In a study funded by a grant from the National Center on Child Abuse, Williams and Finkelhor (1992) found that there are five distinct types of incestuous fathers:

Type 1: a sexually preoccupied offender who is characterized by a special interest in his victim, usually from the time when the victim is very young. This type of offender usually begins molesting a child before the child is 6 and continues the molestation past the victim's puberty.

Type 2: the adolescent regressive offender. This type of offender has conscious sexual interest in the victim but usually does not begin molesting until a victim approaches or reaches puberty.

Type 3: the instrumental sexual gratifier. He will use the victim as a vehicle for his sexual fantasy. These types of offenders are separate in their offending and they often associate their actions with remorse.

Type 4: an offender that is emotionally dependent and often lonely and depressed; sex is not the primary motivator. These individuals will often romanticize about the need for closeness and intimacy.

Type 5: often considered in angry retaliators. This offender demonstrates a very low sexual arousal toward the victim and instead uses a sexual assault to focus on his anger. The victim will be assaulted in retaliation for a spouse's real or imagined infidelity or because the offender was abandoned by a spouse.

The effects of incest can cause a child possibly (perhaps intentionally) to forget or block out what has been done to him or her. Children exposed to incest may experience the following:

- Nightmares, flashbacks, or regressive behavior
- Confusion because of the physical and mental abuse and because of what has happened
- Substance abuse and/or addictive behavior
- Prostitution and/or promiscuity
- Depression, loneliness, or withdrawal from normal or daily activities
- Cognitive, reasoning, physical, and behavioral problems
- Delinquency or dropping out of school
- Anxiety, apprehension, or age-inappropriate sexual behavior
- Cruelty and/or self-injury
- Posttraumatic stress disorder
- Secretiveness, trust issues, and low self-esteem

The trauma of abuse often has a devastating effect on a male victim. These victims will keep the manipulation to themselves and will seldom report the exploitation to anyone because it may question their masculinity. Valente (2005) stated that sexual abuse is a serious problem and boys and men who have been abused rarely report this experience unless asked during a therapeutic or counseling session. The fear of reprisals, stigma against homosexuality, and loss of self-esteem make boys less likely to disclose the abuse than girls. According to Valente, "Supporting self-esteem is a critical intervention because these abused children believe they are damaged, unlovable, and worthless."

In some instances, male children who survive sexual abuse struggle with guilt and anger. This anger manifests itself in frustration and revenge. Retaliation eventually motivates the child to abuse others when he grows older. Valente (2005) said that most boys that are sexually abused may have impaired social relationships and self-destructive behavior. These children will often feel betrayed and may often question why this terrible experience is happening to them. Victims often experience—at the time of the incestuous act and later as adults—a sense of shame, a feeling of powerlessness, and the loss of self-worth.

Williams and Finkelhor (1992) indicated in their review of 45 studies that two common patterns of psychological responses to incest are posttraumatic stress symptomology and an increase in a sexualized behavior. This behavior may include playing with dolls in a sexual manner, putting objects into anuses or vaginas, excessive or public masturbation, seductive behavior, and age-inappropriate sexual knowledge and behavior. Incest can be considered a traumatic incident that will affect a child's growing up in a number of ways. A child subject to incest can experience anxiety, depression, or alcohol or drug abuse and may attempt or commit suicide. A child may often feel that she will be punished or blamed if the sexual abuse is revealed and often thinks that no one will believe her anyway. Statistics have shown that children victims of incest have a difficult time dealing with the anxiety of not being able to divulge the injustice of what happened to them and living with the guilt and shame for the rest of their lives.

A child victim of incest may experience different aggregates of abuse by a parent, sibling, or family member. Contributing to this are

- Frequency of abuse
- Severity of abuse
- Duration of abuse
- Type of sexual abuse
- Age of the victim at the time the abuse started
- Age difference between the victim and the perpetrator
- Use of force or penetration
- Relationship with the abuser
- Emotional and psychological impact of keeping a secret
- Punishment for revealing abuse

Recent studies have also indicated a rise in older brothers abusing younger siblings. The incestuous act of a brother toward a sister is more likely a display of power over his siblings. Boys who commit incest with their siblings often come from a home that has only one parent or in which both parents are absent. Victims often experience—both at the time of the incestuous act and later as adults—a sense of shame, a feeling of powerlessness, and the loss of their childhood.

Many incest offenders often have distorted views of their relationship with the family member whom they are abusing and they

> claim a true and deep love for the child;
> say that the love experienced was mutual;
> take advantage of the trust the child has in the relationship, which makes it easy to abuse his power over the child; and
> often block out the criminal ramifications of the crime and the effect that it will have on the victim.

Incest is considered a statutory crime and is often a felony in most jurisdictional courts in the United States. The purpose of incest statutes, laws, and legislation is to prevent sexual intercourse between individual family members. Laws vary from state to state regarding extended family relationships such as stepparents and a child (stepparent and stepdaughter, stepparent and stepson), and brothers- and sisters-in-law. Some countries allow consensual adult incest, which is most often considered a victimless crime because it is rarely reported.

The Illinois criminal code states that a person who commits incest will receive a much lighter sentence than if he or she molests a stranger's child. In Illinois, if the abuser molests a stranger's child, he or she may receive up to 30 years in prison. If the abuser molests his or her children, a much lighter sentence than expected or even probation may be the result.

Many cases of incest are difficult to prosecute because they are generally the hardest cases to prove. There is seldom any physical evidence unless the victim comes forward or the case is reported by someone. In this case, a physical examination may be needed to substantiate the sexual penetration. A child who is at the mercy of incestuous abuse will more than likely hold on to this dark secret and never come forward. Even if the child does come forward, there is always a possibility that he or she may not be believed because it is the child's word against the perpetrator's word. It is difficult to imagine, but jurors hearing an incest case may be somewhat reluctant to convict a family member if there is not sufficient evidence and the case is based solely on the testimony and statements of the child.

There has always been controversy within the judicial system when it comes to charging offenders who are related to their victims. Some states have discounted the charges because of the hardship the families may experience and other issues that may prevail due to incarceration. Prosecutors give some offenders probation because of the relevancy of the family situation. Some judges have returned the guilty adult family member, oftentimes the father of the child who was abused, to the same home where the abuse originally occurred. The severity of the sexual assault and the chance of the abuse recurring could be the only deciding factor that would prevent this from taking place. State Rep. Jay Hoffman, D-Illinois, said that "a predator, regardless of whether he's related to the victim, is still a sexual predator. The victim suffers as much, if not more, if the individual is related."

Sexual Violence

The Centers for Disease Control (CDC) and Prevention (2006) defines sexual violence as

> nonconsensual completed or attempted contact between the penis and the vulva or the penis and the anus involving penetration; nonconsensual contact between the mouth and the penis, vulva, or anus; nonconsensual penetration of the anal or genital opening of another person by a hand, finger, or other

object; nonconsensual intentional touching, either directly or through the clothing, of the genitalia, anus, groin, breast, inner thigh, or buttocks; or nonconsensual noncontact acts of a sexual nature such as voyeurism and verbal or behavior sexual harassment.

All these acts also qualify as sexual violence if they are committed against someone who is unable to consent or refuse.

Stockholm Syndrome

In terms of sexual offenders, the Stockholm syndrome is a unique phenomenon in which a victim becomes sympathetic and shows compassion for the abuser. This condition often affects females more than it affects males. This book highlights female victims but male victims do exist. In the case of a female victim, the physical and emotional duress experienced goes beyond comprehension. The only contact that the victim has is with her abuser because she is continuously isolated from society. After a while, the victim will develop loyalty to and empathy for her abuser and see this as a strategy for survival. This is often the victim's way of coping with the situation. She may even feel that she has caused the abuse and is always worried about retaliation if she were to seek help. It is not uncommon for a victim to suffer posttraumatic stress disorder. For example, Phillip Garrido kidnapped Jaycee Lee Dugard and held her captive for 18 years. She was believed to have been affected by this experience because she had ample opportunities to escape but never did. Other victims often traumatized by this behavior are sex trafficking victims.

Profile of a Female Sex Offender

Mandy was a 35-year-old gym teacher in a small city in California. Rumors had been circulating throughout the school of how friendly Mandy was with her students, especially the boys. She was verbally warned to act more professionally by the principal, who put her on probation for the rest of the year. She rented a motel room and partied with three teenage girls and a few of her son's 14-year-old friends. Police were called when someone reported suspicious activity in the room. When police arrived, they found a few of the kids, undressed, and marijuana, liquor, beer, and discarded condoms on the floor.

When Mandy was first arrested she denied doing anything wrong. Later, in the police interview room, she admitted having sex with at least two 14-year-old runaways and her son's 15-year-old boyhood friend. At court

Mandy apologized to the judge for her actions and said that the children would never be the same because of what she had done. She admitted that she needed counseling and knew that she had been addicted to sex for years. The judged sentenced Mandy to 4–7 years in prison. Her son was sent to live with a family member.

Profile of a Male Sex Offender

Rich, a 160-pound, 6-foot white male with black hair and brown eyes, was born in Brooklyn, New York. He was placed on the FBI's Ten Most Wanted Fugitives List as a sexual predator. He was sought for engaging in lewd acts in Long Beach, California, with several girls under 10 years old. Rich had also produced and possessed pornographic images of these sex acts, and most of them were found on his computer. He would often gain the trust of his victims' parents and then befriend their children. Rich would ultimately become the greatest friend to the children he met; he entertained the girls by allowing them to play with his pet, watch television, and use his computer to play games. A few of these girls also took short trips with him.

In July 2001, a state arrest warrant was issued in California charging Rich with six lewd acts upon a child and two counts of possession of child pornography. He took pictures of himself with the young girls and stored them on his computer, with a strong possibility that he would disperse the pornography through the Internet. In November 2002, a federal arrest warrant was issued charging Rich with the production of child pornography and unlawful flight to avoid prosecution. In mid-April 2007, a friend received a call from the fugitive. The friend instantly alerted the authorities and told them that Rich was hiding out in Montreal, Canada. Unfortunately, that was all the information they had on his whereabouts.

This tipster alerted the authorities, who knew, based on earlier information, that this tip sounded strong. The FBI agent in Ottawa contacted Interpol Ottawa, as well as the Montreal Police SWAT team and the Canadian Border Services Agency to descend on Rich. Authorities found Rich and he readily admitted his true identity. Fingerprints later confirmed that they had, in fact, nabbed one of the FBI's 10 most wanted sexual offenders. In May 2007, the Canadian authorities arrested Rich in Montreal, and he was extradited to the United States to face federal and state charges of sexual exploitation of children, unlawful flight to avoid prosecution, lewd acts upon a child, and possession of child pornography. At his sentencing, Rich bowed his head and said, "I never did anything to be mean to anyone." In a letter to the court, he said that the children he preyed on had set him up. The US district judge said that Rich was a "deeply disturbed individual" with a "lack of remorse beyond belief." At age 62, Rich pled guilty and was sentenced on December 10, 2007, to 20 years in federal prison.

In My Opinion

Dr. Elena Azaola

Dr. Elena Azaola, a noted researcher in child molestation, has written many journal articles on sexual predation. In an interview, she presented her professional opinions regarding sexual abuse, pedophilia, sex offenders, and sexual predators. Dr. Azaola (personal communication) spoke about quasiprotocol during the interviewing process and how it can ultimately improve sexual abuse case outcomes and conditions. Dr. Azaola noted that law enforcement detectives seem to be more objective and have a better understanding in gathering collaborative information in the interviewing process than social workers. It is in this interviewing process that the information is presented that adversely affects the reliability of the child.

In regard to predatory pedophiles, Dr. Azaola said that many of them adapt to certain proclivities in their attempt to entice young boys into more direct experiences. Sexual predatory offenders are opportunistic and have particular sexual preferences. Boys present a special challenge to sexual predators and they often facilitate many different approaches in gaining access to a desirable victim and grooming him to meet their needs. Dr. Azaola noted the complexity of the situation because boys are reluctant to come forward and almost two out of three victims do not report the offense or what they experienced. She said that predatory pedophiles seek out opportunities, pursue more than one victim, and often desensitize their victim by using sexually explicit material and masturbating each other. Dr. Azaola mentioned that, in the grooming process, these individuals often collect memorabilia of the victim, such as underwear, an article of clothing, or another reminder. When boys become more mature, they will extract more favors from the offender, sometimes exploiting him as well.

In regard to child pornography, Dr. Azaola feels that most of these predatory pedophiles are often motivated by child pornography for two reasons: economic gain (by selling the child pornography they have attained) and sexual gratification. She questioned to what degree child pornography is on the pathway to offending patterns, especially to those who visit the Internet and target their victims. Dr. Azaola described a case of a pedophile priest and pedophile boy scout leader who often shared pornographic pictures. When does it go beyond a passing interest or curiosity? When does it develop into an increased risk and hands-on offense? Dr. Azaola feels that children are inundated at an early age with sexual material and provocative images. Sexual predators have more places to start. This type of polymorphous perversion is often related to lifestyle and premature, underdeveloped sexual interests.

There are many reconstituted families, especially because the divorce rate is high; many remarriages produce more situational stepdad/stepdaughter circumstances. The stepdad/stepdaughter relationship that incorporates weak boundaries, early puberty, impulsiveness, a lack of self-control, and accessibility often poses a risk of sexual abuse. Dr. Azaola goes on to say that the dynamics of pure incest involves a process where a father will "test the waters," especially if the child is emotionally needy. This intentional act often begins with a genuine desire for the child, a seduction process, and presexual innuendos, and it culminates with the probability of not being detected. These intrafamilial episodes often involve alcohol and drugs, which are significant in destroying boundaries and desensitizing the child.

Dr. Azaola acknowledged that the majority of adjudicated sex offenders may not necessarily be classified as a sexual predator. Criminals adjudicated for a sex crime may not necessarily be a pedophile predator or have deviant intentions. Naming someone as a sexual offender (after adjudication) casts the net over a broad number of offenders who may not necessarily pose a risk to society. Sex offenders are always addressing the stigma of recidivism that they will never escape. Dr. Azaola feels there are not enough definitive predictors of sex offenders and predatory pedophiles because most are often grouped under a blanket classification. She says there should be some control to manage the level of risk a sex offender may present to the community. She feels sexual addiction can be compared to alcoholism because it will always be a struggle not to reoffend. Dr. Azaola thinks that age becomes a good deterrent because of the exhaustive energy it takes to endure that lifestyle, the self-control offenders may have acquired over the years, and the realistic anticipated consequences of their actions.

Definitions of Chapter Key Terms

Child abuse: Mistreatment that includes sexual abuse, physical abuse, emotional abuse, and neglect.
Child sexual abuse: Mistreatment of children in a sexual context with an adult who is predominantly sexually attracted to children.
Coercion: To put pressure on or persuade someone to do something against his or her will. This is seen in many families that have experienced incest with a family member.
Copulation: To engage in sexual intercourse.
Cycle of violence: Often thought of as repetitive acts of physical violence against a submissive person through intimidation and forced sexual encounters. These recurring acts of violence accompany elevated emotions and acts of reprisal and revenge.

Dyadic abuse: Most common type of sexual abuse that involves one victim and one offender.

Fondling: Touching, caressing, or stroking breasts and genitalia to provoke arousal and sexual stimulation.

Incest: Unacceptable and inappropriate sexual activity between one family member and another family member or relative. The most common cases of incest involve father and daughter (sometimes referred to as intrafamilial child sexual abuse) and stepfather and stepdaughter relationships. This type of crime is often underreported due to the unwillingness of the child to cause dissension in the family and the secrecy, and privacy of the crime. The victim often experiences low self-esteem, unhealthy future sexual activity, contempt for other women, and emotional problems. This type of crime is considered taboo in most societies.

Molestation: The act of imperiling or subjecting a person to unsolicited and inappropriate sexual advances.

Predatory behavior: Obsession or passion often targeting an innocent victim to satisfy the predator's needs.

Self-gratification: Manual contact other than sexual intercourse with the intent of satisfying one's own desires or sexual pleasure.

Sexual assault: The illegal sexual contact or unwanted sexual act against a person's will that frequently involves force. This type of statutory offense is often inflicted upon someone who may be incapable of giving consent because of age (child) or mental or physical incapacity. It may also be considered conduct of a sexual or indecent nature accompanied by actual or threatened physical force that induces anxiety, shame, humiliation, and mental and psychological problems. Many states have replaced the common term "rape" with the term "sexual assault."

Sexual exploitation: Taking advantage of or manipulating a person sexually.

Sexually transmitted disease (STD): There are eight forms of this disease or infection that rely on sexual transmission to survive and endure. The common forms of this condition can be caused by bacteria, viruses, or parasites. The eight noteworthy conditions are chlamydia (bacteria), gonorrhea (bacteria), trichomoniasis (parasite), HIV (virus), genital herpes (virus), genital warts (virus), hepatitis symptoms (virus), and syphilis (bacteria). A few sexually transmitted diseases are often asymptomatic (show no signs or symptoms).

Sodomy: An unnatural form of sexual intercourse often associated with anal intercourse.

Threat: The intentional act of inflicting harm, pain, or injury; instigating panic or fright.

References

Arcus, D. (1998). *Encyclopedia of childhood and adolescence.* Florence, KY: Gale Encyclopedia of Public Health, a part of Cengage Learning, Inc.

Centers for Disease Control and Prevention, National Center for Injury Prevention and Control. (2006). Uniform definitions for sexual violence. http://www.cdc.gov/ViolencePrevention/sexualviolence/definitions.html

Finkelhor, D., Wolak, J., and Mitchell, K. (2004). Escaping or connecting? Characteristics of youth who form close online relationships. *Journal of Adolescence* 26(1): 105–119.

Flora, R. (2001). *How to work with sex offenders: A handbook for criminal justice.* New York: Human Service, and Mental Health Professionals (Haworth Marriage and the Family).

National Children's Advocacy Center. (2010). Huntsville, AL.

Valente, S. M. (2005). Sexual abuse of boys. *Journal of Child and Adolescent Psychiatric Nursing* 18 (1): 10.

Williams, L. J., and Finkelhor, D. (1992). The characteristics of incestuous fathers. US Department of Justice, National Center for Child Abuse and Neglect.

Pedophilia and Sex Offenses

4

We always want to find a person that is our true love, or our best friend; that is human nature. It is online that everyone has this opportunity. It can take a day to build a relationship; they can act like your best friend. They mold you.

A. (a victim)

I was 10 months from probation when I started going online again looking for girls. There is something intriguing about girls 13, 14, 15. I wanted to get with them; I wanted to have sex with them.

W. (a predator)

Pedophilia and Pedophiles

What is pedophilia? It is a carnal attraction to, erotic fondness for, or sexual preference for a child. Pedophiles can target any boy or girl (or both), from an infant to a teenager. The average age that appeals to pedophiles is children between 10 and 12 years old who are just beginning puberty. Pedophiles covet a child who is inexperienced sexually. Their sexual attraction is often characterized by lust or infatuation for a child that may often lead into a variety of sexual acts that include molestation and intercourse, often against the child's will. Pedophiles will try to develop a relationship with a child by enhancing his or her self-esteem. They will try to seek out a shy, withdrawn, and nonconfrontational child who comes from a troubled environment at home. Pedophiles are unique individuals who often work with children or come into daily contact with them—for example, someone who volunteers as a coach, mentor, scout leader, tutor, or in any capacity where he is unsupervised with a child in a normal capacity that does not often raise suspicion.

Paraphilia

There is a difference between enjoying normal sexual activity and thoughts and taking pleasure in abnormal or unusual sexual endeavors. This aberrant attraction to deviant sexual activity is called paraphilia and almost all adolescent and adult pedophiles share this trait. Past history has shown that many children who have suffered excessive abuse or neglect and were once victims themselves have become today's most proliferate sexual predators. Studies have shown that a substantial number of psychologists believe that paraphilia can be traced back to a pedophile's childhood, especially if he or she was excessively sexually abused, punished, or neglected and has found comfort in calculating and opportunist conduct.

Doermann (2002) claims that "paraphilias differ from what some people might consider 'normal' sexual activity in that these behaviors cause" considerable anguish from day to day, especially the inability to resist sexual and intense sexual desires. Many pedophiles with this disorder often become aroused through some form of stimulus such as a fantasy, child pornography, or another graphic item. It is often through these intense sexual urges or fantasies that pedophiles engage in sexual acts with prepubescent children. Sex offenders with paraphilia confront certain problems, such as anxiety issues, legal consequences, additional sexual dysfunction, and problems with normal social relationships. Research has shown that they often have a poor relationship with their parents or close family members.

Paraphilias include fantasies, behaviors, and/or urges that

> involve nonhuman sexual objects such as shoes or undergarments; require the suffering or humiliation of oneself or one's partner; and involve children or other nonconsenting partners.

Paraphilia and Victims with Disabilities

A very sensitive issue is sex offenders who sexually abuse and take advantage of individuals with learning disabilities. A child with a disability could be the main focus and target for any pedophile because he or she is most likely sexually inexperienced and may not be capable of explaining what has happened or how he or she was abused. It is not uncommon to hear that children who are physically handicapped or who have learning disabilities become victims of sexual abuse on a much larger scale. A sexual offender will take advantage of these children because of their inability to communicate effectively the type of abuse they have experienced. They are a prefect target and, because of their disabilities, they become frustrated because they have little or no control over the situation. Valente (2005) noted that sexual abuse in childhood can affect future relationships and the ability to trust.

Sexual Perversion

Doermann (2002) explained that sexual perversion is associated with sexual excitement that often includes abnormal, bizarre, or deviant sexual imagery. A paraphilia (sexual perversion) is a condition in which a person's sexual arousal and gratification depend on a fantasy theme of an unusual situation or object that becomes the principal focus of sexual behavior. Paraphilias can revolve around a particular sexual object or a particular act and are considered "sexual impulse disorders characterized by intensely arousing, recurrent sexual fantasies, urges and behaviors considered deviant with respect to cultural norms and that produce clinically significant distress or impairment in social, occupational or other important areas of psychosocial functioning." The nature of a paraphilia is generally specific and unchanging, and most of the paraphilias are far more common in men than in women.

Rufo (2007) discovered that sexual predators and sexual offenders often have a specific age group to which they are attracted. For instance, a sexual predator that prefers young girls ages 12–15 will rarely have sexual thoughts or fantasies for another age group.

Pedophiles may engage in various sex acts with children:

- Oral copulation with the child
- Masturbating in the company or presence of the child
- Exposing or revealing themselves to the child
- Fondling or playful behavior to touch the child inappropriately
- Taking the child's clothes off
- Penetration of a child's vagina, anus, or mouth

Generally, pedophiles do not coerce children into these erotic activities, but instead rely on various forms of manipulation and exploitation. Pedophiles will often justify their actions through various excuses that include denial, minimization, and fabrication of their devious actions.

All sexual offenses involve the following actions:

- Arousal, stimulation, provocation, or excitement
- Analysis, perception, rationalization, or validation
- Strategy, manipulation, maneuvering, or persuasion
- Secretiveness, intimacy, seclusion, or being discreet
- Exploitation, abuse, manipulation, or influence

Donna Rice Hughes of ProtectKids.com (personal communication, 2010) noted that pedophiles, when not on the Internet, typically operate in isolation. Never before have pedophiles had the opportunity to communicate so freely and directly with each other as they do online. Their communication on the Internet provides virtual validation for their behavior. They share their conquests, real and imagined. Pedophiles discuss ways to contact and lure children online and exchange tips with other pedophiles on seduction techniques. They use the technology of the Internet to train and encourage each other to act out sexually with children. The Internet also serves as a tool for sexual predators to swap warnings on the avoidance of law enforcement detection.

In an investigative study, Middleton et al. (2006) speak about the relationship of the Ward and Siegart pathway model of child abuse as it compares the actions of sexual offenders into five distinct categories. The fact that such a proportion of this Internet offender sample could be separated into the five distinct pathways by their primary deficits suggests that the Internet offender population is not a homogeneous group and is as diverse within itself as other sex offender groups such as rapists or child molesters, and also that the Internet offender sample here shares similar psychological deficits as other sex offender groups. Sex offenders are likely to fall into one of these five categories or to have a combination of signs or indicators that they may share within other classifications.

The first classification is the *intimacy/social skills deficit,* which is the most populated pathway for Internet offenders. A sexual offender in this group often has a problem maintaining relationships and may substitute the intimacy of a child after adult rejection. This group reported high levels of emotional loneliness. The primary mechanism hypothesized by Ward and Siegart (2002) for this group is the formation of insecure attachments leading to low levels of social skills and self-esteem. Ward and Siegert discuss that the primary cause of sexually abusive behavior is the need to engage in a sexual relationship with another person to alleviate loneliness and to compensate for a lack of intimacy. The Internet offender may be attracted to the Internet at times of loneliness and dissatisfaction in more appropriate adult relationships and sees that children are less fearful and more accepting partners. This type of sexual offender will be sexually aroused around children and will offend at specific times of loneliness or rejection.

The next classification is referred to as *distorted sexual scripts.* The sex offenders in this group may themselves have been victims of sexual abuse or been exposed to sex at an early age. An individual exhibiting this behavior often seeks comfort and closeness through sexual contact and uses sex as a soothing strategy. A sex offender who is classified with distorted behavior is sensitive to rejection. The sexual interactions of offenders within this group would be considered or viewed as purely sexual. This individual is fearful of intimacy and tends toward impersonal sexual behaviors that lead to frustration and unhappiness. This can expand to sexual offending at times of rejection, along with relationship difficulties. Individuals with distorted sexual scripts may turn to child pornography to meet their sexual and emotional needs. These offenders seldom display a preference for children, and their use of child pornography removes the risk of rejection. This sex offender does not do well in adult relationships.

Emotional dysregulation is the third category or classification regarding sexual offenders. This type of individual uses sex as a coping strategy and has problems identifying emotions, anger, and personal distress. He may use the Internet to access both adult and child pornography during times of emotional unhappiness and to increase feelings of pleasure. The sexual offender justifies his behavior by externalizing it as "a loss of control" and justifies sexual arousal for the emotional contentment.

Antisocial cognitions is the fourth pathway associated with the classification of sex offenders. This group, as the name indicates, has many antisocial attitudes and beliefs regarding sexual behavior and sexual offending. They feel superior to children and often makes excuses for their sexual contact with them. This type of sexual offender often does not display any deviant sexual preferences, but will fulfill his needs through opportunities that can lead to sexual offending of children. This group demonstrates little regard for the consequences of their behavior, which may add to the perception that they are not responsible for their behavior. Their use of child pornography on the Internet may simply be an extension of their immoral outlook and behaviors. Their impulsive behavior and opportunistic lifestyle enhance their gratification.

The last classification that identifies sexual offenders is *multiple dysfunctional deficits/mechanisms*. This type of offender exhibits antisocial behavior and emotional loneliness as he takes advantage of any opportunity for sexual gratification. Sex offenders who constitute this "pure pedophile" behavior often have a difficult time controlling themselves and their deceitfulness. Children are their preferred sexual partners and these individuals view sexual relationships between adults and children as the "ideal." The use of child pornography on the Internet for sexual gratification could possibly be an addendum to their career as a sexually abusive pedophile. A sex offender (with multiple dysfunctional deficits) has a primary goal of abusing children through direct sexual contact.

Infantophilia

Infantophilia involves a pedophile that is sexually attracted to a child younger than 5 years old.

Hebephilia

Hebephiles are pedophiles who are attracted to or engage in any sexual conduct with young pubescent females who are often between the ages of 12 and 16 and are considered under the age of legal consent. These types of individuals are known to have relationships with their victims, and they have a tendency to be opportunistic when engaging in their sexual exploits.

Ephebophilia

Ephebophiles are pedophiles who are interested in or desire males 12–16 years of age, which is often considered under the legal age of consent. These types of pedophiles are often more interested in children who are post-puberty.

Teleiophilia

A teleiophile is a pedophile who prefers a mature or older companion between 16 and 19 years of age.

Exhibitionism

Exhibitionism is considered a mental disorder that involves the exposure of the genital area of the body to another person. Children are more often the target of this crime, which is often called "flashing." In some cases, the exhibitionist masturbates while exposing himself (or while fantasizing that he is exposing himself) to the other person. Some exhibitionists are aware of a conscious desire to shock or upset their target; however, others fantasize that the target will become sexually aroused by their display.

Frey (2003) noted that an expert who was treating paraphiliacs suggested classifying the symptoms of exhibitionism by levels of severity:

- Mild: the person has recurrent fantasies of exposing himself, but has rarely or never acted on them.
- Moderate: the person has occasionally exposed himself (three targets or fewer) and has difficulty controlling urges to do so.
- Severe: the person has exposed himself to more than three people and has serious problems with control.
- Catastrophic: this would not be found in exhibitionists without other paraphilias. This level denotes the presence of sadistic fantasies that, if acted upon, would result in severe injury or death to the victim.

Because exhibitionism is a hands-off paraphilia, it rarely rises above the level of moderate severity in the absence of other paraphilias. In terms of the technical definition of exhibitionism, almost all reported cases involve Caucasian males, and almost half of them are married. Although the stereotype of an exhibitionist is that of a "dirty old man in a raincoat," it is rarely found in men over 50 years of age.

Martymaculia

Martymaculia is paraphilia that involves the sexual stimulation of having others watch the performance of a sexual act.

Frotteurism

Frotteurism occurs when an individual rubs his or her genitalia against a child. This type of behavior allows the pedophile intrusive and indiscrete physical sexual contact. L. F. Fallon, Jr. (2003), defines frotteurism as a disorder (paraphilia) in which a person derives sexual pleasure, intense sexual urges, and sexually arousing fantasies when rubbing the genitals against another unsuspecting person. Studies have shown that most individuals with this disorder are males and most of the victims are female.

The primary focus of frotteurism is touching or rubbing one's genitals against the clothing or body of a nonconsenting person. This behavior most often occurs in situations that allow rapid escape. Frottage (the act of rubbing against the other person) is most commonly practiced in crowded places such as malls, elevators, busy sidewalks, and public transportation vehicles. The most commonly practiced form of frotteurism is rubbing one's genitals against the victim's thighs or buttocks. A common alternative is to rub one's hands over the victim's genitals or breasts. Most people who engage in frottage (sometimes called frotteurs) usually fantasize that they have an exclusive and caring relationship with their victims during the moment of contact. However, once contact is made and broken, the frotteurs realize that escape is important to avoid prosecution. The most common age group with this disorder generally occurs from 15 to 25 years of age. In older individuals, this type of behavior becomes apparent in those who are shy, withdrawn, and reticent.

Fetishes

Many people (generally males) have fetishes (a physical attraction to some inanimate article that stimulates sexual arousal). Fetishism is a sexual disorder where an individual will develop persistent sexual fantasies that generally end in masturbation and, in some cases, use of an article with a sexual partner. Fetishes, which often develop in teenage years, incorporate fantasy and sexual gratification and can be described as mild to extreme. A fetish could start innocently with the curiosity and fascination of an object that eventually cultivates sexual arousal, urges, and fantasies. Fetishes often progress out of an experience that occurred in a young person's life when he or she experienced a formidable and exclusive sexual rush or charge from that object. Many psychologists believe that individuals who embrace a fetish are trying to reduce the feeling of sexual inadequacy.

Dr. Mark Schwartz, a practicing psychologist at the Masters and Johnson Clinic in St. Louis, said patients who develop fetishes have often been victims of sexual trauma earlier in life (personal communication). "In the first 10 years of someone's life, there is hardwiring of sexual arousals and then, at puberty, it sort of turns on," Schwartz said. "Then, over time, [the fetish] gets cemented through the repetition of masturbation to the arousing object and it becomes relatively permanent." He stated that the permanence of an individual's fetish can sometimes be made worse by the Internet, a place where there is often a group or chat room dedicated to even the most outlandish sexual desires: "I treated a patient who would try to strangle somebody in order to get aroused; he went online and 25 people came back to him and shared pictures of themselves doing the same thing and the fetish became more normative."

Fetishes can be categorized in three areas:

- Sexual urges for anything made out of material such as silk, leather, plastic, rubber, etc.
- Sexual cravings for panties, lingerie, spiked heels, boots, garters, miniskirts, etc.
- Sexual obsession with breasts, butts, feet, hands, hair, etc.

Voyeurism

Voyeurism is an act of watching a stranger through a window, doorway, or anywhere the offender cannot be seen. Voyeurism or being a "peeping Tom" is a criminal offense. A person who commits this crime attempts to watch a stranger disrobe or view the stranger engaging in a sexual act. According to Dr. L. F. Fallon, Jr. (2003), voyeurism is a psychosexual disorder in which a person derives sexual pleasure and gratification from looking at naked bodies and genitals or observing the sexual acts of others. The voyeur is usually hidden from the view of others. Voyeurism is considered a form of paraphilia. A variant form of voyeurism involves listening to erotic conversations. This is commonly referred to as telephone sex, although it is usually considered voyeurism primarily in the instance of listening to unsuspecting persons.

The objective of most voyeurs is to observe unsuspecting individuals who are naked, in the process of undressing, or engaging in sexual acts. The person being observed is usually a stranger to the observer. The act of looking, or peeping, is undertaken for the purpose of achieving sexual excitement.

The observer generally does not seek to have sexual contact or activity with the person being observed. If orgasm is sought, it is usually achieved through masturbation. This may occur during the act of observation or later, relying on the memory of the act that was observed. A voyeur may have a fantasy of engaging in sexual activity with the person being observed. In reality, this fantasy is rarely consummated.

Clergy, Pedophilia, and Sexual Abuse in the Catholic Church

In the last decade, many alleged victims have come forward and said they had been sexually assaulted, sexually abused, or exploited by Catholic priests throughout the United States. According to a research study conducted by the John Jay College of Criminal Justice (2004), roughly 4,392 Roman Catholic priests have been accused of sexually abusing 11,000 children under the age of 18 in the United States between 1950 and 2002.

The distribution of reported cases by the year the abuse is alleged to have occurred or begun shows a peak in the year 1970. However, considering the duration of some repeated abusive acts, more abuse occurred in the 1970s than any other decade, peaking in 1980. Alleged abuse sometimes extended over many years. In 38.4% of allegations, the abuse is alleged to have occurred within a single year, in 21.8% the alleged abuse lasted more than a year but less than 2 years, in 28% it lasted between 2 and 4 years, in 10.2% it lasted between 5 and 9 years, and, in under 1%, it lasted 10 or more years.

This allegation of sexual abuse against innocent victims has brought out a myriad of civil lawsuits against the hierarchy of the Catholic Church for failing to reveal the priests' sexual misconduct. The Catholic Church has been accused of consistently covering up these crimes. Many people of the Catholic faith were dismayed that priests had abused their power and their position of trust in their abuse of children.

Pope Benedict XVI has acknowledged the abuse, but has not explained how he will manage this crisis as many priests have been convicted and sentenced to prison. Psychologist Paul Dokecki (2004) wrote of the reprehensible behavior of church officials and clergy during the slow uncovering of multiple clergy sexual abuse cases around the nation. He says that the Catholic Church must somehow regain the credibility it once held.

Roberts (2010) acknowledged in the *National Catholic Reporter* that bishops worldwide have raised questions on church policy. Roberts questions the reasoning behind the sexual abuse committed by pedophile priests. He suggests that it may be the clerical culture, manner, and exercise of domination and power. Roberts notes that deep-rooted habits have become inherent to clerical and hierarchical behavior that may have contributed to the scandal.

In the United States, bishops argued when the first cases of sexual abuse and cover-ups were revealed in the mid-1980s that they did not understand the illness and that, in reassigning priests, they were acting on the best advice of psychologists and psychiatrists. Later, some of the loudest defenders of the actions of the hierarchy argued that the media were blowing the scandal out of proportion or that the church, unlike other secular institutions, was being unfairly targeted by lawyers who foresaw big paydays for their clients in settlements of civil lawsuits.

Another factor was the Catholic Church's culture of forgiveness, which tends to view things in terms of sin and forgiveness, rather than crime and punishment. But clerical abuse of the young is a crime, and the church has struggled to find the point of convergence between sin and forgiveness, on the one hand, and crime and punishment on the other.

Many critics of the Catholic Church believe that the executive powers have clear-cut evidence that a fair number of their priests are sexual abusers, but they are safeguarding the truth and its reputation through secrecy and denial. Gregoire and Jungers (2004) noted that within the last few years an explosion of media attention has been paid to clergy sex abuse, an issue that quietly lived within the church for decades but that can no longer be ignored. Not only have priests been exposed as pedophiles and ephebophiles, but they are also being confronted for their participation in a broader range of unhealthy sexual behaviors and addictions. The *Boston Globe* (2002) proposed that child abuse by clergy was apparently not a one-time occurrence or isolated incident. This crime was obviously shielded by the church culture of secrecy as some deviant priests preyed upon numerous victims during multiple parish assignments. Four priests in particular stand out for the number of abuse claims or the seriousness of the charges against them.

There have been many priests that have been formerly accused, but not convicted of sexual abuse. Some feel that bishops have done little or nothing to identify them. This poses a significant problem because in some cases the criminal charges of sexual abuse have come too late; the statute of limitations has passed and nothing can be done to the priests that were accused. The priests in question may have already died, become too old and frail to stand trial, abandoned the priesthood, or been expelled from the priesthood. Critics of the church and the alleged abuse have called on the church to do more to monitor former priests. These detractors are upset that the accused child molesters are not incarcerated, do not have to register as sex offenders, and are intermingling and hidden in their communities.

Pedophilia and Sex Offenses

The Survivors Network of Those Abused by Priests

The Survivors Network of Those Abused by Priests (SNAP) is the world's oldest and largest support group for victims of clergy abuse. They organized 23 years ago and have more than 10,000 members. Despite the word "priest" in the title, the group has members who were molested by religious figures of all denominations, including nuns, rabbis, bishops, and protestant ministers.

SNAP's belief is that housing and monitoring dangerous child-molesting clerics is a prudent step toward preventing more sex crimes against children. Its perspective is that it is terribly self-serving for bishops to recruit, educate, ordain, train, supervise, and protect predator priests, but then cut them loose when they are finally exposed as criminals; instead, Catholic bishops should house these dangerous clerics in secure, remote, and independently run treatment centers so that kids will be safer and priests will be supervised. Keeping proven, admitted and credibly accused child-molesting clerics on the payroll but letting them live wherever they want is the worst of all worlds and almost guarantees sexual predation. The group's philosophy is that there should be a moral obligation of each bishop and religious order supervisor to ensure that innocent kids will not be violated.

The Geoghan Case
Now-defrocked priest John Geoghan preyed on young boys in a half-dozen parishes in the Boston area while church leaders looked the other way. He served 9–10 years in prison for fondling a youth at a pool in Waltham; a child rape charge and many civil claims are pending. In the Geoghan case alone, some 150 people eventually came forward, claiming the priest fondled or raped them. The Boston archdiocese reached a $10 million settlement with 86 other alleged victims. More than a dozen civil suits are still pending.

John Geoghan stands out as one of the worst serial molesters in the recent history of the Catholic Church in America. For three decades, despite his disturbing pattern of abusive behavior, Geoghan was transferred from parish to parish for years before the church finally defrocked him in 1998. After a January 2002 report on Geoghan by the Globe Spotlight Team, the case became a catalyst for revelations of other clergy abuse and church cover-ups. Dozens of priests were accused of abuse by hundreds of alleged victims who filed lawsuits, forcing the archdiocese to release damaging documents that showed the church's obsession with avoiding scandal and protecting its reputation.

The Birmingham Case
Until his death in 1989, the late Reverend Joseph Birmingham allegedly befriended and then abused at least 50 boys over a 29-year career as a

priest in the Boston archdiocese, even as archdiocesan officials ignored numerous complaints against him. At least 50 men have come forward with claims they were abused by the Rev. Birmingham during the priest's tour through the Boston archdiocese. Parents repeatedly complained to the church about Birmingham's behavior—to no avail. After admitting to police and church officials on separate occasions that he had molested children, Birmingham, insisting that he had been "cured," was allowed to remain in the ministry. Even after the death of Father Birmingham in 1989, the archdiocese continues to receive complaints and settle lawsuits brought by his alleged victims.

The Shanley Case
In the 1960s and 1970s, the Rev. Paul R. Shanley made his reputation as a Boston "street priest"—a crusader for runaways and drifters, drug addicts, and teenagers struggling with questions about their sexual identity. But those who turned to Father Shanley for comfort and guidance often found themselves in the clutches of a sexual predator. Thousands of pages of documents show that church officials knew of numerous sexual abuse allegations against Shanley and that the priest had publicly advocated sex between men and boys. Despite this, Father Shanley was shuttled from parish to parish in the Boston archdiocese and eventually transferred to a California church with a letter of recommendation from one of Cardinal Bernard Law's top deputies.

In May 2002, Shanley was arrested in San Diego, where he had been living, and returned to Massachusetts to face ten counts of child rape and six counts of indecent assault and battery stemming from his assignment at a Newton parish in the 1980s. After 7 months in prison, Shanley was released on $300,000 bail. He is living in Provincetown while awaiting trial on charges that he raped four boys at a Newton parish.

The Paquin Case
During two decades of ministry, the Rev. Ronald H. Paquin made a habit of befriending young male parishioners and molesting them. Although numerous complaints were made to the archdiocese over the years, Father Paquin was not removed from parish ministry until 1990. Even then, Paquin continued to molest one boy while he was living at a church treatment center.

Unlike most accused priests, Father Paquin has acknowledged his long history of abusive behavior. In December 2002, he became the first Boston clergyman to admit guilt in a criminal molestation case. Paquin pleaded guilty to three counts of raping a boy and was sentenced to 12–15 years in prison. He has agreed to testify against the Boston archdiocese in other abuse cases. At least 28 civil lawsuits are still pending against him.

Sexual Addiction

Sexual addiction is an extreme obsession with sex. A sex addict often has continuous thoughts and fantasies about sex that may include an unusually intense sex drive. Sex addicts have thoughts of sexual encounters that dominate their mind and way of thinking, making it difficult to engage in healthy and personal relationships. According to Carnes and Wilson (2002), sexual addiction is defined as an ongoing pattern of sexual behavior. This sexual behavior exemplifies three principal characteristics: an inability to reliably stop the behavior, a continuation of the behavior in spite of potential and/or actual harmful consequences, and an obsessive quality to the pursuit of the behavior. Sexual addiction can be compared to other addictions due to the many similarities they share. A sex addict will have urges and desires similar to those of an alcoholic who has to have another drink or a drug addict who can only think about getting high. There is a need to satisfy the craving.

Benuto and Zupanick (2009) believe that sex addicts become preoccupied by sexual thoughts and engage in risky sexual behavior. This behavior can lead to discord in conventional relationships. Another term used to describe sexual addiction is *compulsive sexual behavior*. It is not clear how many people have this condition, but general estimates by experts have said that 3%–6% of individuals in the United States suffer from sexual addiction. Compulsive sexual behavior typically begins in late adolescence or early adulthood. Some experts are not sure what makes a person addicted to sex. It could be a sexual experience or sexual incident early in childhood. Studies have shown that it is more common for individuals to become addicted to sex after they have been sexually abused as children.

There may actually be brain impairments in individuals who have a sexual addiction so that they cannot judge the danger and negative impact of their sexual behavior. Alternatively, individuals with sexual addiction may have such impaired impulse control that they immediately gratify sexual cravings without regard to the consequences. Regardless of the reasons, sexual addicts may seek out stimulation by viewing pornography, engaging in cybersex, or having sex with others or prostitutes. This puts them at risk for a number of life-threatening illnesses (e.g., AIDS), legal problems (e.g., purchasing child pornography), and financial ruin.

Sex addicts have a myriad of different thoughts and fantasies they want to explore. They have thoughts of sex or fulfilling their sexual fantasies, mostly by thinking of their victims while they pleasure themselves, often to orgasm. Sex addicts may just replay or act out their fantasies in their minds. It is not uncommon for a sex addict to rationalize and justify his or her behavior, often blaming others in the process. They generally deny they have a problem and make excuses for their actions. Sex addicts are often considered to be risk takers because of the potential for negative and/or dangerous consequences of their sexual activity.

A greater percentage of males is sexually addicted than their female counterparts. This disease has affected many men, most of whom are in denial. Treating this addiction is like treating any other addiction: first, the person must admit and accept that he has a problem. Treatment of sexual addiction focuses on controlling the addictive behavior and helping a person manage his own destructive conduct. This includes education about healthy sexuality, individual counseling, or support groups. These support groups, often known as Sex Addicts Anonymous, are 12-step recovery programs that resemble Alcoholics Anonymous. It is not uncommon for hospitals, community centers, and support groups to have meetings every day of the week. The sex addicts will often sit in a circle facing each other. They start out with announcing their name and admit they are a sex addict to the group. The participants (the majority of which are men) take turns admitting their sexual thoughts and compulsions, and they speak about the problems (urges) that they have encountered since the last meeting.

These sexual addiction meetings can help the sex addict in a few ways. The support group understands what the individual is going through and knows that this is a process and it takes time, dedication, and commitment to be successful. The group is always there for emotional support, especially if the sex addict has sexual inclinations that may cause him to relapse. Many reformed sex addicts volunteer to be a personal sponsor to one individual, especially those newer to the group. A sponsor is the person who checks in on a new sex addict. The new sex addict often relies on direct personal contact with his sponsor—not only for support, but also to prevent any hint of a relapse. It is not unusual for a sex addict and his sponsor to check in with each other on a daily basis. The sex addict realizes that he or she is not alone and that a sponsor and a core support group are only a call away. The support group can help the sexual addict understand the triggers for sexual urges, assist in managing behavior, and control unique actions.

Behaviors Associated with Sexual Addiction

- Compulsive masturbation (continuous self-stimulation)
- Multiple affairs (extramarital affairs)
- Multiple or anonymous sexual partners and/or one-night stands
- Consistent use of pornography (in some cases, child pornography)
- Unsafe sex
- Phone or computer sex (cybersex)
- Prostitution or use of prostitutes

- Exhibitionism
- Obsessive dating through personal ads
- Voyeurism (watching others) and/or stalking
- Sexual harassment
- Molestation/rape
- Feeling a compelling need for some form of sexual satisfaction when stressed or anxious

Sex Rings

Sex rings are often categorized by one or several sexual predators who sexually exploit children through domination and manipulation. The US Department of Justice (2005) acknowledged that there are normally three types of sex rings: solo, transition, and syndicated. Sex ring offenders often seek out children with whom they are acquainted and whom they feel they can influence and control. Availability and access to the child gives the offender in a sex ring the opportunity to molest several children. Sex rings operate under the guise of entrapment and premeditated behavior and they count on secrecy. Often their victims include

- Runaway children or missing children from an incestuous family relationship
- A child who has left home because he or she was a victim of abuse or neglect from the family
- Children that come from an abusive home where there is little if any parental guidance
- A child kidnapped and forced into prostitution
- Children with low self-esteem
- Children who are in need of money or support
- Adolescents seeking modeling careers who eventually are forced or coerced into posing nude

Sex rings are well organized; they control child prostitution and other criminal sexual activity. They will aggressively recruit vulnerable children and teens or they will try to pick up or kidnap young runaway girls at bus and train stations. With the promise of food, shelter, drugs, and money, they lure these teens into prostitution and shoplifting. Children and teens used in sex rings are often exposed to harsh and persistent physical, emotional, and sexual abuse. Sex rings will always have someone who oversees the girls, who will be beaten or punished when they show any type of resistance or do not follow demands made of them.

Solo Sex Rings

The US Department of Justice claims that a solo sex ring is often controlled and operated by a lone male sex offender. He relies on isolation and secrecy, often through fear and intimidation. His victims usually range in age from infancy to adolescence. The abuser selects strategies particular to each child, often isolating the children from those who could help. The offender will attempt to place the burden of guilt and blame for the abuse on the child.

Solo sex ring abusers will often use physical pleasure and excitement to unite the boys to the sex ring. The fear of disclosing their homosexual behavior will keep them from revealing this inappropriate behavior. The solo abuser rarely shares child pornography or child photographs with other adults. He is generally secretive and does not reveal information about his sexual conquests to anyone.

Transition Sex Rings

Transition sex rings usually involve multiple male adult pedophiles, child molesters, or individuals who have a sexual affliction about children. These types of sex offenders usually are involved with adolescents who are runaways, have been abducted, or have had issues with family violence, abuse, or sexual exploitation. Pornography and stories of sexual conquests are often exchanged between members of this type of sex ring. It is not uncommon to see money exchange hands because children are often prostituted for sex. The adults in this group rarely interact sexually with each other, but often have matching sexual proclivities.

Syndicated Sex Rings

The syndicated sex ring involves a different dimension and component than the other two forms of sex rings. It is very well structured, encompasses secrecy, and is very well organized. It involves

- Multiple adult offenders
- Recruitment of children, often with the help of older children
- Inducement of participation by bribery, threats, or peer pressure
- Delivery of direct sexual services
- Children ranging in age from 11 to 16 years of age
- An extensive network of customers
- Items for trade, circulation, sale, and distribution for profit
- Self-regulation (expulsion of members guilty of actions that are not in the best interests of the consortium)

Prostituted Children

When the subject of children and adolescents involved in prostitution surfaces, a majority of people think that it occurs in tiny villages in a foreign country, but it is happening everywhere. In the United States, there are literally tens of thousands of adolescents living this traumatic life—street kids that remain alone and hidden. Children who become involved in prostitution are forced into the situation because of their surrounding circumstances or are coerced or coached into the profession; they still encounter life-changing experiences.

The majority of minors who become victims of prostitution are often children that are runaways, come from an abusive or dysfunctional home, are rebellious, or were abandoned at some point in their life. Childhood victimization may often lead an adolescent into prostitution and promiscuity. Children as young as 12 have stood on street corners soliciting for sex because they have nowhere else to go and this is their only way to survive.

Adolescents and children can be lured into prostitution, often by a person who takes advantage of them with the affirmation that, for their services, they will be taken care of. Children are often provided with simple necessities such as food, clothing, a small room, and drugs. Sexual and physical abuse, poverty, rejection, drug dependence, and manipulative and dangerous adults are some of the experiences that children often report.

Interstate Sex Trafficking

According to the US Department of Justice Child Exploitation and Obscenity Section, it has a federal crime to transport minors over state lines for the purpose of committing illegal sex acts since 1910. The most recent initiative to combat this crime has been sponsored by the FBI Crimes Against Children Program in conjunction with the National Center for Missing and Exploited Children. Operation Innocence Lost, announced in early 2003, is a nationwide initiative that focuses on child victims of interstate sex trafficking in the United States. The interstate sex trafficking of minors is a growing problem. Conservative estimates reveal that 300,000 American youth are presently in jeopardy of becoming victims of commercial sexual exploitation.

Child-Sex Tourism

According to the US Department of Justice Child Exploitation and Obscenity Section, it is a crime for a US citizen or permanent resident to travel abroad for the purpose of having sex with a minor or to have sex with a minor while abroad. Child-sex tourists are individuals that travel to foreign countries to engage in sexual activity with children. The nonprofit organization End Child Prostitution, Child Pornography, and the Trafficking of Children (ECPAT) estimates that more than one million children worldwide are drawn into the sex trade each year.

Thousands of young victims, some younger than 5 years old, fall prey to the sex trade industry. These children have seen very little of what is known as a normal life. Young children are subject to an underground life of cruelty and brutality and callous pedophiles take advantage of their young victims' innocence and naïveté. A majority of children exploited in the sex trade industry are from Thailand, Cambodia, other Southeast Asia countries, Western Europe, and South America. It is estimated that tens of thousands of children have been forced into child prostitution.

Sex tourism has become a family business in which a son's or daughter's well-being is sacrificed for financial gain and the need to survive. The key factor that has propelled the child sex trade is poverty, the laissez-faire attitude of the government, and the minimum involvement by local law enforcement officers. The situation is now worse than a person could imagine because police often make light of the situation due to ongoing corruption and infrequent prosecution. With this type of facade, many Third World countries actually promote sex tourism and welcome the revenue from these traveling pedophiles who seek out sexual gratification with children. Many countries have laws against sexual exploitation of a child, but they rarely enforce these laws on visiting tourists, ultimately giving child molesters free reign and the green light to fulfill their fantasies.

Families with many children are often targeted by "recruiters" that promise the distressed families a substantial income that they desperately need. Children that are forced into the sex trade business have a myriad of fears that they encounter on a daily basis. These children suffer from low self-esteem, depression, and emotional and verbal abuse. The amount of sexual clients a child has, especially a child under the age of 10, can be alarming. There is physical abuse along with exhaustion, infections, and various illnesses, especially sexually transmitted diseases, which are most prominent among sex trade victims. Even though these children get sick, they rarely receive the proper medical attention. A child's small, underdeveloped body is not mature enough to withstand physical and strenuous sexual activity every day. It is not uncommon for kids to be punished, beaten, starved, or drugged because they failed to live up to their daily monetary goal or potential.

The sex trade business has drawn an abundance of pedophiles, especially by way of the Internet. Child molesters will inform other sexual abusers about specific places they can visit where child exploitation is least likely to be discovered or cared about. Many Internet websites promote the sex tourism trade. Over the years, more and more businesses have arranged sex tours that frequent child brothels. Just like child offenders in this country, these types of offenders come from every walk of life, line of work, and income level. Most visitors to these child brothels rationalize their behavior by saying that they are helping a poor family succeed during economic hardship. A majority of child molesters feel there is less chance of being arrested, prosecuted, and discovered if they travel abroad to a lenient and indulgent Third World country. Anonymity plays an important role that continues to help them avoid accountability for their actions.

Profile of a Female Sex Offender

Nancy was born in a small town in Colorado. She had four younger brothers. Her mom died when Nancy was 7. Her father, Frank, was verbally abusive to all of the children, but especially to Nancy. He expected a lot from her and had her take care of her younger brothers. Nancy took care of the cooking and cleaning after school. Frank had been drinking heavily since his wife had died. One weekend, Frank sent all four boys on a church outing. Nancy, who had just turned 15, was home alone with her dad and had no ideas what her father had in mind. Frank had been smoking marijuana and drinking the entire weekend. He went into her bedroom when she was asleep. All she could remember later was her dad's rough hand across her mouth as he fondled her and tried to take off her pajamas. He raped her as tears welled in her eyes. Nancy never told anyone. She finished high school and went to college to become a teacher.

Nancy excelled in college and was soon teaching history in a high school. She became very popular with her students and other teachers. She would invite a few male students to come by her apartment after school and on weekends. Four or five students would visit Nancy on a regular basis, even though she knew that it was strictly against school policy. It did not take long for her to introduce her male students to alcohol and drugs. They would get high together and this eventually led to many sexual encounters. A parent of one of the teens went to the police and told them someone was providing alcohol to teens. Nancy was arrested for alleged sexual contact with underage students and giving them alcohol and drugs. She was charged with nine counts of contributing to the delinquency of a minor and criminal sexual contact with a minor between 14 and 16 years old. In counseling, Nancy blamed her dad for her behavior.

Profile of a Male Sex Offender

Jon was released from prison in Texas in the summer of 1999. He had served his full sentence of 10 years for molesting a young boy. After his release, Jon managed to convince an entire family that he had become a changed man. But, according to officials, he was still the same conniving sex offender that he had been on the day he entered prison. Police said that Jon established a pen-pal relationship with a family in New Hampshire. According to police, Jon wrote letters back and forth with an editor of a student literary magazine at the University of New Hampshire. The charming and heartfelt letters struck a chord with the young woman; she was convinced that he had become a better person. She said, "He's a very eloquent person and he wrote very nice letters, talking about how he was studying in prison and how he regretted the mistakes of his youth."

Jon corresponded with the young woman during his entire prison term. He convinced her through his manipulative writings and poetry that he was a changed man and asked if he could stay with her, her husband, and their 5-year-old son when he got out of prison. The family happily agreed. That was in the fall of 1999, and cops say that it did not take long for Jon to revert to his old ways.

A couple of weeks after Jon moved in, the 5-year-old told his mom, "I have a secret to tell you." The child said that he and Jon had an inappropriate relationship, revealing that the visiting ex-con had been sexually assaulting him. Upon hearing the news, the parents reported the sexual assault to police. Jon was able to leave before the police came to arrest him. A bench warrant was issued for Jon in late 1999.

In October of 1999, Jon was seen boarding a Greyhound bus and heading south. His last confirmed sighting was in a small town in Mexico in 2000. Unfortunately, before US Marshals could arrive, he was gone again, leaving behind allegations of improper sexual relationships with children in that town. Jon had two masters' degrees, one in the humanities and one in literature. He also spoke French and German, was an accomplished pianist, and once worked at a music store where he taught hundreds of kids to play the piano.

In April 2000, a federal arrest warrant was issued charging Jon with unlawful flight to avoid prosecution. Jon was an Oklahoma native who has ties to New Hampshire, Texas, Mexico, and California. On September 7, 2007, Jon became the fourth child predator to be placed on the FBI's Ten Most Wanted Fugitives List. There was a $100,000 bounty to anyone that was able to apprehend and capture Jon. Officials arrested the accused sex offender without incident in San Jose de Gracia, Mexico; he has been returned to Brentwood, New Hampshire, to face charges of child molestation of a 5-year-old boy. After 9 years of avoiding apprehension, the convicted child molester and sex offender was back behind bars.

In My Opinion

Mrs. Barbara Dorris

Mrs. Barbara Dorris, a former Catholic school instructor in the St. Louis area and the outreach director of SNAP, recently shared her views about sexual predators in the clergy (personal communication). SNAP is a volunteer self-help organization of survivors of clergy sexual abuse and their supporters. They work to end the cycle of abuse in two ways:

- Supporting one another in personal healing
- Pursuing justice and institutional change by holding individual perpetrators responsible and the church accountable

Their most powerful tool is the light of truth. Through their stories and their actions, they bring healing and justice. The Survivors Network of those Abused by Priests

- Reaches out to survivors, their families, and supporters
- Builds mechanisms to support the life-long journey of personal healing, including individual contact, peer counseling, support groups, written and web-based information, and materials
- Works through education and persuasion to change the structure and culture of abuse in the church and society at large

Mrs. Dorris said that sexual predators in the clergy are much like the sexual predators in society: They need to be removed and punished for the harm that they have caused. They are extremely dangerous to children. Parents tend to place members of the clergy in a higher realm of trust and respect than they do other members in the community. Mrs. Dorris said that priests are placed in an elevated status because most people see them as a representative of God. This gives priests an enormous amount of power.

Mrs. Dorris also said that, like most sexual predators, pedophiles in the clergy also look for a victim who is vulnerable and least likely to reveal the sexual abuse. They look for a boy or girl that appears to be a loner or is always a problem. A priest may search out a child that comes from a devout family that would never question the actions of a priest. Priests may also look for a child whose family is in turmoil or going through a divorce, or someone that needs a father figure. A child can become vulnerable if he or she has had prior altercations with law enforcement, drug use, or has a tendency to lie. It is all about opportunity and whether the child will be believed if he or she does come forward. Who would question the true intentions of a priest?

Mrs. Dorris became an active member of SNAP after a 1991 incident at her school that involved a priest and a child. She caught the priest in a sexual act with a student. Her calls to the police, Department of Children and Family Services (DCFS), and the authorities in the Catholic Church went unanswered. Each agency gave her the runaround when it came to taking any action following the next 6–10 months. The chancellor for the Catholic Church acknowledged the priest's behavior but said that it would be difficult to prove because the girl was only fondled.

The Catholic Church acknowledged that a small percentage of its priests (5%) have sexually abused a victim at some point in their careers, including rape, sodomy, fondling, etc. Mrs. Dorris said that it is challenging to determine an accurate number of priests who exploit children because victims can go to the police, therapists, or the church itself to report an incident that occurred. It is unlikely that anyone or any one agency actually shares information received. She said that the average person who contacts SNAP is often in the age range of the 40s when he or she comes forward to reveal the exploitation by a clergy member. Because of the many years that have passed since the abuse, it is not uncommon for older priests to be implicated for their past improprieties. Mrs. Dorris mentioned a very informative website regarding the sexual exploitation by priests called *bishopaccountability.com*.

Mrs. Dorris recalls an incident that happened in Wisconsin with a priest named Father Murphy, who was accused of sexually abusing 200 deaf children in a boarding school. The church knew of the sexual abuse but took no action to defrock the priest. The church has kept a blind eye and chosen not to take action in many documented cases. Many children have not revealed that they were abused and have kept the burden of carrying this heavy secret with them for the rest of their lives. Mrs. Dorris said that it is extremely important for anyone who has been a victim of sexual exploitation by a priest or any sexual predator to let someone know about the abuse. The victim can always talk to someone in law enforcement, a therapist, or friend that will listen and take action.

Definitions of Chapter Key Terms

Child molester: A person who commits some form of sexual act with a child.
Ephebophile (ephebophilia): A pedophile who is interested or desires males from 12 to 16 years of age, often considered under the legal

age of consent. These types of pedophiles are often more interested in children who are post-puberty.

Exhibitionism: A behavior that involves the exposure of one's genital area to another person.

Fetish: An attraction of a sexual nature toward one particular inanimate object. An individual may fantasize and/or masturbate about this object.

Frotteurism: Rubbing genitalia against a child.

Hebephile (hebephilia): Pedophiles who are attracted to or engage in any sexual conduct with young pubescent females who are often between the ages of 12 and 16 and considered under the age of legal consent. These types of individuals are known to have relationships with their victims, and they have a tendency to be opportunistic when engaging in their sexual exploits.

Infantophilia: A pedophile who is interested in a child younger than 5 years old.

Martymaculia: Considered paraphilia, this involves the sexual attraction of having others watch the performance of a sexual act.

Paraphilia: Adult and adolescent pedophiles who enjoy abnormal or unusual sexual activity. Children who were often themselves victims now have become the offenders.

Pedophile (pedophilia): A sexual preference for children (boys or girls or both), usually of prepubertal or early pubertal age. A child younger than 11 is in the age group most often associated with pedophiliac behavior. This sexual attraction is often characterized by lust for or infatuation with a child that leads to a variety of sexual acts that include molestation and intercourse, often against the child's will. Pedophiles will try to develop a relationship with a child and will often seek out shy, withdrawn children or a child who may be handicapped because they are least likely to reveal or tell on the offender. Pedophiles will enhance the child's self-esteem, especially if the child is from a troubled home.

Prepubescent: A child who has not reached puberty.

Pubescent: The age at which a young person reaches puberty or the age when sex glands become functional.

Sexual addiction: An obsession with sex that includes continuous thoughts of sex and sexual predispositions. This type of individual has unusually intense sex drive tendencies.

Sexual perversion: A condition in which a person's sexual arousal and gratification depend on a fantasy theme of an unusual situation or object that becomes the principal focus of sexual behavior (another term for paraphilia).

Sexually violent person: Someone who has been convicted of a sexually violent offense, adjudicated delinquent for a sexually violent offense, or found not guilty of a sexually violent offense by reason of insanity and who is dangerous because he or she suffers from a mental disorder that makes it substantially probable that the person will engage in acts of sexual violence.

Teleiophile (teleiophilia): A pedophile who prefers mature or older companions between 16 and 19 years of age.

References

Benuto, L., and Zupanick, C. E. (2009). Sexual desire disorders—Hypoactive sexual aversion disorder. http://www.mentalhelp.net/poc/view_doc.php?type=doc&id=29725&cn=10

Carnes, P. J., and Wilson M. (2002). The sexual addiction assessment process. In *Clinical management of sex addiction*, ed. P. J. Carnes and K. M. Adams. New York: Brunner-Routledge.

Doermann, D. J. (2002). In *The Gale encyclopedia of medicine*. Florence, KY: The Gale Group, a part of Cengage Learning, Inc.

Dokecki, P. R. (2004). *The clergy sexual abuse crisis: Reform and renewal in the Catholic community*. Washington, DC: Georgetown University Press.

Fallon, L. F., Jr. (2003). In *Gale encyclopedia of mental disorders*. Florence, KY: The Gale Group, a part of Cengage Learning, Inc.

Frey, R. (Ed.). (2003). *The Gale encyclopedia of mental disorders*. Farmington, MI: The Gale Group, division of Thomson Learning, Inc.

Gregoire, J., and Jungers, C. (2004). Sexual addiction and compulsivity among clergy: How spiritual directors can help in seminary formation. *Sexual Addiction & Compulsivity: The Journal of Treatment & Prevention* 11:71–81.

John Jay College of Criminal Justice. (2004). The nature and scope of the problem of sexual abuse of minors by Catholic priests and deacons in the United States (http://www.usccb.org/nrb/johnjaystudy/).

Middleton, D., Elliott, I., Mandeville-Norden, R., and Beech, A. R. (2006). An investigation into the applicability of the Ward and Siegert pathways model of child sexual abuse with Internet offenders. *Psychology Crime & Law* 12 (6): 589–603.

Roberts, T. (2010). *National Catholic Reporter*.

Roberts, T. (2010). Some bishops questioning clerical culture. *The National Catholic Reporter*. September 15, 2010.

Rufo, R. (2007). An investigation of online sexual predation of minors by convicted male offenders. Dissertation, Argosy University, Atlanta, GA.

United States Department of Justice. (2005). *Internet crimes against children, office for victims of crime bulletin*. Washington, DC: United States Department of Justice, Child Exploitation and Obscenity Section.

Valente, S. M. (2005). Sexual abuse of boys. *Journal of Child and Adolescent Psychiatric Nursing* 18 (1): 10–16.

Ward, T., and Siegert, R. J. (2002). Toward a comprehensive theory of child sexual abuse: A theory knitting perspective. *Psychology, Crime & Law* 8: 319–351.

Female Sexual Offenders 5

> Sexual predators find it real easy to spot children who do not have security and who do not have a relationship at home. The way they take advantage of a child that does not have security is first talking to the child. If you spend enough time with a child, the child will trust you, and it doesn't take that much time for a child to develop trust for an adult.
>
> **Predator**

> Her MySpace was such an innocent page; it was a little girl with a baseball cap.
>
> **Mom of victim**

Introduction

The myth that females do not commit child sexual abuse has been slowly dissipating. Female offenders are less likely to commit sex offenses than men, but the number of female offenders has been gradually rising. Jacqui Saradjian, a clinical psychologist and author of *Women Who Sexually Abuse Children*, said,

> I think people find it so difficult to see that women sexually abuse children because the whole view of women is of nurturers, care-givers, protectors—people who do anything to look after children—and they see the women as victims rather than enemies or perpetrators of any abuse. Women in our society have been portrayed as recipients of manipulation but somewhere within their victimization they have learned that to abuse children gave them a sense of power, control, agency, and therefore they use the abuse of children to gain those things.

Sandler and Freeman (2008) stated that there have been a few studies that have compared adult male to adult female sex offenders, but there appears to be a general consensus that the two groups differ vastly. It is apparent that female offenders are not as predatory as male sexual offenders, and they normally take fewer risks in soliciting their victims.

Sexual abuse crimes by a female are seldom thought about, believed, reported, or prosecuted—most importantly, they get away with them. Recent studies have indicated that many female sex offenders have suffered emotional as well as physical abuse in their childhood, and they are not likely to admit the abuse to anyone. Female sex offenders who have been sexually exploited contend with a longer lasting and more severe abuse than male sex offenders who have been sexually exploited.

American culture has been slow to acknowledge the fact that women are clever in their attempt to commit sexual abuse of a child. Most female sexual offenders are attracted to their victim because of loneliness, isolation, and the need for an emotional connection. Reports of sex offenses by women are rare, and female sex offenders arouse little public concern. Many survivors of sexual abuse are often not believed when it is revealed that the abuser was a woman. Some studies have indicated that women commit 25% of all child sexual abuse. A few women act alone, while others sexually abuse with their husbands or boyfriends.

Recent studies have indicated that adult female sex offenders possess the following traits:

- More likely to victimize the children in their care
- Generally have more male victims, while male offenders generally have more female victims
- Have a withdrawn or neglected relationship with one or both parents
- More likely to report the physical abuse to authorities than male offenders
- Have experienced more psychological problems and difficulties
- Likely to be victimized more severely, more often, and for longer periods of time
- More likely to be molested at a younger age than boys
- Have experienced more emotional, physical, and verbal abuse after they were victimized
- More likely to have addictive behavior, especially toward alcohol and drugs, after they were victimized
- Have experienced periods of depression, isolation, and separation after they were victimized

Characteristics of Female Sex Offenders

- Women between the ages of 21 and 35
- Have come from an abusive home and have experienced sexual abuse as children or teens
- Are more likely to be victims of abuse than men
- History of alcohol and/or drug abuse
- May experience depression, anxiety, personality disorders, and coping difficulties
- Substantial numbers employed in skilled and professional jobs
- Often struggle with intimate relationships

Compared to male sexual offenders, female sex offenders usually fit into one of five definitive categories:

- A mother who victimizes her own children
- A female who sexually abuses with a domineering male partner
- A female abuser who holds a position of authority
- A female who is curious and a risk taker
- A sibling or relative who abuses someone in her family

Mothers Who Abuse Their Children

The most common type of female sexual offender takes advantage of any sexual situation and has a history of incestuous sexual victimization. Mothers tend to exploit their own children or other young children in their family. Jacqui Saradjian (1996) said, "I think people find it so difficult to see that women sexually abuse children because the whole view of women is of nurturers, caregivers, and protectors."

Daughters are the primary target for the female sex offenders in this category. The children of this abuse will also be threatened verbally. The mothers will threaten that any revealed abuse may cause the family to break up with the likelihood of their mom going to jail. The child will always feel pressured to keep the secret instead of doing the right thing and reporting the incident. The stress of sustaining the abuse and keeping the family together or going to a foster home is often much more than a child can handle. Children will keep the abuse confidential because of these threats and the guilt they have to endure. Female pedophiles that sexually molest children have often been associated with psychological difficulties, various mental illnesses, and deviant sexual fantasies.

Mothers in mother–daughter incestuous relationships have a tendency to be aggressive in their exploitive role and they are less likely to be a caring and nurturing parent. In the cases of mother–daughter incestuous relationships, numerous studies have revealed that there is a greater acceptance of intimacy by the child, who is less likely to reveal the abuse to others. Studies have shown that abuse is more common than what children reveal to therapists and police. Therapists may have a difficult time recognizing the signs of a mother–daughter incestuous relationship because of the daughter's fear in revealing the abuse. It is not uncommon for women who sexually abuse their daughters to be involved in an unsuccessful or deteriorating marriage. Because of this, the child has a difficult time reporting the incestuous abuse by her mother. If the child reported abuse authorities she would more than likely be placed with the Department of Children and Family Services (DCFS) or assigned to a foster family.

Another aspect of abuse that is difficult to detect occurs when the oldest male child in a single-parent home becomes the replacement sexual partner for the female. The male child will take on an adult role and responsibilities. Children are apprehensive about turning in their mother, fearing repercussions from authorities, who might remove the child or children from their homes. It is a double-edged sword. No matter what, children still want to be with their birth parents, abused or not. A child does not want his or her mom getting into trouble and this places the child in a no-win situation in which he or she accepts the abuse instead of jeopardizing the possible breakup or separation of the family. Many sexual abuse cases that involve children within the family home are often under the pretense of custodial care, which is often the reason why many of these types of offenders are so hard to uncover and detect.

A Female Abuser Dominated by a Male Partner

The second type of female sex offender is coerced by a male friend or acquaintance. This is a common form of female abuse. Most of these women are also sexually abused by their domineering male partner. Women in this circumstance are often nonconfrontational and are often threatened or coerced to commit sexual abuse and other sexual offenses in the company of an abusive and dominant male. Studies have revealed that the female offender is forced and pressured, often fearing abandonment if she does not comply with her male companion's demands.

Victims have reported that a woman often played a secondary role and usually was hesitant to engage in the sexual act, but was forced and threatened to do so. The male in this situation often initiates the abusive behavior and the young female adolescents are most often the intended target of these episodes of intrafamiliar abuse. A few studies have indicated that female sex offenders and their male accomplices were more likely to have more than one victim. This kind of couple will abuse their own children together.

An example of a female being coerced by her male partner occurred when a woman let her male friend have sex with a 6-year-old child for whom she was caring. He performed oral sex on the child and penetrated her vagina and rectum. The 35-year-old female did not participate in the abuse, but felt intimidated and threatened with physical harm if she did not comply. The child cried uncontrollably and was taken to the hospital, bleeding and torn from the abuse. Both were arrested and charged with felonies.

A Female Abuser Who Holds a Position of Authority

The third category comprises females that hold a position of authority, which most often encompasses the teaching or coaching professions. Many female sex offenders of this type do not envision their behaviors as exploitation but rather as a romantic and amorous relationship. According to the Center for Sex Offender Management (2007), highly publicized cases involving inappropriate and illegal sexual contact between female high school teachers and their male students are a primary source of this growing concern. These cases are not representative of the full nature or scope of sexual abuse committed by females, however, and they have the potential to promote myths and misperceptions about the broader issue of female-perpetrated sex crimes.

Historically, cases under the teacher/lover classification have been between young female students and male perpetrators. In the last few years, however, young female teachers have been seeking out their adolescent male students. The teacher–student relationship will start out as a casual friendship. The female perpetrator will initiate a gradual grooming process that breaks down initial barriers or guidelines of trust the student may have. The progression often leads to infatuation with an underage student in her school or in her class. The female instructor does not view this as sexual abuse, but rather as a spontaneous and consensual relationship or connection between her and the student.

The teacher more than likely will engage in sexual activity after school or in a secret location (most often, her own home). The female sex offender relies on the young boy or girl to keep their relationship a secret, and the teacher rarely views the repercussions of their harmful relationship. Ramsland and McGrain (2010) said that in joining with a female teacher many boys are willing to have a sexual relationship. They said that it is clear that the superior position of the teacher, her authority, and her seduction tactics have some effect on the male student. Like male offenders, these women apparently feel entitled to do what they are doing and they engage the boy in a shared secret that feels exciting. They target them, use enticements, reshape their thinking about the appropriateness of what they are doing, and isolate them as a way to make them keep the secret. Those who threaten would then be taking the final step in this process.

Psychologist Mic Hunter (personal communication) has said that there is also the cultural myth (exemplified by movies such as *Summer of '42*, *Men Don't Leave*, and *My Tutor*) that sexual contact between an adult female and a young boy is a desirable initiation into manhood. Boys may not feel victimized because they engage in anticipated sexual activity voluntarily and consider themselves lucky or as a part of growing up. There is a serious misconception regarding sexual abuse of boys compared to sexual abuse of girls regarding teacher–student sexual encounters. Girls who are sexually exploited are always seen as victims, whereas boys are often seen as lucky. The sexual traumatization that boys experience can affect future relationships, even though they appear to shrug off the mistreatment. The younger the boy is when he is exploited, the more psychological harm he may experience.

The teacher in this type of relationship seems to have little regard for her reputation; the relationship is almost always revealed. Her careless behavior will ultimately cost her her job and provide the likelihood of serving jail time for her actions. This type of relationship will ultimately leave the boy or girl disconcerted and perplexed by the relationship. Because of the secretive encounters, a child may experience flashbacks and may find future relationships a challenge or problematic. Female sex offenders often make up the same excuses as their male sexual predator counterparts.

The next two profiles are classic examples of teacher/lover relationships that occur throughout the United States. The first example deals with a 43-year-old former physical education teacher at an elementary and middle school in a small town in Texas. She was arrested for an improper relationship with a student. The alleged sexual encounters took place between the instructor and a 15-year-old male student in May of 2008. DNA samples were found in a vehicle that linked the student to the accused teacher. Court documents alleged that the physical education teacher had a relationship with the student for years, keeping in contact through text and phone conversations. Police said that the physical education instructor also provided the student with a cell phone, bought him candy, gifts, and clothes, and gave him money. According to authorities, the physical education teacher resigned from her position after being arrested and is no longer working for the school district.

The second example concerns a 34-year-old former female teacher who taught in a high school. She was sentenced to 4–15 years in prison after she pled guilty to 21 counts of criminal sexual conduct charges. Previously she had pled guilty to three similar charges in another county. The teacher was arrested in June 2010 when she was accused of having sex with a student for over a year. According to court documents, the sex acts between the female teacher and a 16-year-old male student occurred at her home, at the teen's home, at area hotels, and in her two vehicles. They had sex about 100 times. The teacher was ordered to register as a sex offender after her prison sentence.

A Female Abuser Who Is Curious and a Risk Taker

The fourth type of female sex offender will purposely come in contact with as many younger children in her job or daily routine as she can. This type of female abuser is sexually curious and can be considered a risk taker. She is a person who is in a position as a caregiver, nanny, babysitter, daycare employee, ballet instructor, or school bus driver. This type of female sexual offender has the responsibility of caring for a young child; her duties could be watching, dressing, feeding, or even bathing the child. She will molest the child by sexually exploring or sexually experimenting under the guise of carrying out her duties and responsibilities. Many female offenders in this category are often curious and inquisitive, and they try to "test the waters" to see how far they can go and what they can get away with.

This female offender seeks sexual gratification, fulfillment, and pleasure when exploiting a child. She will often exhibit the same behavior as and will most likely have similar characteristics to those of male offenders. The following are two examples of a risk taker's relationship:

- In 2009, a 22-year-old woman sexually abused a 5-year-old girl that she was babysitting. The babysitter has been sentenced to a total of 84 months in prison for the sexual abuse of the child. She also has to register as a sex offender for the rest of her life.
- A 25-year-old woman from New York was arrested for allegedly engaging in sex with a 12-year-old boy with whom she was acquainted. She was charged with two counts of first-degree rape and one count of first-degree criminal sexual act—all felonies. The police were alerted after the boy told his family about the sex acts. She was arraigned and remained in jail for lack of bond.

There are many female babysitters and other females in care-giving occupations whose sexual misconduct has never been reported.

Females Who Abuse Family Members and Relatives

This category of female offender (sibling incest) is often the least common form of female sexual abuse that occurs. This type of female abuser is often the older sister or relative who is viewed as a friend and nurturer. This type of sex offender will take advantage of the moment and often will keep a low profile and secrecy when abusing her victim. She seldom takes chances and her advances are less intrusive and subtle—often fondling or bathing a relative or keeping the bathroom door ajar, or other forms of voyeurism. The victim is often confused regarding the abuser's behavior and his or her own reaction to the incest experience, which is often expressed as the most damaging and shameful aspect of the abuse. The manipulation may have emotional and psychological effects on the victim.

Female Sex Offenders and Major Components in Their Abuse

- Offending
  - With a male partner (forceful, dominant nature)
  - By themselves (often loving, emotional attachment)

- Relationship with a victim
  - Male or female
  - Family member (incestuous)
  - Babysitter, caregiver, teacher, etc. (situational)
- Action
  - Kissing, touching, and hugging
  - Sexual contact

Key Examples of Risk Factors for Women

- Low self-esteem
- Self-injury, suicide attempts
- Victimization during childhood and/or adulthood
- Employment difficulties
- Low educational attainment
- Difficulties in intimate relationships
- Antisocial peers and attitudes
- Mental health difficulties
- Substance abuse (Blanchette and Brown 2006)

Key Examples of Risk Factors for Adolescent Girls

- Sexual and physical victimization
- Dysfunction and instability within the family
- Parent/child relationship difficulties
- Antisocial peers
- Academic failure
- Pregnancy
- Early onset of puberty
- Mental health difficulties
- Substance abuse (Blanchette and Brown 2006)

Many studies indicate that women who sexually abuse children are likely to have had abusive childhoods and are apt to have emotional problems. According to a 2008 University of Georgia study, a large sample of female child molesters were themselves victims of sexual abuse as children. Susan Strickland, author of the study and an associate professor at the University of Georgia (School of Social Work), indicated the findings have the potential to help break the cycle of abuse by improving treatment for offenders and their young victims.

Strickland's study (2008), the largest of its kind, surveyed 130 incarcerated females, 60 of whom were sex offenders and 70 of whom were not sexual offenders. She examined factors such as childhood trauma, substance abuse, emotional neediness, and personality disorders. While the majority of both groups reported being the victims of childhood maltreatment, the sex offenders were significantly more likely to have experienced pervasive, serious, and more frequent emotional abuse, physical abuse, and neglect. Strickland said,

> This study informs us about the pathway to becoming sexually deviant for females. With this knowledge, we can improve treatment and reduce the likelihood of future sexual assaults on children. We've pretty much known that the majority of women in prison have had bad childhoods and that many have suffered childhood sexual abuse. The subgroup of female sex offenders has suffered significantly more abuse, particularly sexual abuse.

Strickland articulated that sexual abuse of minors by women has been largely ignored by the general public, the legal system, and academic researchers. Many people believe that women are not capable of committing such acts, she said, and the abuse of boys by women is often dismissed as the boys sowing their oats or even "being lucky." The truth is that both boys and girls are molested by female perpetrators and these victims often suffer a myriad of consequences affecting their sexuality, relationships, and beliefs about themselves and others. Childhood sexual abuse also has been linked to a host of emotional and behavioral problems, such as substance abuse and eating disorders. The true prevalence of female sexual abuse of children is unknown, but a commonly accepted figure is that 5%–7% of sex crimes are committed by females. Studies on female sex offenders are rare, and most have been descriptive in nature, have used small samples, and have not used valid statistical measures or control groups.

Recent studies have indicated that many female sex offenders have suffered emotional as well as physical abuse in their childhood, and they are not likely to admit the abuse to anyone. Female sex offenders who have been sexually exploited contend that it is often longer lasting and more severe abuse than that experienced by male sex offenders who have been sexually exploited.

Recidivism

A study by Sandler and Freeman (2010) examined recidivism among female sex offenders. The study was based on a sample of 1,466 females convicted of sex offenses in New York state and explored the following:

- Offending prior to the commission of the offender's first sexual offense
- Rates of recidivism following the first sexual offense conviction
- Factors associated with the likelihood of sexual recidivism

Rearrest was used as the measure of recidivism. Due to the fact that a large number of the offenders received sentences other than custodial sentences, recidivism was measured at 1, 3, and 5 years postconviction, rather than release from custody. Results showed the recidivism rates of female sex offenders to be lower than those of male sex offenders for all types of recidivism studied (any rearrest, felony rearrest, violent [including violent sexual] felony rearrest, and sexual rearrest). Several significant differences were found between the group of female sex offenders who sexually recidivated and the group who did not, including the first sexual conviction and measures of prior offending. The analysis revealed that three factors significantly increased the likelihood of sexual recidivism following the first conviction for a sexual offense:

- A greater number of prior child victim convictions
- A greater number of prior misdemeanor convictions
- Increased offender age

Further, the results of this study indicated that female sex offenders are most likely to begin their sexual offending later in life when compared to males, typically following a history of low-level, nonsexual offending.

Treatment for Female Sex Offenders

Recent studies and leading psychologists agree that therapy and treatment for female sex offenders and male sex offenders who exhibit abusive behavior is relatively the same. Counseling for female offenders may include a variety of issues, including:

- Relationship and reunification difficulties
- Trauma issues
- Exploitation and behavioral concerns
- Victimization traits and characteristics
- Intimacy and caring problems
- Alcohol and substance abuse

Several conclusions can be drawn regarding female perpetrators. A great amount of publicity and awareness about women perpetrators of sexual abuse has greatly increased in recent years. Female offenders have particular needs that are different from those of their male counterparts. The sexual contact between female sexual offenders and children is relatively low compared to the number of children that are sexually molested and abused by males. Many people in society are naïve about the fact that child sexual abuse by females is not as sporadic as once thought. Sex abuse by women has increased in frequency and in the method of abuse. Female sex offenders are less likely to fit the classic description of a pedophile or have pedophilic behavior. Research has shown that female sexual offender recidivism rates have increased, but this group is difficult to gather research on because it has such a small number of convicted offenders.

Profile of a Female Sex Offender

Lisa, a 39-year-old woman from Vermont, pleaded guilty to a reduced charge of felony lewd and lascivious conduct with a child, a charge that was amended from felony sexual assault. Lisa was arrested in August 2009 and was at the time accused of allegedly engaging in sex with her friend's 15-year-old son. She was reportedly caught in bed with the teen boy by the boy's uncle.

Lisa has a strict list of 16 special probationary conditions, including a requirement that prevents her from having contact with males under the age of 16 unless approved in advance by her probation officer and under the supervision of an adult that her probation officer also approves.

Lisa must also avoid buying or drinking alcohol and cannot visit places where alcohol sales are a primary business, such as bars. She must also undergo counseling for alcohol abuse and her sex offense. She will also be listed on the Vermont sex offender registry.

Profile of a Male Sex Offender

A 56-year-old Delaware pediatrician has been charged with molesting 103 children, some as young as 3 months old. Dr. Earl Bradley was arrested in December of 2009 for videotaping sex acts with the children and molesting them repeatedly while their parents waited in another room. He had six cameras in his office. Dr. Bradley's office had a carnival-type atmosphere filled with toys and games for children to enjoy. He had been accused of abusing his patients for the past 11 years, but complaints were ignored. A 160-page indictment for sexual abuse, rape, and exploitation of a child from 1998 to 2009 was issued against him.

The doctor is believed to have molested 102 female children and one male child. Some children were allegedly molested continuously over a series of days or months. One of his victims was allegedly raped from June 2007 until February 2009. Authorities were able to retrieve 13 hours of video and many files, computers, and hard drives, along with 7,000 patient files. Dr. Bradley was indicted on February 22, 2010, on 470 counts of sex abuse involving 103 children. He recently was sentenced to life in prison.

In My Opinion

Dr. Erin Basalay

Dr. Erin Basalay, a postdoctoral fellow in Chicago, Illinois, has been dealing with both juvenile and adult sex offenders who are mandated by the court to participate in counseling and treatment. She notes a distinct difference between male juvenile offenders and male adult offenders (personal communication). Most of her clients have been adult child molesters who have exploited their own children or family members. A large number of Dr. Basalay's clients have a trauma history dealing with other problems besides being sexually abused, including neglect, attachment issues, and physical, emotional, and verbal abuse.

Dr. Basalay noted that juvenile offenders (12–17 years of age) experience different behavioral issues comprising outrage and hostility toward their parents or the primary caregiver in the family. The juvenile offenders often believe they are treated differently than other family members. Her experience has found that, generally, older siblings will abuse their younger brothers or sisters.

Dr. Basalay mentioned that juvenile offenders are more apt to express remorse for their victims and the hurt they have caused. This is a much slower process for adult sex offenders because they are initially in denial and rationalize their harmful actions. She feels that juvenile offenders are more readily able to feel remorse because

> they are in early stages of moral development;
> their thought processes are more flexible; and
> they can take on the perspective of their victim.

Dr. Basalay said that a vast majority of, if not all, adult sexual predators are always involved in a grooming process. She disclosed that sexual offenders talk themselves into the process of offending. Dr. Basalay confidently said, "Not only do sexual predators groom their victim but they are grooming themselves into believing their behavior is acceptable."

Dr. Basalay revealed that child pornography is often a stepping-stone for more serious sexual offending behaviors. It reinforces the negative attitudes and the deviant sexual arousal. She feels that consequences for sexual offending needs to be in place and that incarceration and probation may be helpful for ensuring that mandated treatment is completed. The sex offender registry may be helpful for society to keep people safe, but sex offenders hate the restrictions, rules, difficulty in finding housing, and parole and probation mandates. Their behavior is inappropriate and deplorable, but a therapist must be open and objective during the process of treatment.

Definitions of Chapter Key Terms

Emotional abuse: To manipulate a person psychologically in a harsh manner that will cause persistent anxiety.

Isolation: To alienate a person or keep a person alone or concealed.

Verbal abuse: Often associated with a pattern of behavior. A person uses crude and coercive remarks that are meant to hurt, criticize, or cause an individual emotional pain.

References

Blanchette, K., & Brown, S. L. (2006). *The assessment and treatment of women offenders: An integrated perspective.* Chichester, West Sussex, UK: John Wiley & Sons.

Center for Sex Offender Management. (2007). The effective management of juvenile sex offenders in the community (http://www.csom.org/train/juvenile/index.html), accessed March 29, 2007.

Ramsland, K., and McGrain, P. (2010). *Inside the minds of sexual predators.* Santa Barbara, CA: Praeger.

Sandler, J., and Freeman N. (2008). Female and male sex offenders. A comparison of recidivism patterns and risk factors. *Journal of Interpersonal Violence* 23: 1394–1413.

_____. (2010). Female sex offender recidivism: A large-scale empirical analysis. *Criminal Justice Policy Review* 21 (1): 31–49.

Saradjian, J. (1996). *Women who sexually abuse children: From research to clinical practice.* New York: John Wiley & Sons.

Strickland, S. (2008). Study: Most female child molesters were victims of sexual abuse. University of Georgia news release.

Child Pornography   6

The written word for a female is powerful as pornography for a male. Once a predator taps into a female's emotion by flattery and by telling her that she is pretty or nice, or that she has a good sense of humor, then it gets to where the predator wants to make his move.

Mom of a victim

Yeah, I look at the pictures and store them away. Yes, I used them later for trading material, or I would use them as an "icebreaker" for some of the girls I would eventually try to meet. I found it was a good lead-in.

Sexual predator

Sexual predators commit crimes because they think they can get away with it.

Sexual predator

Introduction

Although many people have heard about child pornography, a majority do not fully understand the true meaning of what this crime entails. Child pornography is not just a picture of a naked child; this criminal act also entails the following:

- Lewd exposure of the child's genitals
- Sexual exploitation including rape of a child
- Explicit sexual activities including stimulation
- Replicated or genuine sexual activities
- Masturbation of a child with the intention of sexual arousal and gratification

Child pornography also reveals images of minors engaged in sexual acts. In child pornography, the offender's face is never shown. The difference between child pornography and pornography is that the former reveals sexually explicit photographs or video that depicts a person under the age of 18 involved in sexually graphic conduct such as sexual intercourse, masturbation, or sexual cruelty. Anyone who collects, distributes, sells, or possesses child pornography is often seen as deviant and abnormal, not only in this country, but internationally as well. Child pornography has grown to epic proportions across the nation because of the Internet, and it has become a social and legal problem for our society. Statistics show that the number of cases of child exploitation, child abuse, and child trafficking has steadily increased due in part to child pornography.

There is a difference in taking a picture of a naked child, child erotica, and child pornography. Having a picture of a naked child is not considered child pornography. Child erotica, which is somewhat easier to get via the Internet, has the child posing in a provocative manner, possibly with lingerie or revealing attire. This type of fascination may cross the line of normal behavior but is not considered child pornography. Many sexual predators are stimulated by the sight of children, preteens, and teens with few or no clothes on. Clifford (2008) acknowledged the issue of child porn as a sensitive one and that child abuse continues indefinitely because it will be viewed and circulated by many over the Internet. While the prosecution of pedophiles and the efforts of law enforcement have increased, so has the difficulty in catching these offenders and finding their innocent victims.

It is not uncommon for pedophiles to use photographs to get aroused before they seek out sexual gratification and lower their sexual inhibitions. Child pornography also substantiates a sex offender's interest in children, especially efforts to blackmail victims into further sexual activity. Seto, Cantor, and Blanchard (2006) found that child pornography offenses are a better diagnostic indicator of pedophilia than sexual offenses against child victims. When assessed in the laboratory, the majority of child pornography offenders showed greater sexual arousal in response to images of children than to images of adults. Recent studies have indicated that sexual offenders are persistent in their quest for pictures of potential victims.

Child Erotica

Child erotica does not adequately meet the legal description or characterization of child abuse or child pornography. Child erotica displays a child in a photograph or video in a sexually suggestive manner. The person who creates child erotica will use sensual clothing or sexual material to enhance the child's innocence. A sex offender will gather and use this erotic material along with child pornography to enhance stimulation during masturbation as he fantasizes about past, current, or intended victims. It is this type of arousal and excitement of scantily clad children that fuels the sex offender's desires to go a step further in the quest of child pornography and, eventually, child exploitation. Many sex offenders admit to acquiring material that focuses on children, child erotica, and child pornography.

Child Pornography and Victimization

In my research, I have found that many sexual predators use the Internet to view and distribute child pornography, to meet and befriend young victims, and to manipulate their victims into meeting them for sexual encounters. Not only do they use the Internet to meet their future victims, but they also use it to communicate with each other. Many experts believe that most sexual encounters that involve children directly involve child pornography and there seems to be a clear-cut correlation between child pornography and the likelihood of physically abusing a child. Bell (2003), a writer for the *Guardian* newspaper in Manchester, England, has served 2 years in prison for downloading and storing pornography. Bell believes that a child is a harmless substitute for the real thing and the first step from child pornography to sexual contact is monumental. Bell also says that imprisonment promotes this type of offending behavior.

In 2008, Bourke and Hernandez were involved in a study that dealt with child victimization and child pornography. This study compared two groups of child pornography offenders that participated in a voluntary treatment program:

- Men whose known sexual offense history at the time of judicial sentencing involved the possession, receipt, or distribution of child abuse images, but did not include any hands-on sexual abuse
- Men convicted of similar offenses who had documented histories of hands-on sexual offending against at least one child victim

Bourke and Hernandez's (2008) findings revealed that the Internet offenders in their sample were significantly more likely to have sexually abused a child via a hands-on act.

Law Enforcement and Child Pornography

Lately in the news, we have seen officers coming out of a sexual predator's home with the entire computer system being confiscated and held for evidence for a crime. Computers make is easy to store and conceal information from other people, such as family, friends, coworkers, etc. Sexual predators can store pornographic pictures in files on the computer that are only known to them. Many predators have even acquired in-depth knowledge of computers in order to keep their secret lives concealed.

Today, computer telecommunications have become one of the most prevalent techniques that pedophiles use to share illegal photographic images of minors and to lure children into illicit sexual relationships. The Internet has dramatically increased sex offenders' access to the population they seek to victimize and provides them greater access to a community of people who validate their sexual preferences. Virtually every day, children are lured away from their families by cybersexual predators.

According to Wells et al. (2007), Internet child pornography possession cases involve the use of the Internet or computer technology to possess and/or collect electronic images of child pornography. These investigations present challenges for law enforcement agents throughout the United States and around the world. Law enforcement agencies that investigate Internet child pornography possession incorporate time, money, resources, and manpower using both traditional and undercover investigations.

Traditional methods could include responding to citizen reports about suspected inappropriate behavior and the discovery of child pornography on the suspect's computer. The second method of investigation deals with law enforcement officers posing as sexual offenders interested in trading or buying child pornography. Each state has specific laws regarding child pornography. Therefore, law enforcement personnel have experienced a number of issues and obstacles in prosecuting the sex offender who distributes child pornography from another state. Some problem areas that specifically need to be addressed are the ages of the children that are portrayed in the photographs and the different classifications and variations of child pornography for each state.

Undercover law enforcement officers impersonate eager sex offenders who want to collect, trade, and sell child pornography over the Internet. A hurdle that often occurs is the ability to infiltrate the tight-knit inner circle of child pornographers. They are leery of everyone because of the possibility of the person being a law enforcement officer waiting to seize their inventory and arrest them for their crime. It may be necessary to obtain a warrant in order to access the pornographer's computer equipment and capture digital evidence needed to prosecute. Many jurisdictions and agencies have become involved and proficient in collecting evidence transmitted over the Internet.

The Internet has opened up new avenues of child pornography possession, and law enforcement agencies have developed approaches that facilitate investigations and convictions in these crimes. However, these investigations may pose some dilemmas and require specific resources. It may be necessary to purchase computers or upgrade existing ones for electronic communication, personnel are needed to work online, training in online investigations may be required, and specific digital technology is often useful in tracking suspects. Most law enforcement agencies have expert computer technicians that can retrieve deleted information from confiscated files of Internet sex offenders who are under investigation or have been arrested.

In cases where offenders are reported to possess images of child pornography on a computer, it is possible that images will have been deleted by the time law enforcement investigators examine the computer. Predators often look at many innocent photos of their victims and may even alter them by adding themselves to the pictures in order to satisfy their sexual fantasies and desires. Sexual predators and sex offenders that post pictures on the Internet frequently run the risk of getting caught.

Wolak, Mitchell, and Finkelhor (2003), in "Internet Sex Crimes against Minors: The Response of Law Enforcement," found that 92% of offenders arrested for possessing child pornography had images of minors depicting explicit sexual activity or focusing on genitals. Such images distinctly fit within most states' existing definitions of child pornography. However, some of the borderline Internet child pornography images identified in this study did not clearly match state definitions.

In a study done by Wolak, Mitchell, and Finkelhor (2007), they discovered that 42% of youth Internet users had been exposed to online pornography in the past year. Of those, 66% reported only unwanted exposure. Filtering and blocking software reduced the risk of unwanted exposure, as did attending an Internet safety presentation by law enforcement personnel.

According to Bourke and Hernandez (2008), technological innovations also have enabled offenders to utilize complex methods for avoiding detection by law enforcement. Such methods include using software to erase electronic "footprints," surreptitiously gaining access to wireless networks to download pornographic material, finding secretive locations for data storage (e.g., wristwatches, MP3 players, videogame consoles), and utilizing hardware to bypass a computer's hard drive with the intention of obscuring certain activities from computer records. Although these attempts to outwit and evade detection are an ongoing challenge for law enforcement officials, arrests for online criminality also have increased at an exponential rate. The scope of this problem is worldwide and it is driven, in part, by the fact that child pornography is a lucrative commodity. The primary findings of this study indicated that the majority of so-called child pornographers were, in fact, undetected child abusers.

The FBI has two programs that deal specifically with child pornography. The first one is the Innocent Images National Initiative (IINI), a component of FBI's Cyber Crimes Program. It is an intelligence-driven, proactive, multiagency investigative operation to combat the outbreak of child pornography and child sexual exploitation. The mission of the IINI is to reduce the vulnerability of children, acts of sexual exploitation, and abuse that are facilitated through the use of computers. This division of the FBI tries to

- Identify and rescue child victims
- Deal with online predators in chat rooms specifically on the Internet
- Investigate and prosecute sexual predators who use the Internet and other online services to sexually exploit children for personal or financial gain

- Strengthen the capabilities of federal, state, local, and international law enforcement through training programs and investigative assistance

The IINI is committed to stopping these crimes. It is joined by the FBI and local police by being proactive around the country and working online undercover to stop those who prey on children.

The second program is the Crimes Against Children Program. This initiative focuses on crimes perpetrated against children by

- Trying to decrease the vulnerability of children to sexual exploitation
- Developing a nationwide capacity to provide a rapid, effective, and measured investigative response to crimes against children
- Enhancing the capabilities of state and local law enforcement investigators through programs, investigative assistance, and task force operations
- Working with multiagency teams to investigate and prosecute crimes across the many jurisdictions throughout the country
- Sharing intelligence
- Specializing in skills and services to apprehend an offender
- Incorporating a victim and witness service

The Internet Crimes against Children Task Force Program (ICAC program) helps state and local law enforcement agencies develop an effective response to cyber enticement and child pornography cases. This help encompasses forensic and investigative components, training and technical assistance, victim services, and community education. The program was developed in response to the increasing number of children and teenagers using the Internet, the proliferation of child pornography, and heightened online activity by predators seeking unsupervised contact with potential underage victims....The ICAC program is a national network of 61 coordinated task forces representing over 2,000 federal, state, and local law enforcement and prosecutorial agencies. These agencies are engaged in proactive investigations, forensic investigations, and criminal prosecutions. By helping state and local agencies to develop effective, sustainable responses to online child victimization and child pornography, the Office of the Juvenile Justice and Delinquency Protection (OJJDP) has increased their capacity to address Internet crimes against children. (US Department of Justice, n.d.)

The US Department of Justice acknowledges that not all collectors of child pornography physically molest children and that not all molesters of children collect child pornography. Not all children depicted in child pornography have been sexually abused. Some have been photographed without their knowledge while undressing and others have been manipulated into posing nude. Depending on the use of the material, however, all can be considered exploited. For this reason, those who "only" receive or collect child pornography produced by others play a role in the sexual exploitation of children, even if they have not physically molested a child.

Child Pornography Laws

The May 1982 Supreme Court case of *Ferber v. New York* noted that child pornography was not constitutionally protected free speech. Ultimately, anyone who produces, distributes, receives, or passes along child pornography is subject to federal prosecution. It is illegal to buy, post, or sell child pornography.

Seven Laws Regarding Child Pornography

Seven laws that have been passed that protect children from the dangers of pornography:

- Sexual Exploitation of Children Act of 1977
- Child Protection Act of 1984
- The Child Sexual Abuse Act of 1986
- Child Protection and Obscenity Enforcement Act of 1988
- Communications Decency Act of 1996 (CDA)
- The Child Pornography Prevention Act of 1996 (CPAA)
- Child Online Protection Act 1998

Stanley v. Georgia (1969)

Law enforcement officers, under the authority of a warrant, searched Robert Stanley's home pursuant to an investigation of his alleged bookmaking activities. During the search, the officers found three reels of 8-millimeter film. The officers viewed the films, concluded they were obscene, and seized them. Stanley was then tried and convicted under a Georgia law prohibiting the possession of obscene materials. Stanley's defense brought up the question: Did the Georgia statute infringe upon the freedom of expression protected by the First Amendment?

The Supreme Court held that the First and Fourteenth Amendments prohibited making private possession of obscene materials a crime. In his majority opinion, Justice Marshall noted that the rights to receive information and to personal privacy were fundamental to a free society. Marshall then found that "if the First Amendment means anything, it means that a State has no business telling a man, sitting alone in his own house, what books he may read or what films he may watch. Our whole constitutional heritage rebels at the thought of giving government the power to control men's minds." The Court distinguished between the mere private possession of obscene materials and the production and distribution of such materials. The latter, the Court held, could be regulated by the states.

Miller v. California

Miller v. California dealt with prohibited material that was considered obscene. Mr. Marvin Miller was convicted of mailing unsolicited sexually explicit material. This was in direct violation of California's state statutes. This case reaffirmed that obscene material is not protected by the First Amendment (*Roth v. United States,* 354 U.S.476). The outcome produced a *Miller* test that established what especially constituted obscene material. Law enforcement and government officials began to see child pornography becoming an emergent problem after the Supreme Court began looking at the issues surrounding obscenity. This prompted the US government to formulate the Sexual Exploitation of Children Act of 1977.

Sexual Exploitation of Children Act of 1977

Using the *Miller* standard set up by the Supreme Court, the Protection of Children against Sexual Exploitation Act of 1977 prohibited the use of children in the production of obscene material and criminalized the distribution of such materials for commercial purposes. This was the first federal legislative effort to regulate child pornography and provide funding for victims of child sexual abuse and exploitation. This law considers anyone under the age of 16 a child and makes it illegal for anyone to own, use, sell, or circulate child pornography. This act also extended the federal government's influence and its authority to prosecute anyone who produced, distributed, or transported child pornography across state lines for the commercial purpose of child exploitation.

Ferber v. New York

Ferber v. New York was the first child pornography case that came before the Supreme Court (in 1982). A New York child pornography law prohibited persons from knowingly promoting sexual acts to children under the age of 16 by distributing material that depicts such performances. This case highlighted significant differences between obscenity and the *Miller* test. The Supreme Court voted unanimously to reject the *Miller* test as it pertained to child pornography. It was in response to this famous court case that legislators of Congress took the inappropriate use of child pornography to a new level by implementing the Child Protection Act of 1984.

According to the Supreme Court,

> The States are entitled to greater leeway in the regulation of pornographic depictions of children for the following reasons:
> (1) It is the legislative judgment that the use of children as subjects of pornographic materials is harmful to the physiological, emotional, and mental health of the child easily passing muster under the First Amendment.
> (2) The standard of *Miller v. California* (413 U.S. 15) for determining what is legally obscene is not a satisfactory solution to the child pornography problem.
> (3) The advertising and selling of child pornography provide an economic motive for and are thus an integral part of the production of such materials, an activity illegal throughout the Nation.
> (4) The value of permitting live performances and photographic reproductions of children engaged in lewd exhibitions is exceedingly modest, if not de minimis.
> (5) Recognizing and classifying child pornography as a category of material outside the First Amendment's protection is not incompatible with this Court's decisions dealing with what speech is unprotected. When a definable class of material, such as that covered by the New [p. 748] York statute, bears so heavily and pervasively on the welfare of children engaged in its production, the balance of competing interests is clearly struck, and it is permissible to consider these materials as without the First Amendment's protection. (No. 81-55 Supreme Court of the United States, pp. 756–764; 458 U.S. 747; argued April 27, 1982, decided July 2, 1982)

Child Protection Act of 1984

This act specified that a minor is any child less than 18 years of age. Legislators felt that child pornography was becoming a multimillion dollar industry that targeted innocent and vulnerable children. The act prohibits child pornography from being produced and distributed and greatly increases the consequences for any adult who is involved in this activity. When he signed the 1984 Child Protection Bill into law, Ronald Reagan said,

> There's no one lower or more vicious than a person who would profit from the abuse of children, whether by using them in pornographic material or by encouraging their sexual abuse by distributing this material. For years, some people have argued that this kind of pornography is a matter of artistic creativity and freedom of expression and so on and so on, and they go on with that. Well, it's not. This pornography is ugly and dangerous. If we do not move against it and protect our children, then we, as a society, just aren't worth much. In the last few months, we've seen news reports of cases involving child pornography and child abuse on a large scale. We've seen reports suggesting a link between child molesting and pornography.

The Child Sexual Abuse Act of 1986
This act broadened the definition of child pornography and banned the advertisement of child pornography. It also increased the penalties for offenders who had been previously arrested for child pornography and subsequently reoffended.

Child Protection and Obscenity Enforcement Act 1988
In 1988, Congress enacted the Child Protection and Obscenity Enforcement Act. This act explicitly prohibited a person from using a computer to possess, sell, distribute, or receive child pornography. This also included transmitting advertisements and visual depictions.

Osborne v. Ohio (1990)
According to the US Supreme Court media, after obtaining a warrant, Ohio police searched the home of Clyde Osborne and found explicit pictures of naked, sexually aroused male adolescents. Osborne was arrested, prosecuted, and found guilty of violating an Ohio law that made the possession of child pornography illegal. The question that was asked of the Supreme Court regarding Osborne's case was whether Ohio's ban on the possession of child pornography violated the First Amendment.

> The Court held that Ohio could constitutionally proscribe the possession of child pornography. The Court argued that the case at hand was distinct from *Stanley v. Georgia* "because the interest underlying child pornography prohibitions far exceed the interests justifying the Georgia law at issue in *Stanley*." Ohio did not rely on a "paternalistic interest in regulating Osborne's mind"; rather, Ohio merely attempted to protect the victims of child pornography. The Court argued that regulations on production and distribution of child pornography were insufficient and could not dry up the market for pornographic materials. The Court also found that an error in jury instructions in the lower courts mandated Osborne be given a new trial. *Oyez,* http://www.oyez.org/cases/1980-1989/1989/1989_88_5986)

Communications Decency Act 1996
On February 8, 1996, the Communications Decency Act was enacted into law. The law criminalizes the use of any computer network to display "indecent" material, unless the content provider uses an "effective" method to restrict access to that material to anyone under the age of 18.

The Child Pornography and Protection Act of 1996 and Virtual Child Pornography
Since the 1970s, federal law has prohibited the production and distribution of child pornography. This applied only to visualizations of actual children

engaged in sexually explicit behavior. Congress established that child pornography is the first step in prompting or provoking children into sexual activity. Legislators also determined that virtual (computer-generated) pornography of children engaged in sexual promiscuity can also be an effective way of seducing an innocent child. In 1996, Congress passed the Child Pornography Prevention Act (CPPA). Legislators defined child pornography to include any visual portrayal that appears to be that of a minor engaging in a sexually overt act. This also includes selling, possessing, advertising, promoting, reproducing, distributing, or shipping this type of material.

According to the US Department of Justice, the Child Pornography and Prevention Act of 1996 has expanded the definition of child pornography. The new definition includes not only sexually explicit visual depictions using a minor, but also any visual depictions that have been created, adapted, or modified to make it appear that an identifiable minor is engaging in sexually explicit conduct. This law makes the cases involving manipulated computer images easier to prosecute.

Virtual child pornography is a fairly new phenomenon in child exploitation. Virtual pornography depicts one or more minors engaging in illicit sexual acts even though children are not actually used. This type of pornography is done by generating images that are enhanced by computer and digital technological advances; this has obviated the need to use minors in the production of child pornography. Congress has amended the definition of child pornography under the federal criminal law so as not to include materials that only *appear* to depict minors.

In the court case of *Ashcroft v. Free Speech Coalition*, the prosecution's argument was that the Child Pornography Prevention Act was unclear and unconstitutional The US Supreme Court agreed and overturned this law in 2002. The Court ruled that the First Amendment, which is the right to free speech, protected virtual child pornography, stating that no child is harmed or used in a simulated or generated image. Though it remains illegal to make, show, or possess sexually explicit pictures of children, the court found that there was no compelling reason to prohibit the manufacture or exhibition of pictures that merely *appear* to be of children. There were also stipulations by the Court involving the production of virtual pornography. The Supreme Court ruling bars any depiction or image that appears to be an authentic child or minor or that is promoted in a manner that expresses that a child or minor was included in the creation or fabrication of the image.

Sex offenders who engage in all aspects of child pornography may now gravitate toward virtual child pornography to produce, possess, and distribute legally sexually explicit images that are practically identical to and indistinguishable from images of "real" children. New software, graphics, and computer animation are being used to create "virtual" images from photographic depictions of actual children and adolescents. The primary objection that most people have regarding child pornography is that it puts many children at risk, especially the physical and emotional harm that it causes the child who is filmed or photographed for the sexual gratification of the sex offender. Virtual child pornography will not stop children from being victimized but may instead energize the growth of the child pornography market. Critics of child pornography have also implied that it will have a trickle-down effect on law enforcement and prosecutor efforts to protect children. An overwhelming number of people have said that virtual child pornography still portrays the images of harm and mistreatment and that it should be prohibited for that reason.

For example, Clifford (2008) said,

> I wonder if the idea of "virtual porn" is just a ticking time bomb to bigger things. To me it is like giving a person a teaser, a taste of something naughty, which only has them wanting more…wanting the real thing. Therefore I wonder if by giving people the opportunity to experiment with the idea of child porn, we are allowing them an opportunity to increase their craving for the real thing.

Essex (2009) noted that Congress has realized that the Internet has facilitated the growth of a multibillion dollar global market for images and video of children and has exceeded law enforcement's capacity to respond. This explosion of child pornography trafficking is claiming very young victims and the images and videos being trafficked typically depict graphic and brutal sexual assaults. The Department of Justice has identified millions of child pornography transactions involving images and video of child sexual assault from an abundance of computer IP addresses worldwide. Many federal agencies find it difficult to investigate the overwhelming number of child pornography and child exploitation crimes they have encountered and thus millions of children are at risk.

Child pornography is not only a growing crime in the United States but also an international problem. Child pornography has become a profitable and widely used online computer and website domain. This industry has seen a dramatic increase in child pornography enthusiasts, abusers, and fanatics, and it is growing daily at an alarming rate. The content of child sexual abuse, especially sexual penetration, has become much worse over time.

According to the Internet Watch Foundation (2011), there are 1,351 individual child abuse domains. Many, if not all sexual predators have their own collection of child pornography; they may share it, but they never want to give it up. Many sexual predators will trade in secret or meet up with other sexual predators to trade child pornography. They may meet in a hotel with their laptop computers, trading pictures among themselves.

In a June 2005 study, the National Center for Missing and Exploited Children revealed that 40% of arrested child pornography possessors had sexually victimized children and were in possession of child pornography (also known as "dual offenders"). Both crimes were discovered in the same investigation. Another 15% were "dual offenders" who tried to victimize children by soliciting undercover investigators who posed as minors online. Overall, 36% of "dual offenders" showed or gave child pornography to identified victims or undercover investigators posing as minors online. Of those arrested in the United States for the possession of child pornography between 2000 and 2001, 83% had images that involved children between the ages of 6 and 12; 39% had images that involved children between the ages of 3 and 5; and 19% had images of infants and toddlers under age 3.

Profile of a Female Sex Offender

Not many women are convicted sex offenders, but Char, a mother of two, is. She is California's only female violent sex offender, confined to a maximum-security state mental hospital where she is considered too dangerous for release. Char told psychiatrists that she had molested children, ages 5–8, whom she babysat or enticed into her California apartment to play with her children.

Char, the third of six children, had a good relationship with her father, but complained that her mother regularly beat her with narrow leather straps, sticks, and her fists. Char was born with scoliosis and a deformity in her mouth that caused speech difficulties. School was difficult for her because she was constantly harassed, ridiculed, and bullied by the other children, mostly because of her physical deformities. Char retaliated to the abuse by tormenting and bullying much younger students in her school. She ran away from home several times between the ages of 11 and 16. She told authorities that she was gang-raped at age 15 by four men who grabbed her off a street. Another tragedy that happened in her young life was that she was severely wounded in a random shooting and spent 9 months in a hospital; she never returned to school. At 19, Char married a US Marine and had two daughters. Their marriage ended after 5 years and she won custody of both girls.

The year after her divorce, 27-year-old Char was submissive and admitted to being very promiscuous and having sex with numerous men; she eventually met a man who was 7 years older than she and had two sons from a previous relationship. He ultimately moved into her California apartment. Her new roommate and boyfriend became rough and physical with her. He beat her often, a few times to the point of unconsciousness, and sodomized her as well.

Char's new boyfriend introduced her to having sex with children. She molested his sons and he would often join her in having sex with children. Char and her boyfriend had sex a couple of times a day with children and with as many as five children at a time, she told psychiatrists. The victims were her boyfriend's sons and other children in their apartment complex. During the 8 months in which she molested, Char drank and used methamphetamine, first snorting the drug and later injecting it. "When she was intoxicated, she was sexually promiscuous, violent, and sexually perverse," according to a May 2001 report by the state Department of Mental Health.

Both Char and her boyfriend threatened the children that their parents or siblings would be killed if they told anyone. Eventually, one of the children did tell, and both offenders were arrested. When Char was questioned, she admitted being afraid of her boyfriend and said, "He made me do it." Char also admitted molesting and abusing four boys and a girl because she wanted to get even with their parents. She blamed lashing out at helpless and weaker victims on the mistreatment in her relationships.

Char initially faced more than 50 counts of felony child molesting. She pled no contest in 1988 to five counts of molestation in exchange for a 14-year prison sentence. Char married her abusive boyfriend after their arrests but divorced him while in prison. Her now ex-husband pleaded no contest to several counts of lewd and lascivious conduct upon children and was sentenced to 24 years in prison.

Char began serving her sentence in September 1988 and was paroled in September 1994. She then worked in construction and had what court records described as two "normal" relationships with adult men. In July 1996, she violated her parole by using alcohol, associating with convicted sex offenders, and having contact with children. She returned to prison and was paroled again in March 1998. Within a month, parole was revoked because she had used alcohol. The state began proceedings to commit her as a sex predator, and she did not oppose the effort.

In September of 1998, Char was sent to Patton State Hospital in San Bernardino County. She was registered as a sexually violent predator. During therapy she expressed regret about exploiting her two daughters, who are now adults. Char acknowledged that her daughters had been sexual victims of her husband and emotional victims of her. At the age of 50, Daryl Ball, Char's ex-husband, was released from prison and is on parole. He was evaluated by mental health experts and it was determined that he most likely would not reoffend again. Char does not wish to be released until she is convinced she can "manage" her behavior. According to a May 2000 report, she has "genuine shame for her behavior and remorse for her victims." Char has not shown any interest in being released from the hospital, most likely because she feels safe there.

Profile of a Male Sex Offender

Paul was indicted in 2006 for attempting to solicit sex from an 11-year-old girl. He worked as a school bus driver in Denver, Colorado for 6 years and allegedly came to Oklahoma City, OK to meet the young grade school girl he spoke with through an Internet chat room. Paul used graphic and explicit sexual conversation in his attempt to convince the young girl to meet him. Oklahoma authorities said the 11-year-old child actually was an officer from the Police Internet Crimes Unit. Paul was arrested when he showed up for their meeting at a local fast food restaurant. He was very surprised and disappointed when he found out the 11-year-old girl was a middle- aged policewomen. Paul was charged with attempted aggravated sexual assault of a child and traveling to another state with the intent of having sex with a child. He served 3 years in prison and was fired from his job as a school bus driver.

In My Opinion

Mr. Daniel T. Coyne

Daniel T. Coyne, a clinical professor at Kent Law School, provided this author with a personal interview regarding sexual predators, sexual offenders, and sexually violent individuals. Professor Coyne practices criminal law in the law offices at Chicago-Kent and focuses his representation on defending individuals charged with murder and individuals subject to involuntary commitment pursuant to the Illinois Sexually Violent Persons Act. Mr. Coyne said that sexual predators are a target population different from typical sex offenders (personal communication). He spoke about sexually violent offenders and said that 90% of them had been sexually victimized when they were younger. Professor Coyne feels that if these victims of sexual exploitation were provided treatment or counseling they might not have reoffended.

Professor Coyne began the interview stating the Sexually Violent Persons Commitment Act was enacted in Illinois in 1998. This act is rarely used because it is procedurally awkward. After an offender has been convicted of a crime and has served his or her time, the law allows the state of Illinois to sue offenders after a summons is served. The case is then referred to the criminal court, where probable cause is determined. This step is referred to as "commit to sentencing." This is where evidence is introduced that indicates if the offender did indeed commit the sexual violent act, but even more important is understanding the reason why he or she did it. To be considered a sexually violent person, three factors must apply:

- The individual is convicted of an enumerated sexual offense.

- The offender suffers from a mental disorder according to the *Diagnostic and Statistical Manual of Mental Disorders* (DSM IV-TR).
- The result of the individual's evaluation is considered "substantial probability"—the offender is more likely to reoffend than not.

Professor Coyne said that the Sexually Dangerous Persons Act was originally adopted in 1938, but it essentially became popular in 1955 because of public uproar over the Schuessler case, where three young boys were sexually assaulted and killed in a forest preserve in Chicago. The case was finally solved in 1995, 40 years after the fact. An informant in the murder case of candy heiress Helen Brach also disclosed that the Schuessler boys had been killed by Kenneth Hansen. A sexual predator, Hansen worked for Silas Jayne, a wealthy stable owner with reputed mob ties. Hansen allegedly lured the boys into the woods with the promise that they could ride the prize horses that were kept at the stables, which were only a short distance from Robinson's Woods. Hansen admitted to the crimes and he is thought to have preyed on hundreds of boys. Ken Hansen died in prison in 2007. Mr. Coyne stated, "Mental illness comes into play because these offenders do not have normal criminal minds, but are imprinted with a specific profile of the victim."

According to Blair (2005),

The Illinois Sexually Dangerous Persons Act was established with a two-pronged objective:

1) To protect the public by civilly committing the sexually dangerous until their recovery and release.
2) To treat the sexually dangerous in order to remove their propensity to commit sexual offenses.

When criminal charges of a sexual nature are filed against a person and the prosecutor feels that person meets the criteria of a sexually dangerous person within the meaning of the act, a petition set forth with the facts is filed. The court then appoints two qualified psychiatrists to examine the accused to determine whether he or she is sexually dangerous. In order to commit a person deemed to be sexually dangerous, the state of Illinois is required to prove beyond a reasonable doubt the person suffers from a mental disorder for over one year in duration and has demonstrated propensities towards sexual assault or molestation of children. Additionally, the respondent has a right to trial by jury and representation by counsel.

If found to be sexually dangerous, the accused is committed to the custody of the Director of Corrections, who will provide care and treatment designed to effect recovery. The accused remains committed until recovery. There is no limit on the time a sexually dangerous person can spend in a treatment program, and the program is not limited to those with curable disorders. Those committed under the Illinois Sexually Dangerous Person Program must disclose a full sexual history. They must then sign an "Acknowledgment of Limited Confidentiality and Waiver" form, and agree to a polygraph test in order to guarantee full and truthful disclosures by those committed. If the sexually dangerous person refuses, they cannot start the treatment program and will remain jailed indefinitely. Some sexually dangerous persons have done just that and have never received treatment. While treatment is not technically a prerequisite to being released, participation increases the likelihood of release. Upon completion of all goals of the program, in order for the sexually violent person to be discharged, an application must be filed before the committing court. The application must be followed by a psychological evaluation report from which the hearing court must find the person no longer dangerous. Releases are conditional, and violation of any of the conditions constitutes recommitment. Upon discharge, outstanding information and the indictment which was the basis of detention are quashed.

Professor Coyne spoke about the sexually violent person (SVP) and the programs that are meant to help him recover. This program allows the sexual deviant person to seek help at a treatment and detention facility. These individuals go through a cognitive five-phase restructuring program. The main goal is for the individual to restructure his thinking and to be able to process why he committed these heinous sexual crimes. This program gives those in treatment tools or resources to recognize triggers for their actions. It is meant to end the offending cycle. After this treatment, SVPs may be placed into a conditional release program. This program monitors their whereabouts through GPS and surveillance agents.

A sex offender registry allows society to know what sexual offenders have done and where they live. Professor Coyne stated, "They should not be able to drop off the radar." He also acknowledged that the government has possibly overreacted and is probably overreaching when it comes to the sex offender registries. He said that some people do not fall under the sexual offender category. An offender who commits a vicious sexual crime should have to register for life; juveniles with sexual charges should have to register for 10 years. The government wants to make all offenders register for a lifetime. If individual states fail to uphold a lifetime requirement, then they may lose federal money that would have been allocated to them. A sex offender registry is really a political issue. Professor Coyne said, "A politician will never lose votes for being tough on sex offenders because most people do not want them [predators] on the street."

Professor Coyne mentioned two specific cases that deal with sexually violent individuals: Floyd Durr and Brad Lieberman.

The Floyd Durr Case

According to Professor Coyne, "The Durr family has spawned an entire generation of sex offenders." Floyd's father and family sexually exploited Fred, his siblings, and other family members.

Floyd Durr pleaded guilty to killing an innocent 11-year-old girl named Ryan Harris and agreed to a life sentence plus an additional 30 years for that crime. Ryan Harris had been visiting a relative in the Englewood area of Chicago before her body was found in an overgrown lot on July 28, 1998. The girl died from asphyxiation and blunt trauma to the skull. Her underwear was stuffed in her throat, and leaves were jammed into her nostrils, according to a Cook County medical examiner.

Prosecutors and defense lawyers said they decided on a plea deal because tests had determined that Durr's IQ qualified him to be considered mentally retarded. In 2002, the US Supreme Court barred people with IQs lower than 70 from facing the death penalty. Durr's defense lawyer was Daniel Coyne. He said that tests revealed abnormalities in Durr's brain and that, from the time Durr was 7 until he was last tested in school at 15, he ranked in the bottom 1% of people tested. Over 8 tortured years, evidence led to a brutal and hardened criminal from a family of violent offenders. Interviews and court records depicted a band of brothers whose fury had simmered and boiled over onto the lives of victims through the years.

Before his plea, Floyd Durr was serving 125 years for his previous sexual assaults of girls. His brother Eddie, 38, has been convicted of committing eight sexual assaults and is serving a life sentence without the possibility of parole. Their youngest brother, Eric, 36, was convicted at age 17 of involuntary manslaughter in the death of a man and has been in and out of prison on other charges since then. The list of crimes sheds little light on how a family came to be so violent. In a previous court hearing, Floyd Durr blamed it on past family abuse and an addiction to marijuana. "When I'm sad, I get high and bad things happen. I rape and I run," Durr said in court documents.

The Brad Lieberman Case

Brad Lieberman still insists he is innocent, nearly 30 years after he was convicted of a series of rapes. Lieberman became known as "the plumber rapist" because he got into his victims' apartments by claiming to be a plumber checking for leaks. Lieberman was convicted of six rapes but had an estimated 17 victims in all, according to court documents. In April and May 1980, while out on bond, Lieberman raped two more women. He has had several disciplinary problems in prison. Lieberman's lawyers filed a petition for his release, saying he was no longer a threat. Throughout his incarceration, Lieberman maintained his innocence and refused to participate in sex offender treatment.

In 2000, he was due to be released from prison after a 20-year sentence, but the Illinois attorney general asked a court to hold him as a sexually violent person. He remains in the custody of the Illinois Department of Human Services in downstate Rushville. In November 2007, the Winston Law Firm filed its petition to have Lieberman released. The petition cited a Rushville psychiatric report that Lieberman's mental disorders were in "full remission." But the attorney general's office said the report was not authentic.

Brad Lieberman appealed the order of the circuit court of Cook County denying his petition for discharge or immediate release from the care and custody of the Illinois Department of Human Services (DHS). Lieberman contended that the denial of his petition was an abuse of discretion and violated his right to the due process of law.

Definitions of Chapter Key Terms

Child erotica: Displays a child in a photograph or video in a sexually suggestive manner.

Child pornography: Not just a picture of a naked child, it involves the lewd exposure of the child's genitals, sexual exploitation including rape of a child, explicit sexual activities including simulated or replicated or genuine sexual activities including masturbation of a child with the intention of sexual arousal and gratification. Child pornography also reveals images of minors who are engaged in sexual acts. In child pornography you will never see the offender's face. The difference between child pornography and pornography is that the former is sexually explicit photographs or video that depicts a person under the age of 18 involved in sexually graphic conduct, such as sexual intercourse, masturbation, and sexual cruelty.

First Amendment: "Congress shall make no law respecting an establishment of religion, or prohibiting the free exercise thereof; or abridging the freedom of speech, or of the press; or the right of the people peaceably to assemble, and to petition the government for a redress of grievances."

Mouse trappings: A commonly used technique by pornography sites where a user gets "locked" into a website. While surfing the Internet, it is possible to click on a website where multiple undesirable websites then open. When this happens a person cannot close or back out of the sites and must close the web browser completely.

Multimedia: A combination of different types of programs that allow a person to see graphics, animation, and text.

Virtual child pornography: A relatively new phenomenon depicting minors engaging in illicit sexual acts, even though no children are used.

This type of pornography is produced by generating images that are enhanced by computer and digital technology.

References

Bell, J. (2003, January 23). I cannot admit what I am to myself: The news that 7,000 men in this country had used a US child porn website shocked Britain. *Guardian*, Manchester, England, p. 2.

Blair, W. W. (2005). The Illinois Sexually Dangerous Persons Act: The civilly committed and their Fifth Amendment rights, or lack thereof. 29 S. Ill. U. L. J. 461.

Bourke, M. L., and Hernandez, A. E. (2008). The Butner study redux: A report of the incidence of hands-on child victimization by child pornography offenders. Published online December 10, 2008, Springer Science + Business Media, LLC.

Clifford, C. (2008). Virtual child porn. Foreign Policy Association (http://children.foreignpolicyblogs.com).

Essex, D. (2009). From deleting online predators to educating Internet users. Congress and Internet safety: A legislative analysis. *Young Adult Library Services I, Internet Dangers and Child Exploitation*, Spring 2009.

Federal Bureau of Investigation (FBI). Innocent Images National Initiative, online child pornography/child sexual exploitation investigations (www.ojp.usdoj.gov). Internet Watch Foundation. (2011). Annual report.

National Center for Missing and Exploited Children. (2005). Virtual child pornography: The impact of the Supreme Court decision in the case of *Ashcroft v. Free Speech Coalition*.

Oyez. (n.d.) http://www.oyez.org/cases/1980-1989/1989/1989_88_5986

Seto, M. C., Cantor J. M., and Blanchard, R. (2006). Child pornography offenses are a valid diagnostic indicator of pedophilia. *Journal of Abnormal Psychology* 115:610–615.

US Department of Justice. (n.d.). Office of Juvenile Justice and Delinquency Prevention (http://www.ojjdp.gov/programs/progsummary.asp?pi=3).

Wells, M., Finkelhor, D., Wolak, J., and Mitchell, K. J. (2007). Defining child pornography: Law enforcement dilemmas in investigations of Internet child pornography possession. *Police Practice and Research* 8 (3): 269–282.

Wolak, M., Mitchell, K., and Finkelhor, D. (2003). Internet sex crimes against minors: The response of law enforcement. US Dept. of Justice Office of Juvenile Justice and Delinquency Prevention.

———. (2007). Unwanted and wanted exposure to online pornography in a national sample of youth Internet users. *Pediatrics* 119 (2): 247–257.

The Internet and Sexual Predators

7

So you end up spending a lot of time on the web (Internet), and some of the friends that you did have in school, you are going to lose contact with them. You are going to go away from your parents a bit, because your parents have their own lives, and you do not want to be attached to their hip all of the time. They [parents] will let you grow a little—that is what they are supposed to do at that age.

Victim of a sexual predator

Sex is the number one searched-for topic on the Internet.

Robert Weiss, Sexual Recovery Institute

Display of an Internet Chat Room Conversation

SexyGirl97: I've been depressed w/school and my parents just don't understand me.
ShyGuy69: I'll listen.
ShyGuy69: Did you say you were a cheerleader 4 the Panthers?
SexyGirl97: How did u know that?
ShyGuy69: I read ur profile.
SexyGirl97: Yeah, I love it.
ShyGuy69: Any chance of seeing u cheer, I should be in ur area after school. We can go for a ride L8R???
SexyGirl97: I guess, how old are u?
ShyGuy69: I have my license, do u wanna go. I'm a little older. Do u like older men?
SexyGirl97: I guess, I'll have 2 let my Mom know.
ShyGuy69: Y, she doesn't need 2 know, let's have fun, it will be exciting!
SexyGirl97: Kewl.
ShyGuy69: I'll take you 2 the mall, I want 2 buy u stuff so u won't be depressed, we can hang out.
SexyGirl97: I've been dreaming of a guy like u.
ShyGuy69: Here I am. It was nice talking w/u tonight.
SexyGirl97: It was nice, see u 2mrw?
ShyGuy69: Great, I can't wait!!!
SexyGirl97: Me 2, By.

The Internet and Sexual Predators

Prior to the Internet, sexual predators hung around parks, schools, and playgrounds. With the arrival of technology, the sexual predator no longer needs to venture from his home to find or meet his victims. The Internet has aggressively developed into a playground of sexual predatory exploitation. Internet exploitation has reached epidemic proportions in today's society, and law enforcement officials have been inundated with the enormity of the problem and have only recently touched the tip of the iceberg in their attempt to control the growth of this deviant population. Now, with a click of a button, a world of potential victims is at a sexual predator's fingertips. It is possible that offenders can access a child more easily online than through conventional social networks because anonymity and secrecy over the Internet give the sexual predator a tremendous advantage in luring young victims.

It seems that the Internet has become a virtual Sears catalog for sexual predators; they can browse from a multitude of profiles to select their next target and fulfill their out-of-the-ordinary needs and desires; they might have had these desires for many years, such as fantasizing about having sex with a child, but might not have carried them out without the Internet. Their fear of getting caught might have kept them from victimizing a child. The Internet, however, has lessened this fear and exposed them to millions of young children and teens and pornographic images. The advent of the Internet created a venue where innocent victims are often enticed into a sexual predator's interaction of deceit and manipulation. The Internet not only allows men who are tempted to venture into this world of cybersex, but also allows convicted male offenders to continue to engage in criminal predatory sexual behavior toward their victims.

Sexual predators are now able to take advantage of the Internet by using it to communicate with each other, sharing and distributing child pornography and other interests. The more offenders meet and share their sexual desires, the more they begin to justify and reinforce their behavior of sexual victimization. By communicating with other sexual predators and sexual offenders, they can justify their abnormal behavior as normal because so many others are doing the same thing as they are—proving they are not alone. With the assistance of community awareness, parents should always be informed and educated about the dangers of the Internet and online sexual offenders.

Wolak et al. (2008) noted that the Internet may facilitate child molesting by making youths more accessible to offenders and creating opportunities for molesters to be alone with victims. The Internet allows the curious person who is just thinking about exploiting a child the opportunity to take a chance on something that they might not have otherwise acted on. Sexual predators that use the Internet will often misrepresent their age, the reason for their inquiries, or their true intentions by trying to lure as many victims as they can at one time and establish relationships with them. Sending pictures of a different person or a photograph that depicts a younger individual is not uncommon.

Bowker (2005) did an extensive study as to why sexual predators commonly choose to use the Internet to carry out their deviant acts. Bowker noted four specific reasons why the Internet is used:

- The Internet provides anonymity. They can provide a fake name, misrepresent their age, and even change their appearance by sending fake pictures to children and teens to whom they talk. The Internet makes it easy for them to keep their real identity a secret.
- The Internet works to the advantage of these sexual predators so that they can bait many victims at one time.
- Computers make is easy to store and conceal information from other people, such as family, friends, co-workers, etc. Sexual predators can store pornographic pictures in files on the computer that are only known to them.
- Predators can find innocent photos of their victims and alter them into sexually explicit ones, even adding themselves to the pictures.

Online Child Enticement

Online child enticement is the conduct of or an attempt or conspiracy to commit:

- Criminal sexual abuse of a minor
- Sexual exploitation of a minor
- Abusive sexual contact with a minor
- Sexually explicit conduct with a minor or any similar offense

Online Behavior

Various polls, surveys, and studies have indicated detailed online behavior:

- Teens have established a significant presence on networking web pages.
- Among 13- to 17-year-olds, 61% have a personal profile on a site such as Facebook or MySpace and half of them have also posted pictures of themselves online.
- Older teens, especially girls who are 16 or 17 years of age, use the Internet for interaction, meeting friends, and networking.

Risks of the Internet

- Of respondents, 71% reported receiving messages online from someone they did not know.
- Of respondents, 45% have been asked for personal information by someone they did not know.
- Of respondents, 30% have considered meeting someone that they have talked to only online.
- Of respondents, 14% have had a face-to-face meeting with someone with whom they have spoken only over the Internet (9% of this group are 13–15 years of age; 22% are 16 or 17 years of age).
- When teens receive messages online from someone that they do not know, 40% reported that they usually reply and chat with that person.
- Only 18% of respondents said they would tell an adult about such contact.

Perceptions of Internet Safety

Children and young adults that use the Internet are curious and seem to seek out adventure and the thrill of the unknown; unfortunately, they are naive to the dangers that it may cause in their lives. Finkelhor, Mitchell, and Wolak (2003) indicated in their study that two problem characteristics associated with close online relationships are high parent–child conflicts and children that are extremely troubled. Girls with high levels of parent–child conflict reported parents yelling at and nagging them and taking their privileges away. The group of highly troubled girls had levels of depression, victimization, and troubling life events. Girls in either of these categories were more than twice as likely as the other girls in the sample to have formed close online relationships. Boys who had less communication with their parents had a compelling tendency to be associated with close online relationships. Girls and boys who reported high levels of Internet use and home Internet access were more likely to report close online relationships.

Other facts from the Finkelhor et al. (2003) study include the following:

- Twenty percent of teens report that it is safe (i.e. "somewhat" or "very" safe) to share personal information on a public blog or networking site.
- Thirty-seven percent of 13- to 17-year-olds said that they are "not very concerned" or "not at all concerned" about someone using information they have posted online in ways they would not want it to be used.

- Fourteen percent of youth reported close online friendships and 2% reported online romances.
- Girls were slightly more likely than boys to have close online relationships.
- Girls 14–17 years of age were twice as likely as girls age 10–13 to form close online relationships.

KINSA (Kids Internet Safety Association) is a not-for-profit, nonpartisan organization that has expertise in the criminal justice field. Its members are committed to thwarting the unwanted solicitation of children online and they assist in finding and rescuing child victims of abuse whose images are shared on the Internet. KINSA reaffirmed that "children and young adolescents lack the ability and experience to recognize the behavior of those who prey on youth online."

Most parents should realize that their children's actions on the Internet are very similar to their day-to-day routines. The Internet will not change their habits, but it will broaden the spectrum of the people they meet. The vulnerability of a child on the Internet may cause a parent to become concerned and worried because children do not recognize the potential danger of the Internet. Parents need to listen to their children and educate them regarding the dangers concerning the different people with whom they will come in contact, especially the sexual predator who may just wait for them.

In an article in *PC Magazine*, Cohen (2006) talked of David Frey's views on sexual predators. Frey, who is an assistant district attorney in Staten Island, New York, and the chief of the technology investigations, contends that most sexual predators are clever and they use adolescents' information to befriend them. Frey also mentioned that a sexual offender would groom a child to his advantage by earning the child's trust: "It is not sexual at first, but [sexual predators] gradually push a little bit further until it is completely sexual and they accomplish what they set out to do."

A major concern that has been voiced by most parents is the lack of communication they have with their children, especially when it comes down to people with whom they are conversing over the Internet. The biggest fear is that they are communicating with online predators or strangers that could befriend them by way of chat rooms, instant messaging, or e-mails. The fact is that many parents do not know their children's passwords, who they are conversing with, who their Internet friends are, and the websites they frequent.

Recent studies and surveys have indicated that

- A vast majority of parents said they are confident in what their children will tell them about their online activities.

- Three out of four parents admit that knowing what their children are looking at on the Internet is more important than respecting their children's privacy.
- Most parents concur that the benefits of the Internet offset its hazards and dangers.
- An overwhelming number of parents said they worry about their children's exposure to online sexual predators and online strangers.
- There is a very good chance that teens have accidentally found inappropriate and unsuitable material while conducting an online search or exploring the Internet.
- A substantial number of parents said the Internet exposes their kids to questionable morals and ethical behavior.
- A number of parents feel their children have not reached the level of maturity needed to understand some of the concepts on the Internet.

Triple A Theory

The triple A theory incorporates the accessibility, affordability, and anonymity of the Internet. A study by Hecht Orzack et al. (2006) indicated that the easy access of the Internet and individuals' continued use of a computer can give rise to symptoms that can be described as Internet addiction as well as other related psychological issues. In "An Ongoing Study of Group Treatment for Men Involved in Problematic Internet-Enabled Sexual Behavior," the authors compare Internet addiction to that of other behavioral and substance addictions such as gambling and alcohol abuse.

Internet Addiction Symptoms

Hecht Orzack et al. (2006) explained symptoms that are indicative of addiction or dependency on the Internet. A few of them are

- Experiencing pleasure, excitement, or relief while on the Internet
- Spending an ever-increasing amount of time or money on Internet activities, with diminished returns
- Buying the newest and fastest computer hardware
- Experiencing dysphonic moods while away from the Internet
- Becoming anxious, angry, or depressed when not on the Internet
- Feeling a loss of control or being overwhelmed while away from the Internet

- Being preoccupied with thoughts about the Internet while away from the Internet
- Repeatedly attempting, unsuccessfully, to limit Internet use
- Using the Internet to escape current problems
- Negating daily obligations due to Internet use
- Losing significant relationships due to Internet activities
- Lying about the amount of time spent on the Internet
- Lying about the content of the websites visited
- Experiencing financial difficulties due to time spent on the Internet
- Experiencing academic difficulties due to time spent on the Internet
- Experiencing physical health problems due to Internet use

Internet Enabled and Sexual Behaviors (IESBs)

An individual's fascination with the Internet can and often will adversely affect that person's life, both at home and at the workplace. Employees have taken advantage of computers in the workplace to satisfy their sexual curiosity. Cooper, Mansson, and Daneback (2005) noted that many corporations are potentially losing hundreds of work hours and thousands of dollars per day due to IESB. Cooper et al. noted that "upwards of 2½ hours per day may be spent in engaging in online sexual activity."

Chat Rooms and Instant Messaging

Online predators are out there lurking and scanning chat rooms, waiting for the right opportunity to join a conversation. It may be tough to spot them and it is difficult to track the virtual and rapid messages in chat rooms, bulletin boards, or news groups. Chat rooms are online, real-time sites where anyone can communicate interactively. The transmission is immediate with the person on the computer at the other end receiving the message. Once two people meet in a chat room, they can quickly move their conversation to yet another private chat room.

Many young people and adolescents use open communication forums such as instant messaging (IM'ing) and chat rooms. Chat rooms allow sexual predators easy access to seek out their next victim. It can be compared to throwing out a fishing line and waiting to lure the fish (child) in. Instant messaging often makes it difficult for police investigators to track real-time dialogue. Dombrowski and colleagues (2004) stated, "Essentially there are two ways for a predator to use the Internet to establish a relationship for the purpose of solicitation: e-mail and instant messaging."

Unfortunately, for most adolescents, IM'ing is a well-known target that entices most sexual predators; they often visit chat rooms specifically looking for young females with provocative, sexually explicit, and stimulating screen names. Detective Dan Jackman of Louisville, Kentucky, has determined that a sexual predator is more likely to look for female names when searching through websites and that sexual offenders have a tendency to move toward female victims (personal communication). They can tell through Internet conversation if a teen or young adolescent is lonely, crying for attention, or just needs someone to talk to or confide in that will listen and not judge.

Wolak et al. (2008) mention that online communications such as e-mail and instant messaging allow frequent, swift, and private exchanges. These online molesters will develop a quick and intense relationship, seducing the child online, often unbeknownst to the child's friends, parents, or caregivers. Online predators have quickly learned and are adept at finding identifying information on any posted online profile. Recent studies have indicated that 50% of teens talk in chat rooms or use instant messaging with Internet strangers. Lewis and Miller (2009) acknowledged that adults generally use technology only as a tool but that adolescents consider technology, including text messaging and chat rooms, to be an essential part of their lives.

The following are some of the techniques predators use:

- They will seek out provocative user names.
- They will investigate and study the child profile online.
- They want to be indiscreet and go to a private chat room.
- The conversation will start innocently. They will ask personal questions and then the conversation will turn sexual.
- They want seductive photos.
- They want to send gifts or money.
- They eventually would like to meet face to face.

Sexual predators are more inclined to gravitate toward female victims and explore the Internet and chat rooms looking for sexually suggestive and expressive screen names such as "Sexygirl97" or "Sexygirl14." The number behind the screen name may indicate the year she was born or her age. In this case, it would be 1997 or that she is 14 years old. Either screen name makes her a prime target. Crisanto (2006) noted that female adolescents who spend a considerable amount of time online in chat rooms may become vulnerable to solicitations by sexual offenders, especially if they give out personal information, such as their home address and telephone number. Finkelhor et al. (2003) stated, "Adolescents, rather than children, seem to be more likely targets of on-line solicitation, owing in part to their greater mobility, sexual curiosity, and autonomy."

Media Information and Newsgroups

While searching for interesting items on the Internet, adolescents access newsgroups by using specific keywords. Sexual offenders often rely on popular websites and newsgroups to obtain a wealth of valuable information about their next innocent victim. According to the Federal Bureau of Investigation (FBI) (2003), newsgroups are similar to a bulletin board with posted messages and allow users to post messages and information by topic. Each newsgroup can hold thousands of postings that may contain text, images, or other files. Anyone accessing public newsgroups can view the postings or post their own responses. The FBI also stated that there are over 29,000 public newsgroups. Users can create private newsgroups; however, these newsgroups require an invitation for access.

Popular Websites

Internet providers often fail to provide ways to protect young adolescents from online predation. Many different websites cater to preteens, teenagers, and young adults. Dombrowski and colleagues (2004) noted in their article, "Protecting Children from Online Sexual Predators," that the Internet supplies sexual offenders with access to a multitude of young adolescents and a new means to engage in the grooming process. The US Sentencing Commission indicated that relationships between sexual predators and young adolescents are enhanced by meeting online in a private setting without pressure or barriers.

Facebook

Facebook was started in February of 2004 and it has become the number one networking site in the nation. Its popularity grew especially as a way of communicating with family and friends. An overwhelming number of children and teens are speaking to one another, exchanging information, and adding to their profiles and lists of friends daily. Online profiles, recent pictures, and experiences are easily viewed, discussed, and accessed. This has become an excellent opportunity to express themselves, experience independence, and explore the world.

It is estimated that Facebook had 450 million users as of May 2011, and it continues to grow daily. In the United States, Facebook is the third most popular website accessed (after YouTube and Google). It is the third most active website of the top 100 websites for children under 18. One of the features of this popular online community is that it allows its registered users to create several albums so that they can organize their photos, which can be viewed by their friends.

Many teens feel that Facebook is safer than MySpace. A Facebook user who does not want his or her information or contacts seen can click on "control your privacy settings." This setting will limit the people who can view the person's profile and photos. It can also choose which part of the Facebook profile is viewable. The individual can choose which part of the profile can be viewed by family and which details are viewable by friends. Facebook has a relatively good security record. Reports have shown that it has had fewer sexual predator attacks than its competitors. Facebook relies on its users to flag or point out any inappropriate content they come across.

Facebook has become proactive by trying to protect its customers against sexual predators; it does not allow its subscribers to share personal information with everyone on the Internet. Chris Kelly has been hired as Facebook's chief privacy officer. Under his leadership, he has set up a number of controls and privacy precautions that have promoted a safer environment for the site's younger users. Since these new safety measures have been implemented, Facebook has seen fewer complaints regarding sexual predators. However, not enough manpower, security, and technology are available to stop every threat.

The goal of networking sites is to connect with as many people as possible with the intent always to attract more customers. Facebook has indicated that out of 150 million subscribers, fewer than 1% are impersonators or use different names on their sites, but that is still 1.5 million people who are deceiving people and have the potential to do harm. Site growth also increases the list of potential victims a sexual predator will try to befriend. Sexual predators will create a false profile to lure potential victims into their world. As teenagers get older, they may seek out their own independence and identity, often looking for an outlet to become independent and explore the world around them. Many teens do not realize that sharing information and pictures can be fun until someone gets hurt.

MySpace

MySpace was founded in 2003 when its management saw an opportunity to create a social website with more options and less restrictions for its users. MySpace was purchased in 2005 for $580 million by Rupert Murdoch, creator of a media empire that includes 20th Century Fox and the Fox television stations. MySpace was the leading website before Facebook was created. It was very popular with young children and teenagers. It has been estimated that MySpace has accumulated 54 million users in just 3 years of existence, with dangers heightened by the unregulated nature of the Internet and the ready availability of personal information online. Many users liked user setup accounts because they were free and easy to set up. The user had to be at least 14 years old and the following was necessary:

- Valid e-mail address
- First and last name
- Password for the account
- Country
- Zip code
- Date of birth
- Whether or not to make the date of birth public
- Agreement to terms of service and privacy policies

MySpace invited its clients to create personalized profiles that could include pictures, music, and videos. Members had the opportunity to create buddy lists that included friends and people they were interested in. MySpace invited trouble because profiles could be read by other MySpace members and, at first, anyone could have access to a MySpace profile. Even to this day, children reveal too much information, and sexual predators seize the opportunity to find their next victim.

Most parents do not know where to find information that may protect their children from online predators. Many parents are concerned about the influence that the Internet and social websites may have on their children, especially teens who are very trusting. MySpace has hired a new chief security officer, Hemanshu Nigam, who will focus on new and innovative ways to prevent sexual predators from infiltrating this popular site. Mr. Nigam helped launch efforts with Sentinel Tech to create a database that will allow a real-time safety system that will assist MySpace in identifying sexual predators that may access the site. Since its inception, Sentinel Tech has kicked 90,000 sexual offenders off the MySpace website.

MySpace has created a database that will allow parents to control their children's activities and movements when they are on the Internet. The safety team at MySpace developed a program that will allow parents to submit their child's e-mail address to them. They in turn will process the child's e-mail so that the child will not be allowed to set up any profiles that an unwanted intruder can view. The concept is for parents to be proactive in their approach and be empowered in their child's life where Internet safety is concerned. Over the past few years, MySpace has implemented over 100 safety and security projects and innovations, including the use of new and improved technology to identify and remove registered sex offenders from the site. MySpace has also been instrumental in pushing for tougher and more stringent laws and standards in its industry.

Security on Social Websites

Many social networking sites have incorporated their own security teams. They are challenged by the ever-changing technology and are always in the process of finding ways to provide a safe Internet environment. The main focus of these social network security teams is to share ideas and new innovations in a joint effort to prevent any unwanted solicitations to their clients by Internet predators.

A few proactive ideas suggested by social networking sites include the following:

- Respond faster and more steadily to any inappropriate content or behavior
- Strengthen software that could be used to find underage users
- Create a special section for children and teens in high school
- Generate a strict verification of all Internet addresses and ages that would ultimately have a check-and-balance backup system
- Have parents become more acclimated to and involved in their children's Internet sessions through training and workshops
- Devote more staff to classifying photographs as unsuitable or unacceptable

Pedophiles are not reluctant to share stories or information regarding the children who have become their victims online and in person. Sexual predators usually work alone, but they can infiltrate an immense online support network. This support network encourages:

- Adult–child sex
- Rationalization of the pedophile's behavior
- Identification of vulnerable children
- Exchanging advice about their successful exploitation
- Sharing information about what does and does not work in seeking out victims
- Law enforcement tactics and warning signs

Webcams

Webcams are cameras that use the computer to display and project the image of a person in real time. Webcams are a standard feature of most newer name-brand laptops. A person with an older home or work computer can place a portable webcam on top of the computer. Most websites, especially those geared toward adolescents, make it easy to post pictures, video clips, and personal data that anyone can download. Teenagers have begun to incorporate webcams to display revealing pictures of themselves to their friends. Many pedophiles will eventually try to entice victims who have a webcam to send pictures of revealing and sensual poses of themselves. Most often, gifts of clothes, jewelry, and money will be offered for more intimate pictures.

Sexting

Many adolescents and children in today's society have cell phones with the capability to take pictures and record video. A relatively new practice called "sexting" has evolved where a person can virtually send explicit sexual pictures of himself or herself or friends via the cell phone. This practice is becoming more popular and common among adolescents.

Newspapers and local news stations have reported a recent trend that involves children as young as grammar school age through high school teens sending nude or sexually suggestive pictures of themselves and acquaintances over the cell phone. Legislators, police, prosecutors, and school officials are faced with a dilemma regarding sexting and are considering invoking child pornography laws on children who send sexual content through their cell phones. Some school officials see sexting getting out of hand, especially when sexual photographs are circulated around school campuses with the possibility of being viewed by tens of thousands of people. Sexting can cause anguish, humiliation, and embarrassment—not only for the person in the pictures, but also for those who distribute the pictures The person sending the sexually explicit or suggestive pictures over the phone may be charged with harassment and possibly be sued in civil court.

Cybersex

Cybersex is sexual communication with another person via the Internet. Weiss and Schneider (2009) said that cybersex is the latest and most addictive form of acting out by sex addicts in a world where computers are ubiquitous at home and in the workplace. Cooper et al. (2005) say that "cybersex is a subcategory of online sexual activities (OSA) and is when two or more people are engaging in sexual talk while online for the purposes of sexual pleasure and may or may not include masturbation." Cybersex allows a person to express sexual fantasies aggressively through an open and descriptive forum. A sexual offender can start out flirting with someone, testing the waters to see how far he can take the conversation, or proceed to "talking dirty" to the person on the other end. A few significant reasons for this compulsive behavior may be low self-esteem, loneliness, a troubled relationship or loveless marriage, the thrill of meeting new people, or the excitement of infidelity.

- The cybersex industry generates approximately $1 billion annually and is expected to grow to $5 billion–$7 billion over the next 5 years.
- Cybersex is an addictive behavior that is propelled by the Internet.

Cappers

"Cappers" is another term for a sophisticated and well-organized group of young online sexual predators who are attempting to seduce teenage girls on their webcams. These young men will secretly record females whom they persuade to disrobe, partially or fully, in front of the camera. They entice these young girls by saying that they could be models or actresses.

The Internet and Schools

Principals, teachers, and parents understand the significance of the Internet in the classroom, as well as at home. Nearly every school and its students throughout the United States are taught to use the Internet and technology wisely. Bradley (2008) noted a growing concern among many school administrators and principals about the safety of the Internet.

The National Association of Secondary School Principals (NASSP) board of directors reiterated that "findings reveal a new social and academic environment with enormous potential for innovation in teaching and learning; unfortunately, they also represent a safety minefield for students and the adults who care for them." NASSP suggests that school officials need to be familiar with all aspects of the Internet, including blogs, cyberbullying, and networking sites. It also feels that it is important to educate staff and students on the boundaries of the law and to use the Internet as a teaching tool.

Recent studies have shown that many parents view the Internet as a valuable teaching and research tool but they are concerned about its safety and the dangers to which their children may be exposed. Many parents love the Internet and encourage their sons and daughters to use it; however, as beneficial as the Internet is, a majority of parents feel that it is extremely important for them to know and approve what their children are doing online.

Today, many schools are confronted with a serious dilemma: teaching a sound and commonsense approach to computer technology in an educational forum without crossing the line into popular social networking sites. A number of middle schools and high schools have blocked their students from accessing social networking sites in school. An article written by Dave

Montgomery of the *Fort Worth Star-Telegram* (2006) stated that Michael G. Fitzpatrick, state representative from Pennsylvania, had initiated the Deleting Online Predators Act on July 26, 2006. This act passed by Congress would require schools and libraries that receive federal funds to limit or ban access to networking sites that could expose minors to sexual advances from adults, with a specific ban on entry to chat rooms when using public school and library computers. Texas Attorney General Greg Abbott called the measure a good step in combating Internet trolling by sexual predators who try to exploit the surging popularity of networking sites such as MySpace, Friendster, Facebook, and Xanga.

With the rapid development of the Internet, there have been concerns about protecting children from viewing pornographic and other destructive images through cyberspace. Congress has passed several acts to censor Internet sites available to children, but only the Children's Internet Protection Act (CIPA) has received Supreme Court endorsement to date. In short, public libraries and schools must install filtering software on their computers as a condition of receiving the federal subsidies. CIPA does not specify which filters must be used and stipulates that the filters can be disabled in certain situations for adult patrons.

The Supreme Court's endorsement of CIPA, although clearly a victory for groups trying to shield children from cyberspace pornography, does not resolve all the legal issues. Challenges involving the Internet seem destined to increase, and the Court recently agreed to review a case involving a federal law that imposes penalties on creators or transmitters of indecent Internet materials for commercial purposes if the materials are known to be accessible to minors. The legal questions go beyond concerns about freedom of speech and the protection of minors; there also are significant privacy concerns related to the increasing ease of cyberspace access to personal information about individuals. Undoubtedly, courts will continue to be confronted with complicated legal issues pertaining to sending and receiving transmissions via the Internet. This is an area of law that school personnel should carefully watch.

Davis (2008) has written about a program called EGuardian. About 750,000 parents are enrolled in this program, which provides a security site for networking sites and ensures that users are age appropriate. Davis also explains that Identity.net, which was established in 2007, has since partnered with i-Safe Inc. This group is a nonprofit-based group that provides an Internet-safety curriculum for about 6.2 million students in public and private schools. Through this new digital privacy curriculum, students can create profiles through Identy.net and learn to share less or more personal information on the Internet. Classroom teachers are instrumental in verifying and keeping a watchful eye on the students' information.

Today, school officials seem to be proactive in their approach to limiting their students' access to networking sites on computers that are used in their schools and to disciplining a child who uses a computer inappropriately away from school. Many school boards have taken the initiative to protect students in and out of school by implementing certain guidelines and restrictions aimed especially at protecting students because of the proliferation of technology. Students can be disciplined for launching inappropriate threats, messages (harassment), or pictures over the Internet on or off campus. School handbooks often emphasize zero tolerance for anyone threatening or endangering the safety of any student over the Internet.

CIPA was enacted to protect school children from gaining access to graphic pictures that are considered harmful or obscene or that contain any type of pornography. This law applies to all federally funded libraries and schools. These institutions must block this material from coming across the Internet through a filter or firewall. The term "harmful to minors" represents any sexually perverted acts, nudity, or any display of a person's genitals.

Profile of a Female Sex Offender

Wendy, a 34-year- old single mother of two from the New England area, had been ordered to serve 120 days behind bars, and was told to stay off the Internet on her home computer after admitting to having sex with a 15-year-old boy. In addition, Wendy was prohibited contact with the victim or any male under the age of 18. Prosecutors said that Wendy first met the boy in an online chat room. Wendy admitted that it was her intention to find and meet a young, energetic male teen online that she would be able to entice into a sexual relationship, even though she feared getting caught in a sting operation by law enforcement. The first meeting occurred at a local mall, where she bought her victim new clothes and video games. The teenage boy admitted to his parents that he felt pressured and scared after a few sexual encounters with the older woman. He knew what she was doing to him was wrong. His parents called police to file a report and to have Wendy arrested. Wendy knew when the police arrived at her door that her escapade with the teen was over, and that her life would be filled with turmoil. The presiding judge sentenced Wendy to 5 years probation that included periodic and random searches of her home computer.

Profile of a Male Sex Offender

In 1991, Mike was convicted of beating three boys with an aluminum baseball bat. He had a violent criminal history toward children and reports indicated that he had nearly killed the children. One victim even "flat lined" on his way to the hospital; the other two children were left unconscious. Mike went on the run immediately after the crime, but police caught up with him a month later as he was trying to reenter the United States from Canada. Mike served 9 years for committing aggravated assault, but was released in the summer of 2000.

On January 31, 2002, Mike became the second child predator to be placed on the FBI's Ten Most Wanted Fugitives List (470th overall). Mike was being sought for repeatedly molesting a 9-year-old female in hotels in Vermont and Massachusetts in September of 2000. He was also wanted on state charges of aggravated sexual assault in New Hampshire. Mike rented a video camera and videotaped the young girl being molested. The victim told one of her family members about the sexual molestation that she had endured. With a warrant to search his home on April 6, 2001, the police recovered computer disks and videotapes depicting Mike and the victim engaging in sexual acts. According to officials, there were more than 90 minutes of videotape. The videos were converted to computer files that would ultimately be destined for other child predators to view on the Internet.

When Mike discovered that the police had been at his residence, he fled in his mother's car and then rented another car. The rental car was recovered a little over a week later at the Los Angeles Airport. The television program *America's Most Wanted* helped take down an accused child molester: After the program aired a 30-second profile on February 9, 2002, agents and cops working the case got their break.

Numerous tips had come in, but it was a call that night from an anonymous tipster that was right on the money. The caller said that Mike worked in construction at a hotel in Los Angeles. As a result of that information, agents in LA learned that Mike was still there and looking for work at a hotel. They found out that Mike had recently contacted Nutel Motel, where he worked as a handyman for a short time in October of 2001. A multiagency law enforcement team set up a sting operation to take him down. Mike was arrested without incident at 5:30 p.m. on April 23, 2002, and was charged in Vermont with 11 federal counts related to the sexual exploitation of children. Mike pled guilty to all 11 counts on June 2, 2003, and was sentenced on February 18, 2004, to 22 years in federal prison followed by 5 years of supervised release. His capture marked the 700th case that *America's Most Wanted* had helped to solve.

In My Opinion

Ms. Anne Collier

Anne Collier, codirector of ConnectSafely.org, has spoken about sexual predation and the Internet (personal communication). For the sake of parents, educators, and young people, it is important that we rely on the research that has emerged since the first youth-online-risk study from the Crimes against Children Research Center (CCRC) in 2000. Before that study, which was sponsored by the Department of Justice and National Center for Missing and Exploited Children, we were operating from the basis of some common sense but also a lot of concern and hyperbole (because so often we fear what we do not understand), which was not a very sound foundation for educating the public. Because of that lack of research, out of necessity, law enforcement stepped in, filling the vacuum created by our lack of research. Police departments, state attorney generals' offices, and the growing number of state Internet Crimes against Children task forces (usually called ICACs) were often asked by schools to provide Internet safety education. Naturally they spoke from their experience with criminal activity online, which research has found to be extremely rare where online youth are concerned.

Through no fault of law enforcement, of course, the public discussion about youth online safety therefore got off on the wrong footing. It was dominated by a criminal-law perspective rather than that of child and adolescent development, which is the proper context for any discussion about online youth. This is why:

- The CCRC has found that Internet-related sexual exploitation of minors represents 1% of overall sexual exploitation of minors. Other more recent key findings in the youth online risk literature include:
  - Not all youth are equally at risk online.
  - The youth who are most at risk online are so-called "at-risk youth" off-line.
  - A young person's psychosocial makeup and home and school environments are better predictors of risk than any technology that he or she uses.
  - Harassment and cyberbullying, not predation, are the most common risks young people face online.

We have also learned from the growing body of social-media research that young people's online activity is embedded in "real life" and cannot be treated as a separate, unrelated experience. What is becoming clearer and clearer from both the youth-risk and social-media bodies of research is that the risk spectrum online maps to the "real life" risk spectrum. This means that expertise in law and criminal activity is a small subset of the expertise needed for youth safety online, and a broad spectrum of expertise (parents, school counselors, school safety officers, social workers, risk-prevention specialists, and mental health care practitioners) is needed to support and protect youth online just as it is off-line. We are now coming to understand that online safety is more a public health issue than a new "field" that would deal strictly with the online part of children's lives, which we had at one time seen to be something new added onto their lives.

The research also shows that young people's behavior and treatment of others online has a lot to do with their own well-being when they use digital technologies and media. A study published in *Archives of Pediatrics and Adolescent Medicine* in 2007 found that aggressive behavior online more than doubles the aggressor's risk of victimization online. Embarrassing and harassing others clearly increases a young person's risk of being treated in the same way, or "what goes 'round, comes 'round," as the saying goes. The Internet is just another "place" or "hangout" where youth socialize and where conflict can be expressed—not a special environment where a new form of conflict called cyberbullying occurs. So the context for young people's behavior—good, bad, or neutral—is largely the school social scene wherever it is manifest, on whatever device, and in whatever environment. Online, just as off-line, bullies and targets can switch roles rapidly when young people get into downward spirals of aggression and retaliation.

So it follows that there is actually no such thing as an online safety expert. On the prevention end, what is needed, instead, is experts in modeling and teaching respect for self and others, empathy, and civility—all the adults in children's lives, at home and school. On the intervention end, we first need to determine the nature of the aggression or conflict—whether it involves typical social rivalry or at-risk behavior—and then decide what expertise is needed, from that of a parent or school counselor to that of law enforcement. For most youth, this is a child- or adolescent-development issue. This is why there is growing emphasis on people's behavior online and off-line, including in the 2010 report to Congress of the Online Safety & Technology Working Group, which recommended making instruction in new social as well as traditional media literacy.

We now understand from what the research has shown us in the past 11 years that the Internet has never been the primary problem, whether we are talking about the sexual exploitation of youth by adults or peer victimization. In fact, it is important to put youth risk online in the context of *all* social problem indicators, which David Finkelhor, director of the CCRC, has done. In a fall 2010 talk, he said that "it's one thing to say that the Internet has dangers on it; it's a very different thing to say that the Internet *increases* dangers." In fact, "the remarkable and jarring thing," he said, is that, in the very period the Net has become pervasive in the past 15 years "we've been observing a dramatically contradictory, positive pattern to the social problem indicators." Here are the changes in the social indicators for the past 15 years, as Finkelhor related:

- Sexual abuse of minors is down (58% from 1992 to 2008), he wrote in a 2010 article.

- Teen sexual intercourse and pregnancy are down.
- Bullying is down, as is the number of kids reporting getting into physical fights.
- The number of kids reporting being targeted by hate speech is down.
- The teen suicide rate "has dropped dramatically."
- The number of teens who say they have contemplated suicide or felt sad or hopeless is down.
- The number of crimes committed by young people has "gone down dramatically in the United States."
- School violence is down.
- Teen drug use is down, too.

Certainly the Internet presents challenges in the way it can amplify and instantly distribute mistakes or malicious behavior. But it is essential that we understand that, only to a degree, does it change the realities with which we have been dealing for a very long time, and we need to understand what that degree is and what impact it has. We cannot get to that if we continue to view the Net as an entirely new and uniquely dangerous phenomenon that has been added to young people's lives. They do not view or treat it as such; to them it is just another "place" to hang out, social tool, entertainment medium, and vehicle for creative expression. Until we stop portraying youth always as an undifferentiated mass of potential victims, we will have no credibility with the very people who are supposed to be beneficiaries of our online-safety messaging.

Increasingly, the Internet is becoming a mirror of and platform for virtually all of human life—updated constantly in real time, from both computers and mobile devices, by its users in every country of the world. The understanding of that needs to be the foundation of "online safety" education going forward if it is going to have any impact at all.

Definitions of Chapter Key Terms

Address: A series of letters and numbers that identify a location. On the Internet, typing in an address lets a person send or receive information from a specific source.

Attachment: A file that has been added to an e-mail.

Blog: Short for web log; a web log is usually classified as a personal or noncommercial website that uses a dated log format (usually with the most recent at the top of the page) and contains links to other websites along with commentary about those websites. A web log is updated frequently and sometimes groups links by specific subjects, such as politics, news, pop culture, or computers.

Bookmark: A way to access a favorite website quickly.
Browser: A program that allows users to view web pages.
Bulletin board service (BBS): A place where people can post messages on a particular topic.
Cappers: Another term for a sophisticated and well-organized group of young online sexual predators who are attempting to seduce teenage girls using their webcams. These men will secretly record females whom they persuade to disrobe partially or fully in front of the camera. They entice these young girls by saying that they could be models or actresses.
CD-ROM: Contact disk, read only memory.
Chat: Informal real-time communication over the Internet. A person can type and send messages that appear almost instantly with other individuals participating in the chat room.
Chat room: An interactive forum on the Internet where a person can engage in real-time discussions with other participants. The chat room is where the chat is taking place and where common interests are often discussed. A person can freely broadcast messages in this venue.
Cyberbullying: Sending or posting harmful or cruel text or images using the Internet or other digital communication devices.
Cybersex: The exchanging of explicit sexual messages, activity, discussion, display, or information via the Internet. This is the counterpart of a telephone sex line that typically takes place in an online chat room.
Cyberspace: All the computer networks on the Internet. The term distinguishes the physical world from the virtual or computer-based world.
Cyberstalking/harassment: The online enticement of children; rude or threatening messages, slanderous information, or repeated and/or unwanted messages.
Discussion group: A group of people who exchange information about a common topic
e-Mail (electronic mail): A service that allows people to send messages with pictures and sounds from their computer to any other computer in the world. An e-mail account and the recipient's e-mail address are needed to send a message.
Emoticons: Animated faces that a person can send in an e-mail when chatting with another person online or when using instant messaging (IM). Emoticons are a way to show feelings to someone online.
Enticement: To seduce or lure a person into a desired behavior.
Flaming: Sending out deliberate confrontational messages to others on the Internet.
Hacker: A popular term for someone who accesses computer information either illegally or legally.
Hard copy: This is the printed/paper copy of a file from a computer.

History: A list of websites that people have visited using a particular computer.

Homepage: A web page that a browser displays when it starts up or the main page of any website.

Hyperlinks: An image or a portion of text that, once clicked, allows electronic connections. These connections access other Internet materials such as images, sounds, animations, videos, or other web pages.

Instant messaging (IM or IM'ing): A service that allows people to send and get messages almost instantly. This is real-time communication that is private and allows the user to transfer video as well as text from one computer to another computer.

Internet: A global system of interconnected computer networks that facilitate data translation and information via telephone lines, fiber optic cables, and satellite links. It is often referred to as the "Net."

Internet protocol (IP) address: A numerical label that uniquely identifies a node on the Internet and is assigned to any device participating in a computer network.

Internet relay chat (IRC): A system that enables people to join online in live discussions to engage in real-time conversation. Instant relay chat is a virtual conference where people from all over the world can meet and talk.

Internet service provider (ISP): A company that provides Internet access to customers.

Navigate: Moving from page to page or website to website when online; also called browsing or surfing.

Netiquette: A term for courtesy, honesty, and polite behavior that should be practiced on the Internet.

Network: Created when computers are connected; allows people to share information. The Internet is an example of a large network.

Newsgroups: Subject-specific virtual message boards or discussion groups on the Internet. Participants in a newsgroup conduct discussions by posting messages for others to read and respond to. User groups are similar to a community bulletin board where a person can post and read messages.

Online: Having access or being connected to the Internet or a computer network.

Online grooming: Using the Internet to manipulate and develop trust of a minor as a first step in gaining information a predator may use eventually to meet the intended victim. This type of grooming often involves developing the child's sexual awareness and may take days, weeks, months, and, in some cases, years to manipulate the minor. The final triumph is for the predator to be able to sexually manipulate the victim when that meeting occurs.

Password: The secret word a person uses when signing on to the Internet or an online service that helps to confirm that person's identity.

Pharming: An online scam that attacks the browser's address bar. A person may type in what appears to be a valid website address and be unknowingly redirected to an illegitimate site that steals personal information.

Phishing: An online scam that uses e-mail to "fish" for the user's private information by imitating legitimate companies. People are often lured into sharing user names, passwords, account information, or credit card numbers. The phishing e-mail contains a link to an illegitimate site.

Post: An electronic message on a newsgroup or bulletin board.

Profile: Exhibits diverse characteristics about a person's lifestyle and an account of the series of events making up a person's life.

Search engine: A program that searches for information on the World Wide Web by looking for specific keywords and returns a list of information found on that topic.

Sexual predator: Often describes a person with an obsession and passion to sexually target an innocent victim to satisfy his or her needs for sexual gratification.

Social networking sites: Mostly web-based services that provide an outlet for people to interact; a collection of various ways for users to interact. A few examples are by chat, e-mails, and sharing pictures and videos. Social networking has revolutionized the ways that members of society communicate and share information with one another. Millions of people use numerous social networking websites every day.

Spam: Unwanted and unsolicited e-mail from an unknown person, company, or source.

Spamming: Mass mailings often sent as instant messages to users that often feature explicit sexual pornography sites.

Streaming (media): The exchange of video clips, sound, or other types of media over the Internet.

Surfing the web: Searching for information via the Internet.

Virus: A computer program that can destroy files. Viruses can be sent via e-mail or through other file-sharing programs.

Webcam: A camera, often on top of a computer, that is used to transfer live video on the Internet.

World Wide Web (web): A vast network of electronic files and a collection of Internet sites that serve an extensive user community over the Internet.

References

Bowker, A. (2005). The cybersex offender and children. *FBI Law Enforcement Bulletin* 74 (3): 12–17. Retrieved from ProQuest Criminal Justice Database.

Bradley, A. (2008). *Education Week* 27 (20): 4.

Cohen, A. (2006). Do you know where your kids are clicking? *PC Magazine* 25 (12): 88–96.

Cooper, A., Mansson, S., and Daneback, K. (2005, June). An Internet study of cybersex participants. *Archives of Sexual Behavior* 34 (3): 321–328.

Crisanto, A. (2006). Female adolescents and sexual behaviors on the Internet (doctoral dissertation, Alliant International University, Fresno, CA). *Dissertation Abstracts International: Section B: Science and Engineering* 66 (11-B): 632.

Davis, M. R. (2008). Firms verify online IDs via schools. *Education Week* 28 (12): 1–2.

Dombrowski, S. C., LeMasney, J. W., Ahia, C. E., and Dickson, S. (2004). Protecting children from online sexual predators: Technological, psychoeducational and legal considerations. *Professional Psychology: Research and Practice* 35 (1): 65–73.

Federal Bureau of Investigation. (2003). *10 Years of protecting our children: Cracking down on sexual predators on the Internet.* Retrieved from www.fbi.gov/page2/deco3/online120203

Finkelhor, M., and Wolak, J. (2003). Internet sex crimes against minors: The response of law enforcement. US Department of Justice and Deliquency Prevention.

Hecht Orzack, M., Wolf, D., Hennen, J., and Voluse, A. (2006). An ongoing study of group treatment for men involved on problematic Internet-enabled sexual behavior. *Cyber Psychology and Behavior* 9 (3): 348–360.

Lewis, M., and Miller, P. (2009). Internet crimes against children: An annotated bibliography of major studies. The Library of Congress Federal Research Division (http://www.ncjrs.gov/pdffiles1/niji/grants/2288/3.pdf).

Madigan, L. (2006, April 3). Madigan observes sexual assault awareness month: Releases quiz to increase public knowledge of sexually violent crimes. Illinois Attorney General Press Release.

Montgomery, D. (2006). Lawmakers target Internet pedophiles. *Fort Worth Star-Telegram*. Retrieved from Newspaper Source database.

Schmalleger, F. (2006). *Criminal law today*, 3rd ed. Upper Saddle River, NJ: Prentice Hall.

Weiss, R., and Schneider, J. (2009). *Untangling the web: Sex, porn, and fantasy obsession in the Internet age.* New York: Alyson Publications.

Wolak, J., Finkelhor, D., Mitchell, K., and Ybarra, M. (2008). Online predators and their victims: Myths, realities and implications for prevention and treatment. *American Psychologist* 63 (2): 111–128.

Law Enforcement on the Internet

8

> I am always searching for young teenage girls, but I am always worried about getting caught by the police.
>
> **Sexual predator**

> My intention is to meet as many young, innocent teenage girls online as possible. I am a charmer, I know the right words to say, and I have money to buy them nice things. All it takes is to show them a little attention.
>
> **Sexual predator**

Law Enforcement Involvement in Investigating Internet Crimes

Law enforcement is faced with two dilemmas: alerting kids and their parents about safe practices on the Internet and trying to slow down the mistreatment of kids by zealous sex offenders. Sexual exploitation against children has given rise to new levels since the advent of the Internet. The daily list of targets continues to grow as victims are harassed, subjugated, and abused throughout this country. Two of the most damaging and detrimental hazards that the Internet provides are online sexual solicitation and the proliferation of child pornography. In light of the rampant emergence of sexual predators infiltrating the Internet, law enforcement agencies and legislators have been forced to develop and implement new laws and tactics to protect children from danger. Law enforcement agencies have been given the green light to intercept sexual advances of predators via the Internet. It has been estimated that 500,000–550,000 convicted registered sex offenders currently live in the United States. What is frightening is the tens of thousands of sex offenders and sexual predators that have never been caught.

A substantial number of law enforcement agencies have established and trained their own task forces that specifically target Internet predators and sexual predation. The Illinois State Police has created its own statewide Internet Crimes Unit (ICU). This specialized unit is one of the largest Internet crime units in the country and currently has 10 officers, eight crime analysts, and seven computer forensic investigators. The creation of the ICU is one of four goals of the state of Illinois's fight to combat sexual predators on the Internet. The other goals include increasing the penalties for Internet crimes and creating a special website so that the public can get information about Internet crime as well as Internet safety. This site can also be used to report any suspicious behavior or activity a person may come across. The last objective of the ICU is to create a partnership with NetSmartz and the placement of Illinois State Police in classrooms across the state to make children aware of the dangers associated with the Internet.

In 1995, the Federal Bureau of Investigation created the Innocent Images National Initiative (IINI), which combats sexual victimization on the Internet and deals exclusively with children and teens. The US Department of Justice indicates that 50,000 predators are on the Internet prowling for children at any given time. A substantial number of law enforcement agencies are experiencing problems due to a weaker economy. There is a lack of the additional funding needed for additional manpower, especially in carrying out sexual offender exploitation initiatives and projected goals.

Police departments and law enforcement agencies have been diligent in their efforts in apprehending sex offenders and sexual predators as they try to travel to visit their victims. According to the US Department of Justice (2009), law enforcement agencies in each city throughout the United States need to develop additional programs that will help to limit or prevent sexual predators accessing the Internet. Extensive manpower is the main concern for most law enforcement agencies, especially when they are trying to apprehend a sexual predator.

Undercover operations that include law enforcement officers who pose as teens take diligence and patience in apprehending sexual predators who are trying to meet underage children and teens online. Law enforcement officials who work this covert detail are diligent regarding every detail in their efforts to capture the traveling sex offender at the intended location for the meeting with the child. When the "traveler" (the name often associated with a sexual predator that tries to visit a victim) arrives, he is immediately arrested and read his Miranda rights. Catching the traveling predator takes hours of patience and extensive personnel to effectively get a conviction. Most cases often end up in guilty pleas and it is not often that a case is dismissed. About a quarter of all sex crime arrests are associated with these secret encounters related to the Internet. "What we are doing is preventing them from meeting someone else," said Andrew Donofrio, a retired lieutenant who headed the Computer Crimes Unit at the Bergen County Prosecutor's Office in Hackensack, New Jersey. "We see men who masturbate on camera and speak sexually to kids. They are doing awful things, and that is happening to real children every day. What are we going to do—wait for them to abuse a child?"

Lieutenant Andrew Donofrio

Andrew Donofrio is the owner of Cyberology Consultants, a company that provides educational and technology investigative services and tools in the fight to curtail the activities of sexual predators. He has experience and knowledge regarding sexual predators and is considered a leading expert in the field. Andrew acknowledged that sexual predators use grooming techniques to take advantage of their victims (personal communication). However, he stated that in today's society children are exposed to sexual content at a very young age. Kids today are exposed to pornography and sexually explicit material a lot sooner than past generations were. Consequently, many children are not shocked when a sexual predator uses brazen language or transmits pornography or nude pictures of himself, especially in chat rooms on the Internet. It is not uncommon for a predator to start talking about sex three or four lines into the conversation. Andrew said that this is a "sign of the times" and increases the vulnerability to victimization for today's child.

In regard to the Internet, Andrew said this venue just gave people, especially sexual predators a perceived safe medium to use to contact children, out of the view of watching parents or other civic-minded adults. Parents have always taught their children not to talk to strangers on the street, but they unwittingly let their child speak with a stranger online while they are in the next room. The child feels comfortable because mom or dad is nearby. The combination of children who are not put off by discussions of sex and the ubiquity of the Internet in their lives makes for a target-rich environment for sexual predators.

Andrew feels that sex offenders try to justify their actions when caught with child pornography. He stated they frequently claim that the interest in child pornography started with "accidental exposure." Andrew tends to dismiss that notion and feels that seeking out child pornography is very much about the sexual charge an offender gets from objectifying another person for his sexual desires. Moreover, Andrew stated that many offenders try to play down the heinousness of child pornography, citing that there was no real contact with a child. Andrew feels that each time an offender views child pornography, which is essentially picture or video documentation of a child rape, the child is victimized. Oftentimes, kids subjected to this will suffer physical and emotional repercussions the rest of their lives. Andrew expresses concern that an offender who views child pornography will be fueled to act out against a vulnerable child and that fantasy will not sustain the sex offender for too long. A few sex offenders may be satisfied masturbating to child pornography, but if presented with access to sex with a child, planned or not, they would most likely act out to achieve sexual gratification. Sex is a powerful form of motivation.

Andrew came into contact with many sexual predators who, after engaging and enticing their victim online, traveled (sometimes great distances) to meet their victims. Andrew has arrested a variety of offenders including a high school physical education teacher; a 37-year-old network engineer from Las Vegas, who flew across the country for what prosecutors said was an intended rendezvous with a 13-year-old girl; and a 48-year-old physical therapist from Philadelphia, who authorities said drove up from South Jersey expecting to meet a 14-year-old. Sexual predators are prevalent in our communities and often portray themselves as trustworthy, productive members of society.

In the early days of the Internet, typical travelers were often white, upper middle-class males. These were the people who could afford access to technology. After technology became less expensive and accessible to a great cross section of the population, "typical" no longer exists. Today, there are no general categories; sexual predators come in every age, race, religious affiliation, and social/financial demographic. Andrew did mention that the one common denominator was that they were almost always male, regardless of the victim's gender.

Andrew said that safety and education are important. He states that parents were really not prepared for this much technology this quickly. Additionally, children often know more about and are far more comfortable using technology than their parents. This places parents at a significant disadvantage. Further exacerbating the problem is the fact that children today are quick to reveal who they are and intimate details about themselves, their friends, and all aspects of their lives. Parents must put monitoring software on their computers at home, tell their kids that it is there, and be diligent about monitoring their children's online activity.

Detective Alan Kruk

Law enforcement is continually striving to stop Internet predators from meeting with and sexually abusing young, innocent children. Detective Alan Kruk, a noted Chicago police detective specializing in sexual predators throughout his career, has arrested many sexual offenders who travel to meet their intended victims. He often poses as a young teenage girl in various chat rooms. Detective Kruk said, "It does not take long for a sexual predator to start asking intimate sexual questions" (personal communication). It is when the sexual predator travels across state lines to have a sexual encounter with his victim that he is arrested. Travelers will often deny their true intentions. Detective Kruk keeps a detailed log and will bring the transcripts of his Internet conversations of the sexual predator to court. These Internet transcripts, along with other acquired evidence, will prove the sexual intent and motivation of the offender and will always show the sexual predator initiating the sexual encounter.

An assistant US attorney was arrested at the Detroit Metropolitan Airport because he had crossed state lines to have sex with a 5-year-old girl. He had arranged a meeting with a woman over the Internet whom he believed to be the girl's mother. The woman was a detective with the county sheriff's Internet sting task force and was posing as the decoy.

Commander Michael Anton

Law enforcement has faced an uphill battle trying to arrest sexual predators. Michael Anton, commander of the Illinois Cook County Sheriff's Police Department Criminal Intelligence and Special Investigations Unit, specifically deals with sexual predator cases. His team converses daily with potential sexual predators that are online in various chat rooms on the Internet. His investigators pose as teens in hopes of hearing from men looking to meet and have sex with young, naive victims. Commander Anton's unit boasts a 100% conviction rate for over 365 captured Internet predators due to their detailed and diligent efforts in gathering substantial evidence against the offenders. The convicted offenders have traveled from as many as 30 different states. Predators have come from countries such as Sweden, Ireland, and Mexico to meet their intended victims. Commander Anton noted that 40% of these travelers had admitted upon arrest that they were successful in previous attempts to seduce and sexually abuse young children (personal communication). There is a "wall of shame" with a picture of every sexual predator that has been caught, processed, and convicted by this unit. In some instances, the end results after conviction have been five offenders who have attempted suicide and 10 offenders who have committed suicide.

Commander Anton and his team, Special Investigators Tiffany Ruffoni and Anthony Stack, have been a part of over 500 hands-on investigations of sexual offenders, child molesters, and sexual predators. Anton categorizes sexual offenders into two groups: traveling sexual predators, called preferential predators, and situational predators. In his opinion, the preferential predators are the more dangerous type of predator; they fall into the distinct parameters of offending by the age of the victim. If the predator only likes 12-year-olds, that is most likely to be the age of the intended victim, and he will do whatever it takes to find someone in that age group. Anton goes on to say that most sexual predators were abused themselves. Many sexual predators have acknowledged that if they were abused by the age of 10, this is most likely the age they prefer their victim to be because development of their sexuality stopped at that age. He describes the situational predator as a watered-down version of the preferential predator. This type of offender takes advantage of any situation where he can get away with some form of sexual abuse—touching, voyeurism, etc. In Anton's opinion, this type of predator more readily responds to therapy or counseling.

Anton gave an example of one traveling sexual predator that originally set out to meet a 14-year-old girl. Prior to this, the offender sent many pictures of child pornography over the Internet. After many months of investigation and with substantial evidence against the offender, a warrant was issued to confiscate his home computer. The evidence found on the computer's hard drive revealed that the sexual predator had child pornographic pictures of himself performing oral sex on his infant daughter and other pictures of him attempting to sexually penetrate her. The sexual predator was arrested and found guilty of sexual exploitation of a child along with distributing child pornography. He was sentenced to a 39-year prison term, with 18 years of that sentence doing federal time.

The Regional Computer Forensics Lab (RCFL) is a computer task force that is funded by the Federal Bureau of Investigation (FBI). These specialists review any data within the computer, mirror any pornographic images on the hard drive, and crack any evidentiary encryption that has been configured or transposed.

Commander Anton discussed the new grooming law implemented in Illinois. The Grooming Law, 720 IlCS 5/11-25, states that

> (a) A person commits the offense of grooming when he or she knowingly uses a computer on-line service, Internet service, local bulletin board service, or any other device capable of electronic data storage or transmission to seduce, or entice a child, a child's guardian, or another person believed by the person to be a child or a child's guardian, to commit any sex offense as defined in Section 2 of the Sex Offenders Registration Act or to otherwise engage in any unlawful sexual misconduct with a child or with another person believed by the person to be a child. (b) Sentence. Grooming is a class 4 felony. (P. A. 95-901. Eff. 1-1-09)

Anton feels that grooming is a slow progression that starts out with finding an intriguing screen name. The sexual predator will initiate a conversation and ask for detailed information about the child with the hope of receiving a picture, especially if any interest is generated. The predator is apt to send a real picture of himself or the car he drives. He will send any pertinent information he thinks will help the child feel comfortable and keep the conversation going. The ultimate progression of the conversation is to get the child eventually to talk about sex. The predator may then send a link to a pornographic website and he will ask if the child likes the site and how it makes him or her feel—trying to get a reaction or a read from the child that will indicate whether this potential victim may be a willing sexual participant. By getting the child to speak about sex, the predator will attempt to lower his or her sexual inhibitions. Anton's investigative team said that kids are very trusting and often give more information than they should. Kids do not feel threatened because they live in Chicago and the person to whom they are speaking is in California. The goal of the predator is to make the child feel in control.

Commander Anton revealed that most predators want some sort of proof that the person to whom they are speaking is not in law enforcement or from an agency that guards against sexual predators. They will even ask if they are speaking with a police officer. Investigators Ruffoni and Stack said that before the hit television show *To Catch a Predator* was created, it was not unusual to see five men masturbating in front of a webcam that was attached to the offender's computer. It is now a class 4 felony to send explicit sexual pictures using a webcam, the Internet, or any other electronic means.

Child pornography is not just a picture of a naked child; it is the lewd exposure of the child's genitals, rape of a child, simulation of sex with a child, or masturbation of a child. Commander Anton said that the general public really does not understand the true meaning of child pornography. There is a difference between taking a picture of a naked child, child pornography, and child erotica. Having a picture of a naked child is not considered child pornography. Child erotica, which is somewhat easier to obtain, has the child posing in a provocative manner, possibly with lingerie or revealing attire; this is not considered child pornography. In child pornography, the offender's face is never seen. Many, if not all, sexual predators have their own collection of child pornography; they may share it, but they never want to give up their collection. Many sexual predators will meet other sexual predators in a hotel with their laptop computers in order to trade pictures. An interesting fact noted by Anton and his team is that most, if not all, of the sexual predators with whom they have dealt may be considered hoarders. They not only collect child pornography but also do not throw any of it away.

Commander Anton and his investigative team spoke about how manipulative pedophiles are. They said that 99% of pedophiles know their victims and what they look like and will take the time to find out about the child. The pedophile preys upon a child that comes from a divorced home or one who is timid, shy, or weak. Pedophiles will first try to get to know the child in a nonthreatening manner and eventually try to have some sort of relationship. Pedophiles are the types of people who smile when they are committing the offense or hurting someone. In Commander Anton and his team's opinion, most pedophiles find a profession or put themselves in a position to be around or with children—for example, a priest, teacher, Boy Scout leader, or daycare worker.

Detective Mark DiMeo

Mark DiMeo is a 24-year veteran of the Chicago Police Department and a lead investigator for 11 years with the Special Investigations Unit of the Chicago

Police Department's Detective Division. He has solved many sexually related crimes involving children. He said that sexual predation is a "gift that keeps on giving." DiMeo explains that the offense of sexual abuse against children has a ripple effect: It continues to progress every day and it has the potential to be uncontrollable (personal communication).

Detective DiMeo mentioned that the bulk of cases start out with the sex offender grooming the victim. He said that many times sex offenders look for perceived weaknesses in children with whom they come into contact: "They often target the weak and withdrawn child." He noted that the abuse starts out gradually—kissing, touching, and using inappropriate comments—to see how far the offender can go before being turned down. DiMeo stated, "There is no one face to a child sexual predator; they are all unique." The sexual predator knows what he is doing is wrong; a few feel bad and show uncontrollable regret, but others will put the responsibility for the abuse on the child.

Detective DiMeo discussed one shocking case that involved a victim's mother's boyfriend. The mother and her boyfriend were both in their early 30s. The mother asked the boyfriend (not the baby's father) to change her 1-year-old daughter's diaper while she attended to chores in another room. The boyfriend removed the soiled diaper and measured his penis against the baby. He then penetrated the baby with his penis. The baby screamed and continuously cried as blood spurted from her vagina profusely. The boyfriend hurriedly put on a new diaper, handed the crying baby to her mother, and left the apartment. The mother tried to console the baby and noticed the flow of blood when she removed her diaper. She called police and took the baby to the emergency room, where the baby's injuries of a torn vagina were documented. The boyfriend was eventually arrested and confessed to sexually assaulting the baby and is currently serving time in prison. In his confession, the offender wanted it known that the reason he measured his penis against the victim was that he "cared" and was "not an animal."

DiMeo said that sexual abuse by strangers does occur, but the majority of sex offenders with whom he and his staff have come in contact are intrafamilial predators. He calls this "the enemy from within" because the offenders are cousins, uncles, stepdads, and other trusted family members.

The subject regarding the accusation of a child being sexually abused and the turn of events afterward was also discussed. The well-being of any child that has been sexually abused is always taken into account. The child will not be revictimized by putting him or her on a witness stand in a court of law. DiMeo said that one of the most important segments at the start of the investigation is called the forensic interview. This is an official interview for a law enforcement purpose that is performed by a forensic interviewer. This interview documents the victim's account of whether or not a crime occurred. The forensic interviewer typically holds a master's degree or better in child psychology. The interview takes place with the abused child in a friendly, comfortable, and tranquil environment and is observed through a one-way mirror by a police detective, a member of the prosecutor's office, and personnel from the Department of Children and Family Services. The forensic interviewer asks nonleading questions in order to obtain factual responses from the victim regarding the alleged assault or abuse. The police detective is responsible for writing down what the child says about the crime and the abuse. In some locales, the interview is videotaped. DiMeo stated that Chicago is currently in the process of implementing videotaped interviews.

The police will not charge the offender based only on the testimony of a child but rather after they have a confession from the offender stating that he has committed sexual exploitation of a child. The sad fact is that if the offender does not confess, he may never be charged. A polygraph is sometimes used to obtain a confession, but entrapment is never the focus or intent. In many cases, polygraphs are a great investigative tool, even though such evidence is not admissible in court. The polygraph exam has a twofold advantage in this type of investigation. If the accused passes the exam, this proves that he was not being deceptive and that the victim may not have told the truth. If the offender does not pass the polygraph exam, this documents his deceptiveness. His statement is often recanted, admitting his guilt. DiMeo states, "The truth never changes; only lies change." Any mention of the polygraph test during a trial is grounds for a mistrial.

Crime scene processing is also an important factor in the investigation. The police try to locate evidence left behind by the offender. This could be any discarded items, condoms, and semen identified in a rape. A reality is that some victims become pregnant with the offender's child. DNA testing is done on the child's mother, the child, and the offender; if the offender's victim has an abortion, DNA from abortion fetal tissue is collected. A judge may have to issue a search warrant to extract DNA from an offender (typically by swabbing the inside of the offender's mouth) if the offender refuses to give it voluntarily.

DiMeo identified the medical exam as a very important segment of the investigation. There are doctors that are experts in the field of child sexual abuse who exclusively examine child victims. A doctor will use a culpascope. This machine takes detailed pictures of the affected and injured area of the child. The pictures are kept as evidence and eventually used in a trial against the offender. If a person can picture a clock, a tear at the 12 and 6 locations in comparison to a child's vagina is fairly consistent with the fact that a sexual assault most likely has occurred. This documented evidence oftentimes results in a conviction. Detective DiMeo said a key ingredient of his successful cases deals with DNA and medical evidence. He noted that some sexual offenders are careful not to leave any evidence, while others seemingly do not care.

Another important component in the investigative process is documenting what witnesses know or remember. There are different types of witnesses. The first is an eyewitness; that is, this person actually observed the offender committing the crime. The second is an outcry witness. This witness is the first person to whom the victim tells the story. The last type of witness is a situational or circumstantial witness, which is someone that, due to circumstances, has knowledge of the crime.

Detective DiMeo explained that an interview of an alleged offender is crucial to a good sexual assault investigation. The offender must be advised of his Miranda rights initially and understand them, but DiMeo explained that guys like to talk about sex. Great care is taken to ask open-ended questions so as to allow the offender to provide the details that only he would know and to safeguard against a false confession. All of these steps are designed to corroborate the victim's account and clearly show that a crime occurred, what exactly occurred, who the offender is, and how law enforcement knows all of these things.

In conclusion, DiMeo believes that the sexual registry laws work. They help people feel safe. It is important for people to know where in their neighborhoods sex offenders live and who they are. DiMeo went on to say that he admires the Children's Advocacy Center in Chicago because it incorporates the police, prosecutors, premier experts in the medical and psychological field, and the Department of Children and Family Services under one roof. He said it makes it less stressful for the victim and his or her family regarding the alleged abuse or assault. There are children advocacy centers in every state. They offer these needed services for children that are the victims of sexual abuse or sexual assault.

Detective Bob Collins

Bob Collins retired after 28 years with the Chicago Police Sex Crimes Unit. He said that Internet predators that travel to see their victims are looking for a naïve person (personal communication). He said, "Sexual predators are like the lion at the waterhole looking for the weakest animal or prey, the one who is the most vulnerable." The predator will look for the right opportunity, even if the victim is disabled—anyone that the predator can groom. Detective Collins said that most Internet predators are between the ages of 20 and 35 and are not typically the "old" people that most people conceptualize. It does not take long for a sexual predator to lock onto an adolescent, especially when he knows his victim is underage.

Sexual predators are found in all races, cultures, and socioeconomic groups, with a common thread being child pornography. Detective Collins mentioned that most, if not all, sexual predators hoard and trade child pornography. He mentioned one specific case where a sexual predator had over

10,000 images of children ranging from young children to teens; the offender, in this case, actually took pictures of himself molesting family members and young children. Detective Collins called child pornography the stepping stone to committing the actual crime. He said, "Sexual predators live in a fantasy world where they feel their actions are perfectly acceptable. They are slow and manipulative individuals and want to be a buddy or pal to the child; they want the child to need them."

Detective Collins feels the sexual offender registry is a good tool to keep track of offenders who commit sexual crimes and exploit children. He feels that DNA evidence is a godsend and has made his job as a sex crimes detective easier. He thinks that sexual offenders will never stop offending, regardless of how many times they are incarcerated or how many counseling sessions they participate in.

DNA Evidence

DNA is another name for deoxyribonucleic acid; it is contained in virtually every cell in the human body and is considered the building block for the body. According to the National Commission on the Future of DNA Evidence, the DNA in people's blood is the same as the DNA in their saliva, skin tissue, hair, and bone. Importantly, DNA does not change throughout a person's life and no two people have the same DNA, except for identical twins. DNA evidence has played an important role in solving criminal cases—both to convict the guilty and to exonerate those wrongly accused or convicted.

A trained evidence technician can collect DNA evidence from many different sources at the crime scene. If the crime is a sexual assault, DNA can be collected from the offender's sweat, saliva, blood, hair, cigarettes, condoms, semen, clothing, or any pertinent articles in possession of the offender. The collection of DNA evidence and how it was obtained are critical in identifying the possible offender and proving who was and was not at the scene, with a greater likelihood of solving the crime.

DNA Testing

According to the National Commission on the Future of DNA Evidence, the most common form of DNA analysis is called polymerase chain reaction (PCR). PCR has allowed investigators to analyze evidence samples of limited quality and quantity successfully. The PCR process makes millions of copies of very small amounts of DNA. This enables the laboratory to generate a DNA profile, which can be compared with the DNA profile from a suspect. A statistic is then generated to reflect how often one would expect to find this particular DNA profile in the general population.

Possible location of DNA	Source of DNA
Bite mark or area licked	Saliva
Fingernail scrapings	Blood or skin cells
Inside or outside surface of used condom	Semen or skin cells
Blankets, sheets, pillows, or other bed linens	Semen, sweat, hair, or saliva
Clothing, including undergarments worn during and after the assault	Hair, semen, blood, or sweat
Hat, bandanna, or mask	Sweat, skin cells, hair, or saliva
Tissue, washcloth, or similar items	Saliva, semen, hair, skin cells, or blood
Cigarette butt, toothpick, or rim of bottle, can, or glass	Saliva
Dental floss	Semen, skin cells, or saliva
Tape or ligature	Skin cells, saliva, or hair

Source: National Commission on the Future of DNA Evidence.

When a sexual assault victim has a forensic medical examination, the evidence collected from the victim's body and/or clothing, which may include the offender's DNA, is packaged in a sexual assault evidence kit (sometimes referred to as a "rape kit"). Additional evidence, such as body fluids left at the location of the crime (e.g., on bedding, furniture, or the rim of a drinking glass), may also be collected. The rape kit and the crime scene evidence samples are usually sent to a crime lab for analysis. If biological evidence is found, the crime lab attempts to obtain a DNA profile. If a profile is found, it can then be compared with a suspect's DNA sample. If there is no identified suspect, DNA offender databases that contain the archived DNA profiles of known offenders throughout the United States, as well as DNA profiles from crime scenes in other unsolved cases, can be searched.

As with fingerprints, the effective use of DNA may require the collection and analysis of human samples. Because extremely small samples of DNA can be used as evidence, it is important for police and evidence technicians to ensure that it does not become contaminated. DNA evidence can become contaminated when DNA from another source gets mixed with DNA relevant to the case. This can happen when an evidence technician sneezes or coughs over the evidence when collecting it. In investigating sexual assault cases, it may be necessary to collect and analyze the DNA from the victim's consensual partner to eliminate the partner as a possible suspect.

CODIS

According to the National Institute of Justice, the *Combined DNA Index System* (CODIS) is an electronic database of DNA profiles that can identify suspects. This process is similar to the Automated Fingerprint System database (AFIS). Currently, every state is beginning to implement a DNA index of individuals convicted of certain crimes. Upon conviction and sample analysis, perpetrators' DNA profiles are entered into a DNA database. Just as fingerprints found at a scene can be run through the automated fingerprinting search, DNA samples can be run through CODIS. This gives law enforcement officers another tool to identify possible suspects.

Police Reports

How police officers document and describe a sexual attack is an important part of the judicial process. Their report on sexual misconduct, abuse, or an assault may be the difference between a sexual predator's being convicted and staying in prison or released to be free to offend again. Experts in law enforcement and prosecutors in criminal court cases have indicated that a poorly written police report can cause problems for a victim if the victim pursues the matter and it is presented in court. An inadequate narrative can have a detrimental effect, especially if it generates disbelief, uncertainty, and skepticism. The more exact and accurate the storyline in referencing a sexual assault is, the greater the probability of a successful conviction. Specific wording such as "give," "participate," "engage," or "perform" may imply that the sexual act was consensual instead of a forced, involuntary, or coerced act.

The Entrapment Defense

The entrapment defense is based on the belief that someone should not be held accountable and convicted for a crime derived from communication that the government originally instigated. According to *West's Encyclopedia of American Law* (2008),

> Entrapment is a defense to criminal charges when it is established that the agent or official originated the idea of the crime and induced the accused to engage in it. If the crime was promoted by a private person who has no connection to the government, it is not entrapment.

Shestokas (2008) said entrapment is a defense to criminal prosecution if a government agent induced a person to commit a crime that the person was otherwise unlikely to commit. If a person is ready and willing to break the law and the government agents merely provide an opportunity for the crime, there is no entrapment. It is not entrapment for an undercover agent to offer to engage in an illegal activity with the person. A person is not a victim of entrapment if he was ready, willing, and able to commit the crime if an opportunity presented itself, as long as law enforcement did no more than offer an opportunity.

West's Encyclopedia of American Law (2008) notes:

> When an officer supplies an accused with a tool or a means necessary to commit the crime, the defense is not automatically established. Although this factor may be considered as evidence of entrapment, it is not conclusive. The more important determination is whether the official planted the criminal idea in the mind of the accused or whether the idea was already there. Entrapment is not a constitutionally required defense, and, consequently, not all states are bound to provide it as a defense in their criminal codes. Some states have excluded it as a defense, reasoning that anyone who can be talked into a criminal act cannot be free from guilt. The rationale underlying the defense is to deter law enforcement officers from engaging in reprehensible conduct by inducing persons not disposed to commit crimes to engage in criminal activity. In their efforts to obtain evidence and combat crime, however, officers are permitted to use some deception. Most states require a defendant who raises the defense of entrapment to prove he or she did not have a previous intent to commit the crime. Courts determine whether a defendant had a predisposition to commit a crime by examining the person's behavior prior to the commission of the crime and by inquiring into the person's past criminal record if one exists. Usually, a predisposition is found if a defendant was previously involved in criminal conduct similar to the crime with which he or she is charged.

According to the *US Department of Justice Criminal Resource Manual* (1997),

> Entrapment is a complete defense to a criminal charge, on the theory that "Government agents may not originate a criminal design, implant in an innocent person's mind the disposition to commit a criminal act, and then induce commission of the crime so that the Government may prosecute." *Jacobson v. United States*, 503 U.S. 540, 548 (1992).

The US Supreme Court has recognized that when investigating certain criminal behavior, law enforcement may lawfully use an array of undercover techniques. A valid entrapment defense has two related elements: (1) government inducement of the crime, and (2) the defendant's lack of predisposition to engage in the criminal conduct (*Mathews v. United States*, 485 U.S. 58, 63 (1988)). Of the two elements, predisposition is by far the more important.

The question most often debated is whether entrapment occurs when a law enforcement officer induces a person to commit a crime, by means of fraud or undue persuasion. The entrapment defense protects a defendant from governmental intimidation. In the court case of *Jacobson v. United States*, the Supreme Court overturned a child pornography case based on the entrapment defense.

There are two foundations to the current entrapment defense:

- *Government inducement of the crime:* The government's behavior or performance would instigate or induce a law-abiding citizen into crossing the line and breaking the law. The government actions of inducement may include promises, persuasion, threats, or harassment.
- *Willingness to commit the crime:* One of the main components in the entrapment defense is the defendant's inclination or predisposition to engage in illegal activity or criminal conduct. The person is ready and willing to commit the crime.

The sexual exploitation of a minor is a federal offense. A few ethical and legal questions have been raised regarding who has jurisdiction over the sexual offender once he or she is caught. The problem is that a sexual predator on the Internet can live next door, in the next municipality, or across the country. Many law enforcement agencies and special task forces are specifically geared toward catching the Internet predator and they often will work together, sharing their information and joining forces in the apprehension of the most devious Internet sexual predators. Many attorneys employed by Internet offenders claim their clients have been wrongly convicted of exploiting children based on the defense that undercover officers were used and this is entrapment. Defense attorneys have indicated that the entrapment defense is based on the belief that a person should not be convicted of wrongdoing if the government, especially one of its law enforcement agencies, initiated the action. Legal experts have argued that an individual may not have attempted or committed a sexually related crime if he had not been provoked or led on by the government. Sexual predators who are caught by undercover officers posing as teenagers on the Internet typically try to use this defense to gain an acquittal.

The First Amendment to the US Constitution guarantees freedom of speech. The issue has arisen as to whether someone can be charged for exercising this right over the Internet. There are laws in place that make an adult communicating with a minor over the Internet for sexual purposes a crime that is punishable by law. However, in order for an offender to be responsible, he must know that he is communicating with a minor. That is, only some rights pertaining to freedom of speech over the Internet are protected. If an adult knowingly uses the Internet to convince or entice a minor into sexual relations with him or her, the speech used to commit this act is not protected under the law.

Computer Evidence and the Fourth Amendment

According to the FBI, Division of Criminal Justice Services (2007), all digital investigations, especially Internet-facilitated child sex crimes, rely on forensic analysis to secure evidence needed to obtain a conviction in a court of law. What is important to an investigation is duplicating the image of the evidence, which can be found on hard drives, cell phones, and other external media. Forensic analysis is an effective means in leading to the identification of sexual offenders that create and distribute child pornography. Data and records obtained from digital media and Internet usage can yield important investigative leads. Digital evidence of exploitative images that are seized from computers and other electronic files need to be analyzed to establish the production, possession, transport, and distribution of child pornography. This collection of digital evidence is critical for prosecution.

Dateline NBC

Watchdog group Perverted Justice, along with Chris Hansen (author of the book *To Catch a Predator* and a news reporter with the NBC *Dateline* television show *To Catch a Predator*), teamed up with local law enforcement authorities that orchestrated stings to catch sexual predators visiting young, innocent victims for sex. In 2007, Chris Hansen stated the following:

> Who are these guys? Based on my experience there is no one-size-fits-all characterization. About a third of them, I think, are sick, evil, or wired to want to have sex with young teens. Technically, most are not pedophiles; that term refers to someone who seeks sex with prepubescent children. These guys would probably be trying to meet kids for sex whether or not the Internet existed.
>
> Another third, I think, tend to be younger men who surface in our investigations, the twenty- or twenty-one-year-olds whom I refer to as the opportunists. Some are socially awkward and sexually inexperienced. This group figures that young teens might be having sex anyway and since the girl or boy is really only six or seven years younger, why not go for it?
>
> As for the other third, I believe they would not likely be involved in this behavior without the Internet. For many men the computer provides twenty-four-hour-a-day, seven-days-a-week access to the Internet. And it is anonymous. You can be anyone you want to be online. And it's as addictive as a drug for many men. This mix ends up being a very strong cocktail. The men in this group often start by viewing pornographic websites, and then come to the chat rooms. Their addictions and compulsions develop to the point where men no longer see the line between fantasy and reality. The only thing that will satisfy them is a face-to face meeting with the target of their desire.

Perverted Justice

Many advocacy and vigilante groups and victims of computer predators have tried to educate others about this growing problem. Perverted Justice originally started as a vigilante group against sexual predators and is now an Internet watchdog group that exposes online predators. Perverted Justice volunteers expose sexual predators who try to converse inappropriately with children and young adults. This group also aids police departments and criminal justice agencies by being proactive in online investigations. Xavier Von Erck, director of operations, indicated that Perverted Justice has worked with police on 544 convictions as of April 2011.

The Perverted Justice volunteers pose as minors and try to capture pedophiles in their search for victims. Ms. Del Harvey, the Perverted Justice criminal law enforcement coordinator, explained that most of the people who assist Perverted Justice in investigating online improprieties make sure that the sexual offender's age is confirmed before any inappropriate sexual conversations begin. The Perverted Justice group admitted that the sexual offender will always initiate any Internet dialogue.

Wiretapping

According to the National Academy of Sciences, in April 2003 Congress passed a law that provides wiretapping authority for seven sexual offenses, including child pornography and the sexual exploitation of children. Part of a broader child-protection bill entitled the Protect Act of 2003, which also mandates the Amber Alert system for abducted children, this law expands federal law-enforcement agencies' wiretapping authority to catch online predators before they strike.

The Legal Impossibility Defense

"Impossibility" in criminal law is "a fact or circumstance preventing the commission of a crime"—for example, "the defendant has not committed a crime because no child actually existed to entice for illegal acts." Although the first impossibility defense adopted by the courts was very broad, the courts eventually narrowed the defense and distinguished between two types of impossibility: factual impossibility and legal impossibility.

Factual impossibility, which can never be a defense to the crime of attempt, is "impossibility due to the fact that the illegal act cannot physically be accomplished." Legal impossibility occurs when a defendant's actions, even if carried out, do not constitute a crime because an element of the crime has not been satisfied.

Profile of a Female Sex Offender

Debbie, a 38-year-old married mother of four from California, has pleaded guilty to engaging in a sex with a 15-year-old neighbor that resulted in a pregnancy and birth of child. Debbie pleaded guilty to a felony lewd act with a child 14 or 15 years old, oral copulation with someone younger than 16, and unlawful sexual intercourse, according to court records. Under the terms of the plea deal with prosecutors, three of the same counts were dismissed.

Debbie was married with three children when she had the affair with the boy, who lived nearby. She had been friends with the boy's family and started inviting the victim to her house late at night in early 2009. Debbie was accused of having sex about two times a week with the boy between February and November 2009. She gave birth to the boy's daughter on November 21, 2009.

The boy's mother grew suspicious when she found suggestive handwritten notes between the two; she confronted her son, who admitted the relationship. The boy first had sex with Debbie, who had watched him grow up, before he graduated from elementary school. The boy's family has custody of the girl, but Debbie is battling for visitation rights. In addition to 365 days behind bars, a superior court judge sentenced Debbie to 3 years of probation and ordered her to register as a sex offender. Conviction without the plea deal could have fetched her a maximum sentence of 7 years and 8 months in state prison.

Profile of a Male Sex Offender

According to the FBI, Grant, a convicted sex offender, is currently wanted in Santa Rosa, California, on a felony arrest warrant issued on October 28, 2003. He is charged with nine counts of lewd and lascivious acts with a child under 14 years of age, two counts of lewd and lascivious acts with a child who was 14/15 years old, and two counts of lewd and lascivious acts with a child under 14 years of age by the use of force, violence, duress, menace, and threat of bodily harm. These charges stem from Grant's alleged sexual molestation of a young female family member, which occurred over a period of approximately 8 years. Grant has also been charged with failure to register as a sex offender. A federal arrest warrant charging him with unlawful flight to avoid prosecution was issued on March 31, 2006, in the United States District Court, Northern District of California, and San Francisco, California.

In My Opinion

Dr. Frank Schmalleger

Frank Schmalleger, PhD, distinguished professor emeritus of the University of North Carolina and author of a multitude of criminal justice textbooks, revealed his thoughts on sexual predators and sexual offenders (personal communication):

I think that we need to be careful to distinguish among offender types and to realize that "predators" and "offenders" are not necessarily the same. The term "sexual predator" includes a wide variety of offenders. Nowadays, it seems all who violate laws regulating sexual behavior are seen as "predators." The true predators, however, are those who aggressively victimize others in relatively vicious ways. In particular, those who aggressively and violently victimize children through direct sexual contact are especially stigmatized. As is true with most crimes, however, it is probably true that only a relatively small group of hard core offenders commit most of the crimes that occur within this category. For those who constitute this small group, however, sexual victimization becomes a lifestyle and reform or rehabilitation appears unlikely.

Sex offenders are motivated by a number of things, including physical desire, a need to humiliate their victims, and complex psychological factors. Hence, a single deterrent strategy is unlikely to prevent all crime commission. The anticipation of strict punishment seems to have little effect on many of the most serious sex offenders, although something as simple as public embarrassment may work with relatively minor offenders. It's recently become obvious that sexual offenders use the technology afforded by the Internet to victimize others, or to turn relatively innocent people into co-participants in various forms of sexual deviance. Complicating things is the fact that social websites, or those that facilitate interpersonal interaction, are hard-pressed to be financially profitable. Consequently, self-policing is unlikely to occur, and only social outcry, sometimes through novel forms of legislation, is likely to curtail the opportunities they provide. The sex offender registry works in the sense that it may limit the opportunity for further offending. The more people know of former sexual offenders in their midst, the more able they are to take steps to prevent their own victimization or the victimization of others about whom they care.

Definitions of Chapter Key Terms

Entrapment: Luring or enticing a person into committing a crime and then prosecuting him or her for it.

e-Stop: Allows social networking websites to identify sexual predators and prevents them from harming again.

Exploitation: Taking unfair advantage of an unknowing child or individual, often by coercing him or her into doing something immoral, wrong, or harmful.

Global positioning system (GPS): A service that transmits, via satellites, information regarding positioning and navigation.

Traveler: A term generally used by law enforcement agencies to refer to an online sexual predator who travels (often across state lines) to meet victims that were first met on the Internet.

References

Anonymous. (2007). *Information Today* 24 (5): 3.

Hansen, C. (2007). *To catch a predator: Protecting your kids from online enemies already in your home.* New York: Dutton.

National Commission on the Future of DNA Evidence. Office of Justice Programs. What every law enforcement officer should know about DNA evidence.

Radford, B. (2006). Predator panic: A closer look. *Skeptical Inquirer* 30 (5): 20–21, 69.

Shestokas, D. J. (2008). The entrapment defense for criminal defendants: The government made me do it (http://www.suite101.com/content/the-entrapment-defense-a78198).

United States Department of Justice. (1997). United States Attorney's Criminal Resource Manual, Washington, DC. p. 645.

United States Department of Justice. (2009). Office of Sex Offenders, Sentencing, Monitoring, Apprenhending, Engineering, and Tracking.

West's Encyclopedia of American Law, 2nd ed. (2008). Florence, KY: The Gale Group.

Incarceration, Recidivism, and Rehabilitation

9

I was a resource for questions and answers, not necessarily about sex, but about life in general. To have sex, you have to have acceptance. I wanted to have sex with her.

W. (sexual predator)

A lot of this stuff put on social networking sites is stuff they do not want to tell their parents. It sucks you in almost.

Girls speaking about the Internet

Introduction

The release of convicted sex offenders into society will long be debated by many due to the controversy regarding the moral, ethical, and legal issues that it encompasses. Government officials point out that early release of offenders is a strain on many communities and law enforcement because of the lack of adequate resources and manpower to supervise parolees effectively. Lawmakers face challenges regarding a person's civil liberties and the need to keep society safe from criminals that have been previously arrested for sexual crimes. According to recent studies, convicted sex offenders often struggle with an improper and irrepressible sexual desire for their child victims. The child who was once abused then becomes the offender. A good predictor of this is the harshness and severity the child experienced with regard to the unsolicited sexual exploitation. This chapter will focus on how incarceration and rehabilitation affect recidivism.

Incarceration

A few studies indicate that the majority of registered sex offenders are likely to head back to prison—more so than any other type of offender—and the only way to stop sexual predators is to keep them incarcerated. A simple question concerning a chronic problem regarding sex offenders is how long they need to be incarcerated after they have committed their crime and whether it is safe to release them. Many victims and their families are worried about convicted sexual offenders who have exhibited deviant and unacceptable behavior and who, after incarceration, are returning to start a new life within the community. According to US Bureau of Justice statistics, the Department of Justice (2000) noted that since 1995 one in seven prison inmates in the United States is serving time for committing sexual offenses.

Most legislators may be truly worried about the safety of their citizens, while others weigh the cost of rehabilitation over incarceration. Law enforcement officials have pointed out the various problems that sex offenders pose once they are released back into the community. Community activists and victims of sexual offenders will often blame the entire criminal justice system for failing to provide longer sentences for these offenders. According to recent studies, incarceration has very little, if any, effect on sex offenders that have committed sexually violent acts. Prison alone may not be the most effective treatment to keep a sex offender from reoffending. Freeman-Longo (2000) stated that most incarcerated sex offenders often reoffend but expressed that with proper treatment, there is a strong possibility that the chances of reoffending can be reduced.

A variety of issues that should be addressed after a sex offender is released from prison:

- Monitoring the offender's actions and whereabouts
- Ensuring that court-ordered mental health treatment takes place
- Monitor and adjusting treatment (what works and what does not work)
- Victim protection
- Sex offender registration

Recidivism

What will it take for that deviant behavior of a sexual offender to subside? When it is safe to release a sex offender back into society? Is there a solution to stop repeat offenders from reoffending? A study by Carich, Kassel, and Stone (2001) revealed and warned that a complete and reliable cure for sex offenses does not exist. The consensus of most people is that sexual predators and sexual offenders are destined to reoffend. My study has come to the same conclusion, also illustrating that sex offenders will often fabricate the reasons they were arrested and justify their actions, rarely blaming themselves.

According to most studies, recidivism rates for sex offenses are often far higher than those for other crimes. The Department of Justice Center for Sex Offender Management indicates that recidivism may occur when there is a new arrest, a new conviction, or new commitment to custody. Some studies use the return to prison as the standard for determining recidivism. Two separate and significant reasons why a sex offender is returned to prison are that he or she has been (1) convicted of another sexual crime, or (2) rearrested because of a technical breach that violates conditions of release. This may include staying away from a child or family member or testing positive for drugs or alcohol in the system.

Castration

Many health care experts have concluded that castration is probably the most effective means to reduce recidivism of convicted sex offenders. Grossman, Martis, and Fichtner (1999) said that favorable reports about the effectiveness of castration have been countered by reviews in which it has been disparaged on ethical grounds and scientifically discredited as not 100% effective. With the advent of sexual predator laws, castration as a treatment option is now subject to discussion that includes media attention to individual cases as well as focused state legislation specifying the conditions under which orchiectomy (removal of the testicles) may be performed.

This chapter focuses on two forms of castration: surgical castration and chemical castration. Surgical castration is the permanent removal of the male's testes. This procedure will make the male sterile and will ultimately affect and decrease his sexual desire. Chemical castration is the injection of an antiandrogen drug that will reduce the male's testosterone level and eventually reduce his sex drive.

In September of 1996, California became the first state to pass legislation to authorize castration (either chemical or physical) for certain sex offenders nearing their release dates. Since 1996, six states have voted in legislation to castrate sex offenders either chemically or surgically. Currently, a few states allow both chemical and surgical castration for sex offenders. California, Florida, Georgia, Louisiana, Montana, Oregon, Texas, and Wisconsin are a few of the states that have implemented some form of castration for convicted sex offenders who are very close to being released into society. The states that authorize castration have different viewpoints regarding the behavior that triggers castration and whether castration should be discretionary, mandatory, or voluntary. California, Louisiana, and Florida are the only states that give sex offenders a choice to undergo surgical castration.

The topic of castration will be debated by many because it is often seen as additional punishment for convicted sex offenders. The argument is that sex offenders have served their time in prison, which should be punishment enough. Many feel that to make a sex offender undergo surgical or chemical castration is a violation of the offender's rights because he is being punished twice. According to Findlaw.com, the American Civil Liberties Union (ACLU) criticizes chemical castration because it violates sex offenders' constitutional rights to privacy under the Fourteenth Amendment, rights of due process and equal protection, and the Eighth Amendment's ban of cruel and unusual punishment. Proponents of the legislation argue that castration is justified to help control sex offenders' behavior and to protect potential victims.

Chemical Castration

Sex offenders are constantly challenged with the thought of reoffending and the consequences of what might happen if they get caught again. The problem they face is avoiding tempting situations, keeping their behavior in check, and not acting out. A few doctors have experimented with antiandrogen drugs that will help control frequent masturbation and sexual desire. These antiandrogens are expensive drugs that are known to cause weight gain and breast development as a side effect. Bradford and Pawlak (1993) have found that antiandrogen treatment of sexual offenders has been shown to reduce the recidivism rate. The sex offender experiences a diminished sex drive and desire to reoffend.

A few judges around the country have been willing to explore the possibility of chemical castration as punishment for sexual offenses. A few states have been contemplating legislation that would allow a judge to mandate chemical castration for any deviant sexual act or for any offender convicted of committing certain sexual crimes against children for the second time. Currently, two classes of medications are primarily used in suppressing sexual urges among sexual offenders: Depo-Provera and Depo-Leupron. The problem with chemical castration is ensuring that the convicted offenders keep taking the prescribed medication.

Depo-Provera

The drug that is primarily used in chemical castration is medroxyprogesterone acetate (MPA) or Depo-Provera. This drug has been used to treat sex offenders in the United States since the 1960s. Depo-Provera is commonly used as a birth control drug for women. It restricts the release of luteinizing hormones from the pituitary gland. An injection of Depo-Provera helps to control or deter sexually offensive behavior in males. By reducing testosterone levels, the drug also diminishes compulsive erotic fantasies and lowers male sex drive. Depo-Provera has side effects for a male that may cause swelling of the breasts, loss of facial hair, and nausea. Chemical castration does not permanently alter the sex offender since testosterone levels can normalize once the injections diminish. The drug does not cause impotence during treatment and individuals can still experience erections and ejaculations.

California was the first state to pass a first sexual castration law in 1996 due to an increase in sexual offender activity. This law mandated that any sexual offender who was convicted for the second time and whose victim was 13 years old or younger would have to be injected with Depo-Provera once a week. A number of other states followed California's lead and more than half have either considered or passed chemical castration legislation. There has been a vocal community of critics against chemical castration of sex offenders, including medical practitioners and the American Civil Liberties Union. However, support for this chemical procedure is growing, with 12 states waiting to pass similar laws. The states with chemical castration laws often mandate court-ordered chemical castration for repeat sex offenders, and studies have shown that the recidivism rates are relatively low.

The state of Oregon implemented a pilot program where potentially dangerous sex offenders who were to be released into the community were given weekly injections of Depo-Provera. Collier Cole, a psychologist with the Rosenberg Clinic in Galveston, Texas, who has used Depo-Provera to treat sex offenders since the mid-1970s, said that Depo-Provera presents many long-term side effects. He said that it not only reduces the male sex drive, but also provides a moderate reduction in masturbation and tends to reduce sexual fantasies.

Depo-Leupron

The second drug that is primarily used in chemical castration is called Depo-Leupron (leuprolide). Depo-Leupron is a man-made hormone that reduces the amount of testosterone and also decreases the sex drive in adult males. Given by injection once a month, Depo-Lupron appears to be more effective than Depo-Provera because it causes far fewer adverse side effects, like potential blood clotting and liver problems. In a 2005 study done by Schober and colleagues, they reported that "cognitive-behavioral psychotherapy augmented with leuprolide acetate (LA) significantly reduced pedophilic fantasies, urges, and masturbation; however, pedophilic interest did not change during one year of therapy."

Depo-Provera and Depo-Leupron are not necessarily a cure but, with counseling and therapy, could help recidivism among the most dangerous sexual offenders. Dr. Barbara Schwartz, who is in charge of the sex offender treatment programs at the Massachusetts Department of Corrections, noted that other medications might actually be more effective while having fewer side effects. Dr. Schwartz stated that Prozac could help sex offenders by interfering with their obsessive-compulsive tendencies.

Cyproterone

A synthetic steroid, cyproterone suppresses testosterone in the body and is available in Canada and Europe. According to Bradford and Pawlak (1993), cyproterone acetate is a powerful antiandrogen used in the treatment of paraphilia for at least a decade. Studies have reported that it is effective in reducing the recidivism rates of sexual crimes perpetrated by men. It acts through competitive inhibition of the androgen receptors, blocking the effects of testosterone and dihydrotestosterone. Systematic clinical studies of its effectiveness and its clinical effects on sexual behavior are lacking, however. In Bradford and Pawlak's study, 19 paraphilic men who had also recidivated in a variety of sexual crimes were treated with cyproterone acetate and placebo in a double-blind crossover design. The use of the active drug was associated with a significant reduction of some aspects of sexual behavior, particularly sexual fantasies. There were also significant effects on levels of circulating sex hormones and some effects on physiological measurements and self-reports of sexual arousal.

Triptorelin

Triptorelin (Decapeptyl-Cr) is a synthetic drug that overstimulates the body's production of certain hormones, causing this production to shut down temporarily. Triptorelin lowers the testosterone level.

Surgical Castration

When surgical castration is mentioned, many people assume the male's penis is amputated. Sexual castration (orchiectomy) is an irreversible procedure that involves a small incision in the scrotum to remove the male's testes. Testosterone and dihydrotestosterone are the hormones responsible for maintenance of sexual behavior, and it is the testes that produce testosterone. Surgical castration's primary effect is to diminish the sex offender's physical and emotional ability to respond to sexual stimuli. Proponents of the procedure argue that surgical castration is minimally invasive because it is not major surgery and is often performed on an outpatient basis. There is no risk that offenders will manipulate the procedure, as they could with drug therapy and it produces long-lasting results. Dr. Shawn Johnston, a California psychologist, pointed out that surgical castration could dramatically reduce recidivism rates among sex offenders, particularly child molesters. Fred Berlin (1994), founder of the Johns Hopkins Sexual Disorder Clinic, noted that surgical castration does in fact lower testosterone levels and that this hormonal change has helped some pedophiles to control their sexual desires better.

Surgical castration is rarely used to prohibit sex offender activity in the United States, but some sex offenders are opting for this procedure with the hope of receiving reduced time in prison. Experts claim that deterrence of future sexual offenses depends significantly on whether the sex offender understands that what he did was wrong and whether he has volunteered for the procedure. In 1998, Jeffery Morse of Illinois admitted his involvement in a child molestation case. He voluntarily requested to be surgically castrated before his sentencing in hopes of curing his urges and reducing his punishment. This type of case was a first in Illinois. The judge, Donald C. Hudson, noted Morse's castration and still sentenced him to 26 years at Statesville Penitentiary. Dr. Michael Bailey, a psychologist who teaches at Northwestern University in Evanston, Illinois, provided expert testimony on whether castration cuts the likelihood that a sex offender will strike again: "I believe surgical castration is one of the most, perhaps the most, desirable route for sex offenders like Jeffery Morse."

Others argue that surgical castration is a fitting punishment for heinous sexual crimes. An ardent supporter of surgical castration, Texas district court judge Michael T. McSpadden believes in this justification. In 1992, McSpadden presided over the case of Steven Allen Butler, who sexually assaulted a 13-year-old girl while he was still on probation for fondling a 7-year-old girl in 1989. Butler volunteered to be surgically castrated in exchange for a lighter sentence and McSpadden agreed.

Surgical castration has been used successfully by European countries, including Denmark and Germany, to treat sex offenders. Studies show that those countries have drastically reduced recidivism rates compared to rates for sex offenders who were not surgically castrated. Danish laws governing castration were first enacted in 1929 and stemmed from the government's intent to protect society from recidivistic rapists. However, the law allowed for persons to be castrated if they believed that their sexual drive placed them in danger of committing a crime. The law was amended to include castration of persons whose sexual drive produced considerable psychological suffering or social devaluation. The sexual recidivism rate among the surgically castrated offenders there is extremely low.

The Czech Republic has allowed at least 94 prisoners over the past decade to be surgically castrated. Many of the Czech psychiatrists who supervise the hour-long procedure agree that it is the best way to suppress sexual impulses in even the most dangerous and treacherous sexual predators. The Czech Republic uses this procedure for sex offenders and has found that surgical castration is an effective method of deterring sex offenders.

Should a sex offender who volunteers to undergo surgical castration waive his Eighth Amendment rights not to have to undergo cruel and unusual punishment? Keith Fremin volunteered to undergo surgical castration in exchange for a lighter sentence. The question arose as to whether his rights under the Eighth Amendment were abused by his undergoing surgical castration. Sex offenders who choose surgical castration make a voluntary choice. "Fremin volunteered to undergo castration, a move criminal justice experts called extremely rare" (Gordon 2005).

Emmet Hanger, Jr., a Virginia lawmaker, introduced legislation that would allow some sex offenders to choose to be surgically castrated rather than face indefinite detention in a mental health facility. If a sex offender chooses to be surgically castrated, he will be granted his freedom after serving out his prison sentence. Many civil libertarians have opposed the Hanger Bill, often questioning the procedure's effectiveness. This legislative bill could invoke the constitutional right against cruel and unusual punishment even if presented as a voluntary option. The American Civil Liberties Union has condemned physical castration as cruel and unusual punishment. Mr. Hanger acknowledged that he understood the opposition but introduced his bill as a cost-cutting measure. It costs the state of Virginia $300,000 for each sexual offender who is civilly committed to a treatment facility.

Legislation regarding chemical and surgical castration has not come without legal, ethical, and medical controversy. The recidivism rate for castrated offenders is relatively low and studies have revealed a clear distinction between surgical castration and other forms of treatment. When used in conjunction with therapy, surgical castration can considerably reduce the frequency of a sexual predator's reoffending. The leading controversy of surgical castration can be seen from both legal and medical standpoints. The legal issue concerns whether surgical castration violates a person's civil liberties regarding cruel and unusual punishment. The medical issue is whether surgical castration can guarantee that previous or potential victims will not be sexually victimized.

In Springfield, Illinois, a convicted sex offender attempted to castrate himself because he said that he had felt the urge to touch and hurt children and to offend again. The 59-year-old man had successfully removed one testicle, and the other testicle had been badly damaged, when the police arrived. He was taken to the hospital because he was bleeding uncontrollably. The sex offender said he had flushed his testicle down the toilet. He said that he was not trying to commit suicide but rather to stem his urges and desires.

Sex Offender Treatment Programs

A topic that is highly debated among many professionals, politicians, and police officers is the effectiveness of treatment programs for sex offenders. Heller (2008) stated that although sex offenders are the ones who receive counseling in a group or individual setting, the focus of sex offender treatment programs is on protecting society by providing offenders with the means to help themselves not to reoffend. With a growing number of individuals being confined for sex offenses, many correctional facilities are turning to such treatment programs to attempt to rehabilitate offenders in order to create a safer return to society.

In a study, Buttell and Carney (2002) evaluated treatment providers' perceptions of the impact of the Internet on the treatment of sex offenders. This study surveyed all of the agencies in South Carolina that provide treatment services for sex offenders. Analysis indicated that

- Most treatment providers were unaware of the potentially negative impact of the Internet on their treatment efforts with clients.
- Most treatment providers had no policy restricting their clients' Internet use.
- The overwhelming majority of treatment providers felt that they were poorly equipped to deal with this issue.
- Almost all of the treatment providers felt that probation and parole would be of little assistance in helping them monitor their clients' use of the Internet.

Implications of the findings for improving treatment services for sex offenders were explored and discussed.

There are currently over 2,000 treatment programs in the United States. A vast majority of sex offenders are mandated to participate in a treatment program by way of a court order after their prison sentences have ended. Very few sex offenders willingly participate in these programs, which raises the question: Do they really want to get help and not reoffend again?

Mental Health Treatment

Many health care professionals feel that sex offenders may be in need of mental health treatment and that behavioral treatment and counseling may be the only way to keep them away from children. There is a debate between clinicians and law enforcement. Many clinicians believe that therapy and treatment will ultimately lower the recidivism rate, even if by only a small percentage. Law enforcement contends that tougher sentencing is the only way that sex offenders will stop reoffending and that mandatory therapy issued as probation is just a quick fix—a temporary Band-Aid on a large gash. Sex offenders are bound to do what they know best. Past studies have indicated that those who have not undergone any treatment for their conduct will reoffend 10%–35% more often than those who have undergone some form of counseling.

Researchers who study sex offenders have the offenders talk about their sexual crimes and what they have done to their victims. This is not an easy undertaking. Many researchers find that convicted and released sex offenders do not reveal very much information about their past sexual crimes and experiences, even in therapy. Their entire life is a web of secrecy and illusiveness. English (1997) stated,

A cure for sex offending is no more available than a cure for epilepsy or high blood pressure. But use of a variety of interventions can help manage these disorders. A realistic objective of treatment is to provide sex offenders with the tools to manage their inappropriate sexual arousal and behavior. A therapist can in many cases teach offenders self-management by developing skills for avoiding high-risk situations through identification of decisions. Treatment focuses on recognizing and managing deviant sexual behavior and offenders' thoughts and attitudes to promote it.

Dr. Fred Berlin, a professor at Johns Hopkins University and founder of the National Institute for the Study of Prevention and Treatment of Sexual Trauma, stated, "The best public safety approach on pedophilia is to provide these people with treatment." According to *Washington Monthly* (1994), "Counseling may be the answer for some but most experts feel it is not enough to prevent past sexual offenders from re-offending again." Dr. Berlin noted that a sexual offender's condition is similar to alcoholism: It is incurable, but treatable.

With regard to counseling and treatment for sex offenders, recent studies have indicated the following:

- Treatment may not immediately reduce the risk of reoffending.
- Long-term treatment may be instrumental and effective in reducing the risk of reoffending.
- Offenders are able to cope and manage their life better after counseling.
- Both group and individual therapy are effective for sex offenders.
- Drugs are seldom used in conjunction with concentrated and intensive group therapy.

Group Therapy

Group therapy has been very effective for adolescent as well as adult sexual offenders. It often takes place in a discreet location within a hospital, mental health care, or counseling facility. This environment is where many sexual offenders are able to speak in a relaxed setting where they can share the same issues and problems. They often start the meeting by giving their first name and begin discussing and acknowledging previous incidents in their lives and how and why they committed the crimes. This type of therapy allows the sexual offender to share experiences, express feelings, and be candid knowing that he is not alone.

Profile of a Female Sex Offender

Theresa is a 43-year-old woman from Pennsylvania who pleaded guilty to a charge of harassment. An agreement between the defendant and the victim and his family was reached after Theresa had been charged with corruption of minors under which the state withdrew that charge. The victim's family consented to the agreement.

Theresa was arrested in June on police accusations that she engaged in sexual intercourse repeatedly between March 30 and April 5 with the 17-year-old high school student. She was working as a teacher's aide in special education classes for students in 9th–12th grade at the high school during the alleged incidents.

According to the criminal complaint, the first incident happened in March on a dirt road about a mile from the student's home and was witnessed by children on a school bus. Police said the second incident was reported in a desolate area near a swamp, and that a dump truck driver saw a third incident in April on another desolate road. Later, Theresa and the student exchanged sexual images of each other via texting, police said. According to court documents, the student told police that Theresa would pick him up in her car after class at the high school and they would drive to a secluded area and engage in sex. Theresa corroborated the student's story, adding that the activity occurred inside and outside her vehicle. They both told police that she gave the student $60 to purchase new clothing.

Profile of a Male Sex Offender

Curtis is a sex offender wanted for his alleged sexual activities with a 14-year-old Minnesota girl whom he met on the Internet in February of 2000. Curtis is alleged to have communicated with the victim mostly via the Internet for approximately 6 months. In July of 2000, Curtis allegedly flew to Minnesota, met the teenage victim, and engaged in sex acts with her at a local hotel.

In My Opinion

Mr. Mike Sullivan

Edward Nichols, MSW, LCSW-R, of Nichols Consulting, specializes in working with individuals who are falsely accused of sexual abuse and attorneys who are representing the falsely accused. Mr. Nichols, who is a psychotherapist, indicated that false charges of child sexual abuse, sexual abuse, molestation, and incest are a combination of people seen in divorce litigation and criminal trials (personal communication). He said that when most Americans hear that someone is accused of child abuse, they automatically assume that the accused is guilty—"so what if a few are innocent?"

The individuals who are falsely accused of child abuse are often guilty of poor judgment. They put themselves in a vulnerable position. In today's society, almost anyone can be accused of touching someone inappropriately. Certain populations, such as foster parents, can be the focus of false allegations. Often, the foster child has been in the system long enough to know what accusations can do, especially if the child has been mistreated or does not want to be with the foster family. These foster children are aware of the harm they can cause. Mr. Nichols said, "False allegations are the nuclear weapon in the arsenal of domestic relations."

Mr. Nichols contends that many accused individuals cannot afford a good defense attorney. A $50,000 cost is often not uncommon in defense of sexual abuse cases. Mr. Nichols feels that public defenders cannot devote the quality time and utilize the available resources to defend accused abusers effectively. He reaffirms that the sanctions are just as high. He offered this comparison of competent knowledgeable attorneys to public defenders: "If you have a heart condition, do you want a heart specialist or surgeon to operate on you or would you rather have a really good nurse with a sharp knife?" He noted that it takes a team effort, especially if the accused is convicted of molesting a child, because there is a very good chance that that person will be spending a good portion of his life in prison. Mr. Nichols said it comes down to a trial by experts and that often the focal point is the testimony of the child. In a majority of the sexual abuse cases his firm handles (about 99%), DNA is not used as evidence.

On Mr. Nichols's website, Falseabuse.com, he states seven stages that an accused sexual offender goes through:

- *Shock.* The individual who is falsely accused is shocked by the allegations.
- *Disbelief.* The individual cannot believe what is happening and how he got into this situation.
- *Confidence.* The individual is confident that the truth will come out and others will dismiss the allegation of abuse.
- *Confusion.* This individual will vacillate between the false allegations and the possible jail time he might have to serve.
- *Research.* The individual will begin exploring and learning as much as he can in proving that he is innocent.
- *Fear.* The individual will be labeled and falsely convicted of sex abuse and realize the foreseeable problems in the future.
- *Getting help.* The individual needs to find someone who can help him through this ordeal.

Definitions of Chapter Key Terms

Chemical castration: Injection of an antiandrogen drug that will reduce the male's testosterone level and eventually reduce his sex drive.

This is most commonly accomplished by injection of Depo-Provera, a derivative of progesterone that significantly reduces the testosterone level, sexual fantasies, and arousal. It also believed to reduce the recidivism rates in sex offenders.

Cyproterone: A synthetic steroid that suppresses testosterone in the body; it is available in Canada and Europe.

Depo-Leupron: A man-made hormone that reduces the amount of testosterone and also decreases the sex drive in adult males.

Depo-Provera: A man-made hormone that reduces the amount of testosterone and also decreases the sex drive in adult males.

Group therapy: Sexual offenders are able to speak in a relaxed environment and share the same issues and problems.

Recidivism: Reoffending or committing the same type of crime again.

Surgical castration (orchiectomy): Removal of the male's testes. This procedure will make the male sterile and ultimately affect, decrease, and inhibit his sexual desire.

Triptorelin: A synthetic drug that overstimulates the body's own production of certain hormones, causing the production of these hormones to shut down temporarily.

References

Berlin, F. S. (1994). The case of castration, part 2. *Washington Monthly* 26 (5): 28–29.

Bradford J. M. W., and Pawlak, A. (1993). Effects of cyproterone acetate on sexual arousal patterns of pedophiles. *Archives of Sexual Behavior* 22 (6): 629–641.

Buttell, F. P., and Carney M. M. (2002). Treatment provider awareness of the possible impact of the internet on the treatment of sex offenders: An alert to a problem. *Journal of Child Sexual Abuse* 10 (3): 117–125.

Carich, M. S., Kassel, M., and Stone, M. (2001). Enhancing social interest in sexual offenders. *Journal of Individual Psychology* 57 (1), p. 18.

English, K. (1997). Managing adult sex offenders in the community. *National Institute of Justice Research in Brief (US Department of Justice)*, pp. 1–11.

Freeman-Longo, R. E. (2000). Children, teens, and sex on the internet. *Sexual Addiction and Compulsivity* 7 (1–2): 75–90.

Gordon, M. (2005). Child rapist OKs surgical castration: Rare penalty avoids possible life in jail. *New Orleans Times-Picayune*, July 13, 2005.

Grossman, L. S., Martis, B., and Fichtner, C. G. (2009). Are sex offenders treatable? A research overview. *Psychiatry Services* 50: 349–361.

Heller, M. L. (2008). Sex offender rehabilitation: Educating correctional cadre. *Corrections Today* 70 (6): 42–45.

Schober, J., Kuhn, P., Kovacs, P., Earle, J., Byrne, P., and Fries, R. (2005). Leuptolide acetate suppresses pedophilic urges and arousability. *Archives of Sexual Behavior* 34 (6): 691–705.

United States Bureau of Justice Statistics. (2000). *Criminal justice information policy*. Washington DC: Author.

Tragic Stories That Resulted in Landmark Legislation

10

He was nice to me, always asking about school and my grades. When he wanted to meet at the mall, I thought it would be OK. He seemed a lot older than he said he was. When we left the mall, I should have never got into his car. He tried to kiss me and touch me as soon as I sat down, I was scared, real scared. I remember crying as I ran away. I never told anyone until today.

Victim

She was a cheerleader; I have a thing for cheerleaders. Her profile said she was adventurous, so I took a chance. I did not think she would tell her parents. This was the first time I was ever caught.

Sexual predator

The Jacob Wetterling Story

Jacob Wetterling was kidnapped on October 22, 1989. Jacob (age 11), his brother Travis (10), and his friend Aaron (11) were riding their bikes home from a convenience store. A masked man with a gun approached them and told them to throw their bikes in the ditch and shut off their flashlights. He commanded Trevor and then Aaron to run toward the woods, with the threat of shooting them if they did not. The gunman held Jacob behind. By the time the boys looked back, both Jacob and the kidnapper were gone. Friends, relatives, neighbors, and people of the community searched in nearby remote areas and passed out flyers every day, but to no avail. Jacob has not been heard from since. It is not uncommon that kidnappers sexually exploit the children they abduct.

The Jacob Wetterling Act

According to the US Department of Justice (2008), specific laws directly affect sex offenders. Mrs. Patty Wetterling, Jacob's mom, was instrumental and at the forefront in getting the Jacob Wetterling Act (also known as Jacob's law) passed. This act is a federal law enacted in 1994 that mandated all states to establish sex offender registries and register sex offenders or lose federal funding. Jacob's law was the first undertaking by the federal government to prevent convicted sex offenders from repeating their crimes after release. It was the outcome of Patty Wetterling's unwanted education in sexual violence against children. The Jacob Wetterling Crimes against Children Sex Offender Registration Act was part of the 1994 Crime Bill signed by President Bill Clinton. The goal of this act was to give law enforcement a tool to help build safer communities. All states now have sex offender registries in place. Wetterling says (http://www.dailystrength.org/groups/families-of-sex-offenders/discussions/messages/10631032),

> Are these policies working? Are our "get tough on sex offenders" laws having the desired effect? Human Rights Watch (HRW) has questioned what sex offender policies are working and which ones are not. [It] published a 143-page report, "No Easy Answers: Sex Offenders Laws in the United States." The researchers examined whether communities are safer with these laws and what issues and concerns policy-makers should consider. HRW found that many laws may not prevent sexual attacks on children but do lead to harassment, ostracism, and even violence against former offenders.

The Jacob Wetterling Foundation advises:

Community Notification is not about chasing sex offenders out of our neighborhoods. We all face the challenge of building new communities, which recognize that sex offenders live and work among us. Experts state that sex offenders are less likely to re-offend if they live and work in an environment free of harassment. If we are going to make our communities safer we need to use this law to our benefit. We need offenders to succeed because if they don't that means there will be another victim.

In 1999, for the 10th anniversary of Jacob's abduction, Patty Wetterling decided to write an open letter to the abductor. Minnesota newspapers agreed to print it for her. Wetterling consulted the FBI for advice on how to word the letter. In the letter, Wetterling ask[ed] the abductor if Jacob [wa]s still with him. She offer[ed] compassion for the abductor, and sa[id] that all little boys, including the abductor when he was one, deserve a happy childhood. She t[old] him… that she d[id] not see him as an ugly, dirty old man…She and her family [we]re looking for answers, that only he c[ould] answer them, and that she want[ed] to know what became of Jacob after the kidnapping. The letter generated some tips, but nothing substantial.

…in early 2004, news reports circulated that new evidence was being considered in the abduction of her son. News outlets in the Twin Cities indicated that another boy had been assaulted not long before Jacob disappeared. Police were also ruling out the long-held belief that the abductor had gotten away in a car (Academic Dictionaries and Encyclopedias).

The Jacob Wetterling Crimes against Children and Sexually Violent Offender Registration Act of 1994

Enacted as a part of the Omnibus Crime Bill of 1994, the Jacob Wetterling Crimes against Children and Sexually Violent Offender Registration Act

- Established guidelines for states to track sex offenders
- Required states to track sex offenders by confirming their place of residence annually for ten years after their release into the community or quarterly for the rest of their lives if the sex offender was convicted of a violent sex crime (http://www.ojp.usdoj.gov/smart/legislation.htm)

The Jacob Wetterling Improvements Act 1997

Passed as part of the Appropriations Act of 1998, the Jacob Wetterling Improvements Act took several steps to amend provisions of the Jacob Wetterling Crimes against Children Act. This law

- Changed the way in which state courts make a determination about whether a convicted sex offender should be considered a sexually violent offender to include the opinions not just of sex offender behavior and treatment experts but also of victims' rights advocates and law enforcement representatives
- Allowed a state to impart the responsibilities of notification, registration, and FBI notification to a state agency beyond each state's law enforcement agency, if the state so chose
- Required registered offenders who change their state of residence to register under the new state's laws
- Required registered offenders to register in the states where they worked or went to school if those states were different from their state of residence
- Directed states to participate in the National Sex Offender Registry
- Required each state to set up procedures for registering out-of-state offenders, federal offenders, offenders sentenced by court martial, and nonresident offenders crossing the border to work or attend school
- Allowed states the discretion to register individuals who committed offenses that did not include Wetterling's definition of registerable offenses
- Required the Bureau of Prisons to notify state agencies of released or paroled federal offenders, and required the Secretary of Defense to track and ensure registration compliance of offenders with certain uniform code of military justice (UCMJ) convictions (http://www.

dailystrength.org/groups/families-of-sex-offenders/discussions/messages/10631032)

The Jessica Lunsford Story

Jessica Lunsford, a pretty 9-year-old, lived with her father and grandparents in Florida. She was abducted from her grandparents' home on February 23, 2005, by a registered sexual offender named John Couey. He admitted that Jessica had been bound and gagged for 2 days in his home. Couey eventually raped and suffocated Jessica before burying her in a shallow grave. Her body was found on March 18, 2005, buried under a pile of leaves about 150 yards from her home. Couley's mattress also had Jessica's blood splatted all over. Couley was arrested for the kidnapping, sexual assault, and murder of Jessica Lunsford and sentenced to death in March of 2007. He died in prison of natural causes on September 30, 2009.

Jessica's Law

The Jessica Lunsford Act was enacted in 2005, soon after her kidnapping, sexual assault, and murder occurred. This Florida law is intended to be more stringent in tracking released sex offenders. It enhances penalties for sexual crimes against children, requiring a lifetime of electronic monitoring for the worst offenders and providing for the death penalty for the murder of sexual crime victims. Jessica's law is yet another example of hard-hitting legislation designed to protect children. It was essentially enacted to punish child sex offenders harshly and to reduce substantially their ability to sexually exploit another victim. Jessica's law has a mandatory minimum 25-year prison sentence that includes lifetime monitoring for any adult convicted of lewd molestation of a victim who is under 12 years old.

Similarly to what happened after Megan's law was enacted, a number of states have introduced similar legislation since Jessica's law was enacted. Radford (2006) stated,

> Every state has notification laws to alert communities about former sex offenders. Many states have banned sex offenders from living in certain areas, and are tracking them using satellite technology. If journalists, child advocates, and lawmakers are serious about wanting to protect children, they should turn from the burning matchbook in front of them and face the blazing forest behind them.

Under the act, modern technology will be in place to protect children from sexual predators by making it possible to track them easily.

The Megan Kanka Story

Maureen and Richard Kanka lived in a quiet town in New Jersey for 15 years. They were a typical American family, raising three children and enjoying the American dream. All of that changed on July 29, 1994, when their daughter, Megan, was lured into neighbor Jesse Timmendequas's home. Mr. Jesse Timmendequas was born April 15, 1961, and in 1969 allegedly saw his father "brutally rape" a neighborhood girl. As a child, Jesse was repeatedly sexually abused by his father. The Timmendequas family moved often; by the time Jesse was 17, they had reportedly moved 21 times. In 1979, when Jesse was 18, he pled guilty to aggravated sexual assault of a 5-year-old girl and began his 9-month prison term the following year. Soon after his release from prison, he pled guilty to sexually assaulting a 7-year old girl, this time serving 6 years behind bars. Once again, Jesse was released from prison and moved into a quiet neighborhood in Hamilton Township in New Jersey with two other convicted sex offenders whom he had met at the Adult Diagnostic Treatment Center.

Jesse used the excuse of showing Megan his puppy as he led her to his bedroom. He confessed that he tried to molest her soon after she entered his bedroom. Megan tried to fight him off as she screamed for help. Jesse admitted that he knocked Megan to the floor as he continuously punched her in the head. He strangled her as he brutally raped her. Jesse put her lifeless body in a box and dropped the box off in a remote area about 3 miles from his home.

Megan's parents called police to report that Megan was missing. Many local residents, neighbors, family, and friends assisted the many police officers and firefighters combing the area near the Kanka family home for any trace of Megan. The outpouring of sympathy and support was extraordinary as volunteers went door to door passing out flyers in hope of securing any lead. Jesse Timmendequas even stopped by the Kanka home and offered to circulate flyers. Maureen Kanka went on television asking for the safe return of her daughter: "Please, please help us find our daughter. We want to bring her out safely. Whoever out there has her, she's a wonderful girl…she's only 7. Let her come back." After an extensive search, Megan's body was eventually found by Hamilton Township Police on July 30, 1994. It had been dumped on the West Windsor side of Mercer County Park.

Jesse Timmendequas was arrested at 7:00 p.m. on Saturday, July 30. On August 1, Timmendequas was arraigned for the murder of Megan Kanka. On October 19, he was indicted. His trial for the murder of Megan began on January 13, 1997, and he was eventually found guilty of sexual assault and murder on all counts. Jesse was sentenced to death for the murder; however, in 2007, New Jersey abolished the death penalty and sentenced him to life in prison without parole.

Megan's parents led a crusade to help change the law regarding sexual predators. Maureen Kanka said, "We knew nothing about him; if we had been aware of his record, my daughter would be alive today." It is because of her rape and murder that Megan's law now exists. Richard and Maureen Kanka worked tirelessly to create an atmosphere of awareness of the danger and exploitation of children by sexual predators. They started the Megan Nicole Kanka Foundation. Megan's parents obtained over 400,000 signatures on petitions urging new laws to be enacted that would make people aware of sexual predators that move into a neighborhood and community. The Kankas explained that "every parent should have the right to know if dangerous sexual predators move into a neighborhood." On October 31, 1994, nine bills known as Megan's law were passed by the New Jersey State Senate and signed by Christine Whitman, governor of New Jersey.

Megan's Law

The entire notification law identification program came to the attention of many, especially after the brutal rape and murder of Megan Kanka. Megan's law is a federal law enacted in 1996 that requires public notification when a sex offender is released from prison or when a convicted sex offender moves into a new area or neighborhood. On March 5, 2003, the US Supreme Court ruled that information regarding potential sexual offenders could be publicly posted on the Internet.

According to the Megan Nicole Kanka Foundation, it is a national tragedy that hundreds of families will not be allowed even the small dignity of knowing where their children are because they will never be found. There is a growing body of evidence that pedophilia sex offenders cannot be cured and their behavior cannot be controlled. Therefore, it is urgent that we take lawful steps to protect our children. At the very least, any convicted pedophile released from prison cannot be allowed to reside in neighborhoods without the knowledge of the parents and children in that neighborhood.

Laws created for the protection of children, such as Meagan's law, implemented a registry system in an attempt to track the whereabouts of convicted sex offenders. By law, a person convicted of a specified sex crime is required to register as a sex offender with a local law enforcement agency and law enforcement officials will alert the community when a convicted sex offender moves into a neighborhood. Notification laws fluctuate significantly from community to community. Almost every state attempts to keep track of sex offenders and where they reside and to provide useful information to the public when a sexual offense occurs. Several states have enacted their own legislative versions of Megan's law.

On May 17, 1996, President Bill Clinton signed Megan's law as an amendment to the Jacob Wetterling Crimes against Children Act. Megan's law requires each state in the country to notify the public when dangerous sexual offenders are residing in their area. Some states have developed a three-tiered system for categorizing the offenders by risk to the public. By using this system, each state determines who gets notified of the offender's residence:

- Tier one is a low risk of reoffending.
- Tier two is a moderate risk of reoffending. In some states, tier two notices go out to schools, daycare centers, and organizations that have children under their care.
- Tier three is a high risk of reoffending. Tier three notices go out to families living within a certain radius of the offender's home.

Some states have set up databases of sex offender information through local police departments that can be accessed by the public. Some require written requests for information and others require a fee for sex offender information. Thirty-seven states have developed sex offender Internet registries. Megan's law provides several different avenues of notifying the public across the country. Each state has created the notification system that best suits its state constitution and need. Many proponents of Megan's law feel that the potential benefits of protecting the general public far outweigh a sexual predator's right to privacy. Estimates reveal that 20% of sexual offenders required to register fail to do so. Some may fear retaliation for their crime; others are transient and move from state to state.

Megan's Law of 1996

During the mid-1990s every state, along with the District of Columbia, passed a Megan's law. In January of 1996, Congress enacted the federal Megan's law, which

- Provided for the public dissemination of information from states' sex offender registries.
- Provided that information collected under state registration programs could be disclosed for any purpose permitted under a state law.
- Required state and local law enforcement agencies to release relevant information necessary to protect the public about persons registered under a state registration program established under the Jacob Wetterling Crimes against Children and Sexually Violent Offender Registration Act. (http://www.ojp.usdoj.gov/smart/legislation.htm)

The Adam Walsh Story

Adam Walsh was a 6-year-old boy who was abducted when he went shopping with his mother, Revé Walsh, at a Sears department store in Hollywood, Florida, on July 27, 1981. Adam wanted to stay by the video game section of the store as his mom went to look at lamps not more than 75 ft away. Revé Walsh told Adam to make sure that he waited for her. When Revé returned, Adam was nowhere to be found. She desperately searched for her son. Friends and family began looking and searching for the young boy, but to no avail. Sixteen days later, a decapitated head was found in a canal in Vero Beach, Florida. Adam was identified through dental records and by a family friend. Ottis Toole, a drifter and convicted serial killer, admitted his involvement in the killing but recanted his story twice. Toole died in prison in 1996 before he was convicted of the crime on circumstantial evidence.

After the death of his son, John Walsh became the cofounder of the National Center for Missing and Exploited Children (NCMEC). Since 1984, 160 missing children cases have been reported to the NCMEC and 132,300 children have been recovered. John Walsh is also noted for his television show, *America's Most Wanted: America Fights Back*. Wal-Mart implemented a "Code Adam" in 1994 to assist parents and employees in finding children in the store and monitoring store exits. The US Department of Justice has estimated that 4,600 children are abducted annually by nonfamily members.

The Adam Walsh Child Protection Act

President George W. Bush signed into law the Adam Walsh Protection and Safety Act on July 27, 2006, in a ceremony in the White House rose garden. The act is intended to track sex offenders nationwide and provide stricter registration for offenders. Sex offenders can register through the National Sex Offender Registry, which is an online service that links all state offender websites. Sex offenders will also receive tougher and harsher penalties, especially if they prey on children using the Internet. This is an online service linking state sex offender websites through all states.

If an offender fails to register, he or she could face a 10-year maximum term or a 5-year consecutive mandatory minimum sentence for committing a crime while failing to register. The Adam Walsh Act not only gives sex offenders a mandatory 10-year prison sentence if they assault any child under the age of 18, but also prohibits them from showing or sending child pornography or any other obscene material.

The Adam Walsh Child Protection and Safety Act of 2006 gives specific information about released sex offenders and allows the federal government to prosecute state offenders:

- Promotes a three-tier system (based on severity of the crime)
  - Tier 1: offenders must register in person on an annual basis for 15 years.
  - Tier 2: offenders must register in person on a semiannual basis for 25 years.
  - Recidivism drives offenders into higher tiers.
- Promotes uniformity across public sex offender websites
- Requires sex offenders to register specifically where they reside
- Requires that sex offenders let law enforcement know where they work and where they attend school
- Requires reporting any name change, employer change, or address change within 3 days
- Includes crimes of adult pornography and conspiracy
- Extends registration to include certain juveniles convicted only of the most serious sexual crimes

Adam Walsh Child Protection and Safety Act of 2006

- Created a new baseline standard for jurisdictions to implement regarding sex offender registration and notification
- Expanded the definition of "jurisdiction" to include 212 federally recognized Indian tribes, of whom 197 have elected to start up their own sex offender registration and notification systems
- Expanded the number of sex offenses that must be captured by registration jurisdictions to include all state, territory, tribal, federal, and uniform code of military justice (UCMJ) sex offense convictions, as well as certain foreign convictions
- Created the Office of Sex Offender Sentencing, Monitoring, Apprehending, Registering, and Tracking (SMART Office) within the Department of Justice, Office of Justice Programs, to administer the standards for sex offender notification and registration, administer the grant programs authorized by the Adam Walsh Act, and coordinate related training and technical assistance
- Established a Sex Offender Management Assistance (SOMA) program within the Justice Department

Sex Offender Registration and Notification Act (SORNA) as Part of the Adam Walsh Child Protection and Safety Act of 2006

SORNA requires sex offenders to register and keep their registration current in each jurisdiction in which they reside, are employed, or attend school. A sex offender must also initially register in the jurisdiction in which convicted if it is different from the jurisdiction of residence. Jurisdictions' registration programs must incorporate these requirements to implement SORNA:

> ...A sex offender must, not later than three business days after each change of name, residence, employment, or student status, appear in person in at least one jurisdiction in which the sex offender is required to register and inform that jurisdiction of all changes in the information required for that sex offender in the sex offender registry. This information must immediately be provided to all other jurisdictions in which the sex offender is required to register. Jurisdictions must also require a sex offender to provide notice if he or she is leaving the jurisdiction prior to the move; the sex offender must provide information about the jurisdiction to which he or she is going.

> ...A sex offender must appear in person, allow the jurisdiction to take a current photograph, and verify the information in each registry in which that sex offender is required to be registered not less frequently than:
> - Annually for a tier I sex offender,
> - Every six months for a tier II sex offender, and
> - Every three months for a tier III sex offender.

> Sex offenders must carry out this schedule of personal appearances in all jurisdictions where they reside, are employed and attend school.

> ...A sex offender must, not later than three business days after each change of name, residence, employment, or student status, appear in person in at least one jurisdiction in which the sex offender is required to register and inform that jurisdiction of all changes in the information required for that sex offender in the sex offender registry. (http://www.ojp.usdoj.gov/smart/faqs/faq_registration.htm)

The Dru Sjodin Story

Dru Sjodin was a 22-year-old student who attended the University of North Dakota. She was last seen alive speaking on her cell phone with her boyfriend on her way home from work. Five months later, Dru's body was discovered in a ravine near the home of Alfonso Rodriguez, Jr., a registered sex offender who had spent 23 years in prison. Psychiatrists at the prison where Rodriquez had been previously incarcerated noted that his behavior and conduct seriously implied that he was at a high risk to reoffend again. Studies have shown that about 70% of violent sexual predators are at a high risk of reoffending and many will do so within 6 years of being released from prison.

On August 30, 2006, a federal grand jury deliberated less than 4 hours before indicting Rodriguez for kidnapping and murder. On September 22,

2006, after three decades of committing sexual assaults, Alfonso Rodriguez, Jr., was sentenced to death by a federal jury in Fargo, North Dakota. Rodriguez's attorneys appealed, stating that Rodriguez did not receive a fair trial. On September 22, 2009, the 8th US Circuit Court of Appeals disagreed and upheld the death sentence for the kidnapping and murder of Dru.

Dru's Law

The rape and murder of Dru Sjodin by a convicted sex offender in 2003 prompted Congress to take additional action in the war against sexual predators. Dru's law requires convicted child molesters to be listed on a national Internet database and face a felony charge for failing to update their whereabouts. This database will be the first national online listing available to members of the public, who can search by zip code. It will aid police officers in finding more than 100,000 sex offenders who are unaccounted for. It calls for harsh federal punishment for sexually assaulting children. If a victim is murdered, the offender could face the death penalty.

At the signing ceremony, President George W. Bush said the new law will help prevent child abuse by creating the national child abuse registry and requiring investigators to do background checks on adoptive and foster parents before they are approved to take custody of a child. Giving child protective services professionals in all 50 states access to this information will improve their ability to investigate child abuse cases. Child advocates have called the bill the most sweeping sex offender legislation to target pedophiles in years. The law imposes a mandatory minimum sentence of 30 years for raping a child, a mandatory 10-year penalty for sex trafficking offenses involving children and for coercing child prostitution, and increases minimum sentences for molesters who travel between states.

Dru's law has been instrumental in the creation of a national registry and database of high-risk sex offenders. The law establishes a procedure for assessing the danger of a sex offender offending again. Some politicians hope this law will protect many Americans from being abducted and murdered by offenders who previously have committed violent offenses. Many of these sex offenders are characterized as high risk for reoffending but are often let out of prison with no monitoring or safeguarding of any kind.

Madeline M. Carter, director of the Center for Sex Offender Management, says, "Professionals have long recognized key difference among sex offenders. These relate to the types of crimes they commit, to the victims they target, to their risk for reoffense and to the types of interventions that will most likely reduce their risk." The federal approach puts all of these aside in favor of a single factor: conviction under a specific law. Perhaps the chief reason that states have not come into compliance, though, is cost. The registry is another unfunded federal mandate. Most states just cannot afford it. The registry cannot be completely effective without all of the states in compliance. Some politicians call Dru's law a one-size-fits-all approach.

Dru Sjodin National Sex Offender Public Website

According to the Dru Sjodin national sex offender public website, the public can search all 50 state registries simultaneously. The site gets more than 17,000 visits a day. According to the National Conference of State Legislatures, states have been in a near open revolt over the rules that accompanied its creation: "This law created a one-size-fits-all approach to classifying, registering and, in some circumstances, sentencing sex offenders. If Congress doesn't amend the law, states will continue managing their registries their own way but with less federal money than before."

The Dru Sjodin national sex offender public website, coordinated by the US Department of Justice, is a cooperative effort between the jurisdictions hosting public sex offender registries and the federal government. This website is a search tool that allows a user to submit a single national query to obtain information about sex offenders through a number of search options:

- By name
- By jurisdiction
- By zip code
- By county (if provided by jurisdiction)
- By city/town (if provided by jurisdiction)
- National

The Pam Lychner Story

Houston real estate agent Pam Lychner prepared to show a vacant home to a prospective buyer. Awaiting her at the house was a twice convicted felon, who brutally assaulted her. Her husband arrived and saved her life. She then formed "Justice for All," a victims' rights advocacy group that lobbies for tougher sentences for violent criminals. In July of 1996, Pam Lychner and her two daughters were killed in the explosion of TWA Flight 800 off the coast of Long Island.

The Pam Lychner Sex Offender Tracking and Identification Act of 1996

US Senators Gramm and Biden credited Lychner with helping craft the language of a bill that established a national database to track sex offenders.

Later that year, Congress passed the Pam Lychner Sexual Offender Tracking and Identification Act of 1996 in her memory.

This act requires the attorney general to establish a national database (the National Sex Offender Registry—NSOR) by which the FBI can track certain sex offenders. The law also

- Mandated that certain sex offenders living in a state without a minimally sufficient sex offender registry program register with the FBI
- Required the FBI periodically to verify the addresses of the sex offenders to whom the act pertains
- Allowed for the dissemination of information collected by the FBI necessary to protect the public to federal, state, and local officials responsible for law enforcement activities or for running background checks pursuant to the National Child Protection Act
- Set forth provisions relating to notification of the FBI and state agencies when a sex offender moved to another state

Chelsea King's Story

Chelsea King was jogging through a park in San Diego when she was abducted by a registered sex offender named John Albert Gardner, III. Gardner admitted to sexually assaulting and killing Chelsea. He also admitted to killing a 14-year-old girl named Amber Dubois, who had disappeared a year earlier. Gardner was spared the death penalty but will spend the rest of his life in prison, with no chance of parole.

Chelsea's Law

This law was named after the tragic rapes and brutal murders of Chelsea King and Amber Dubois by a convicted sexual predator. This bill was signed into California law on September 9, 2010, by Governor Arnold Schwarzenegger. Anyone convicted of a violent sex offense against a child in California will get life in prison without parole, and the "one-strike" provision applies to forcible sex crimes against minors, taking into account the victim's age and whether the victim was bound and gagged or drugged.

Profile of a Female Sex Offender

Melinda, 33-year-old woman from New Mexico, was sentenced to 17 months in the custody of the New Mexico Corrections Department after she was found guilty of contributing to the delinquency of a minor. This was to be followed by 1 year on parole with the remaining 3 months of the sentence suspended. Upon release from custody, Melinda will be on 3 months of supervised probation.

Melinda was a substitute teacher at a school where the minor was a student. She was arrested on May 7, 2009, in Louisiana, after 5 days on the run. She was found with a 16-year-old boy with whom she allegedly conducted an illicit relationship. Both had been missing since May 2, 2009, when police had questioned them about the alleged sexual relationship. Melinda and the teen were stopped in Louisiana for a traffic violation on May 7, 2009, and detained by authorities. Subsequent interviews with the pair indicated that on the day before their disappearance, May 1, 2009, after both had spoken with police, Melinda picked the boy up near his home at a school where he was spending time with friends. They allegedly went to a local motel, where they had sex and talked about leaving town. The next day, she picked him up at his home and the two began a 5-day journey that would take them through Texas, Mississippi, Alabama, Georgia, and, finally, Louisiana. While they were in Texas, they broke their cell phones to avoid being tracked through them. At the time, Melinda was married and had children; she planned to retrieve her children and rejoin the young boy.

Profile of a Male Sex Offender

Phillip had a reputation for kidnapping and was accused of kidnapping 11-year-old Jaycee Lee Dugard. Her family reported her missing on June 10, 1991. She was walking toward the school bus, on her way to school, as her dad watched. He turned and witnessed his daughter being propelled into an open door of Phillip's vehicle. Jaycee's dad was too far away to catch up to her and could only watch as his daughter was driven away. A major manhunt ensued, to no avail, and the family feared the worst as days grew into months. Jaycee's dad recalled how investigators viewed him as a person of interest in the months that followed.

Jaycee was found 18 years later in the company of a registered sex offender. She had been held captive by Phillip and his wife in California. Phillip fathered two children with Jaycee while she was held captive. Jaycee and her two children never received any medical attention and were kept under constant supervision in the backyard under two tents surrounded by a 6 ft tall fence. Parole officers never checked the entire property when they visited his residence.

Phillip was eventually caught when his suspicious behavior drew the attention of police officers while he visited the campus of the University of California, Berkeley. During questioning, Phillip admitted to kidnapping Jaycee. He was booked on charges that included kidnapping, rape, conspiracy, and committing lewd acts with a minor. Phillip and his wife were also accused of kidnapping and conspiracy, and were both held on $1 million bail each. Phillip said his undertaking was an act of God.

In June of 2011, Phillip, who is now 60 years old, was sentenced to life (431 years) in prison and his wife was sentenced to 36 years-to life in prison.

In My Opinion

Ms. Kimberly Hart

In a personal interview, Kimberly Hart, executive director of the National Child Abuse Defense and Resource Center (www.falseallegation.org), said that she believes the registry system does not work. The initial intent of the registry was to keep track of the most dangerous sex offenders (i.e., predatory pedophiles). Instead, the registry system is overloaded and has lost its purpose. Hart believes it is often the case that registered sex offenders rarely become or regain the posture of productive members of society because they can never lose that stigma of "sex offender" until they die. The theory of the registry may have some merit for law enforcement, but she questions the benefit to the public at large because there are no facts or details behind the offense. It is not a simple process, but if the registry, public notification, and Internet access are available, so should the facts of the case be available. If the registry is going to stay, Hart believes there should be subcategories of placement. Someone with a history of stranger interaction with the intent of harming a child is, in her opinion, the most dangerous of all sexual offenders (i.e., predatory). These types of offenders are not the same as an 18-year-old man having sexual contact with his 16-year-old girlfriend. She says,

> The registry system is so overloaded that society loses sight of why it was developed. There are so many people on the registry that it does not alarm anyone. There should be a balance of notification and education. Children are taught that child molesters are behind every bush. We are terrorizing children about every stranger; we should be educating them, not paralyzing them.
>
> There are many degrees of child abuse, from the sex offender who grabs a stranger to a father or stepfather accused of molesting a family member. Inappropriate behavior is still wrong, but we should never lose our objectivity. There are some people who make situational mistakes, who can be treated with an extremely low risk of reoffending, and who should not be lumped in the category of the most dangerous predatory pedophiles.

Hart mentioned a case where four teenage girls made false accusations against a homeless man. These girls made up a story and said they were sexually molested by him because they did not want to get into trouble for breaking their curfew. This homeless man would have spent the rest of his life in prison if one of the girls had not confessed and explained that it was all a lie, a made-up story to protect themselves. Hart went on to explain that normally there are no ramifications or penalties for children who lie due to the fear of repercussions but that this will thwart genuine victims from coming forward. There is no test that can prove or disprove that someone was or is a sexual predator. Individuals may have deviant thoughts, but that does not mean they act on them. Some people will lie about being sexually abused.

> We are so quick to judge. We see it on television every day. Innocent people are convicted on the testimony of a child. Everyone passes the buck; law enforcement and forensic interviewers do not fully challenge what the child is saying nor do they explore possible motives for lies. Most people will believe a child and do not believe a child would lie about sexual abuse. Children can and do lie about sexual abuse, which most often creates a serious consequence for any individual accused of sex abuse, which the children might or might not comprehend. A layperson will question why the child is not telling the truth. The burden of proof is on the defendant to clear [himself or herself] of any wrongdoing and try to defend against an accusation that is a lie, or prove [he or she] did not do something while facing the rest of [his or her] life on the registry if [he or she does] not get life in prison.

Hart suggests that any adult aiding a child complainant in a false allegation should be subjected to the same penalty as the person being accused. As a trial consultant, Hart has witnessed kids make a claim of sexual abuse and then ask whether "they can go on Oprah now!"

Hart pointed out that in some states there is a disproportionate penalty for being convicted of child sexual abuse, where a person would receive less time if he or she had killed the child. Hart is an advocate for truth and she feels that a fair trial is not only important, but also necessary. She strongly believes that sexual predators should be locked up if they did the crime, but being falsely accused is wrong. There should be a challenge on both sides; every aspect of investigating child sexual abuse claims should be objective in finding out the truth no matter how painful. Justice is not served by investigating blindly or advocating for either side. Prosecutors are an advocate for the complainant and claim to represent the people. The defense is an advocate for the person accused. In the middle are law enforcement, medical and forensic personnel, and mental health professionals that should be asking the difficult questions and be fully accountable for their involvement. The problem lies in that the prosecutors and child abuse investigators are protected by immunity to err on the side of abuse. Hart feels everyone should be held accountable for what they do or fail to do in any such criminal case, especially when it concerns child abuse.

Hart brings light to another case regarding a man accused of molesting his stepdaughter in Missouri. Everything was documented in the case. His wife and stepdaughter both lied about the incident; Hart believes that it was the wife's intention to frame her husband. Unbeknownst to the defense at the time, but not to the prosecuting attorney and the chief of police, the lead investigating officer had a vested interest in the case because he was sleeping with the defendant's wife. The defendant was originally convicted on the testimony presented, but the affair was shortly thereafter discovered. An appeal was won and a second trial led to a hung jury. The third trial resulted in an acquittal.

Hart believes our system of justice is broken: "We have all of these protections and immunities in place for those supporting the allegation, and until these factors are removed, we will never get to the honest truth." It may feel good to the public to know a person is locked up, but it is a disservice to justice if the person is innocent. By conducting a thorough investigation, reporting all of the facts and relying on peer-reviewed science, the innocent will most often be vindicated and the culpable will most often plea or be convicted. After the Child Abuse Prevention and Treatment Act mandate became reality, child abuse allegations became a financial boon: more prisons for departments of corrections, more sex crimes prosecutors with alleged specialized training, invention of one-stop advocacy centers working under the direction of the prosecution, sex crime law enforcement detectives, special multidisciplinary teams and programs at hospitals, and CPS and the unaccountable child protective services. "All supply and demand requires funding!" Hart said.

References

Academic Dictionaries and Encyclopedias. (2010). Cengage Learning.
Mandelstam, J., and Mulford, C. (2008). Unintended consequences of sex offender residency laws. *Corrections Today* 70 (4): 104–105.
Radford, B. (2006). Predator panic: A closer look. *Skeptical Inquirer* 30 (5): 20–21, 69.
Sandler, J. C., Freeman, N.J., and Socia, K. M. (2008). Does a watched pot boil? A time-series analysis of New York state's sex offender registration and notification law. *Psychology, Public Policy, and Law* 14 (4): 284–302.
US Department of Justice. (2008). Fact sheet: Project Safe Childhood. Retrieved from www.ojp.usdoj.gov/newsroom/pressreleases/2008/doj08845.htm

Sex Offender Registration and Notification Laws

11

Questions I found too risqué or that I think my mom would think were a little too wild or something, I would just go online and ask other people. We talked openly [with Mom]; she always had the answer to the question that I was asking, but I didn't want to ask her everything.

Victim

A lot of my interest that gets my attention comes from the screen name—Tricia 13 Ohio, Young Beauty, Sexy Girl 13—things of that nature. I look at the screen name, check out the profile. If the profile doesn't offer anything, I send them an INSTANT message [IM'ing]. "Would you like to chat, do you like older men? If you are into older men, do you really like older men?" That was pretty much the standard line: "Do you really like older men?"

Sexual predator

Earlier Issues with Sex Offenders

During the 1930s and 1940s, many states adopted a civil commitment procedure for dangerous sexual offenders who had been designated sexual psychopaths; under these laws, offenders were incarcerated until they had been judged not to pose a public danger. In the 1950s and 1960s, many states initiated laws and legislation that allowed commitment of sex offenders to psychiatric hospitals or institutions instead of incarceration in prison to keep them from committing another sexual crime. A surge of sexual offenses throughout the 1970s led lawmakers to believe that therapy, treatment, and rehabilitation were not really the answer. Most politicians thought the only answer would be to ensure that sex offenders were sent back to prison (Jenkins 2010).

In the late 1980s and early 1990s, a series of murders involved children who were sexually assaulted and heinously murdered. This prompted many states to enact new laws that mandated long-term prison sentences for convicted sex offenders who brutally and sexually killed their victims. The idea was to keep them from ever offending again.

Policymakers must contend with many difficult challenges—not only in supervising convicted sex offenders, but also in keeping the public safe and aware of the potential danger the offender brings to a community. A number of enacted laws have helped to educate the community on sex offenders and enforce mandatory obligations for a released sexual offender that help to protect the public. The release of criminals that have engaged in unlawful sexual behavior prompts fear in most people, especially those who live in the criminal's neighborhood.

Registered Sex Offenders

There is not a community in America that does not have a sex offender living or working nearby. Sexual offenders are required to register annually for life—unless convicted of violating the Sexually Violent Persons Commitment Act after July 1, 2005, after which it was necessary to register every 90 days for life. According to the National Center of Missing and Exploited Children, in September of 2008 there were 665,000 registered sex offenders living in the United States (49,000 of them residing in Florida). In January 1993, the Habitual Child Sex Offender Act was amended and renamed the Child Sex Offender Registration Act. This act required an offender to be certified as a child sex offender after his first conviction for a sex crime against a victim less than 18 years old. In January 1996, the Child Sex Offender Registration Act was amended and renamed the Sex Offender Registration Act. This act stated that "any person convicted of a felony sex crime or an attempt to commit a felony sex crime is required to register as a sex offender regardless of the victim's age." A special provision was provided to make this act retroactive to include any person either released from prison or sentenced to probation within the last 10 years.

Sex offender registration and community notification laws were introduced and enacted in the early 1990s, with the intent to deter recidivism of convicted sex offenders. These laws notify a community of a sex offender's release and restrict where a sex offender can live. Lawmakers have endorsed notification and registration laws because they believe they are the most effective way of protecting public safety. The notification and registration laws have improved police effectiveness in preventing sexual abuse and solving previous sex crimes against children. Countless Americans have overwhelmingly supported these notification laws because they promote community awareness and keep track of sex offenders that require scrutiny and supervision.

Prior to the passage of Megan's law and similar notification laws throughout the United States, people did not know when a released sex offender moved into their community. Communities have used these laws to take control of their neighborhoods and assert their right to have safe and secure neighborhoods. Many community activists, politicians, victims' rights advocates, and parents applaud the implementation of notification laws. They feel that this will assist parents not only in protecting their children but also in helping them be aware of sexual predators that have moved into their immediate area. Defenders of these laws note that requiring released offenders to register with the police is an easy way for law enforcement to keep tabs on pedophiles and child molesters. Sex offender registration also gives law enforcement in nearby cities and suburbs the opportunity to locate a suspect or share information on any suspicious activity regarding sexual exploitation.

Recent studies have shown that 95% of all sexual offense arrests were of first-time sex offenders. This figure may cast doubt on the effectiveness of notification and registration laws that target repeat offenders. Many opponents of sex offender notification laws feel that these laws shame a convicted sex offender and make it extremely difficult for him to live a normal life, retain a job, and become a productive member of society. Sandler, Freeman, and Socia (2008) contend that although the federal and many state governments have enacted registration and community notification laws as a means to better protect communities from sexual offending, limited empirical research has been conducted to examine the impact of such legislation on public safety. According to the Illinois State Police's "Guide to Sex Offender Registration and Community Notification in Illinois" (2006), the Habitual Child Offender Registration Act states that a person convicted after August 15, 1986, could be certified as a child sex offender only upon his or her second or subsequent conviction of a sex crime against a victim less than 18 years of age.

Attorney General Lisa Madigan of Illinois emphasized in an article in the *Christian Science Monitor* that all 50 states require convicted sex offenders to register with law enforcement agencies or face varying levels of penalties, including felony charges and prison time. The proposed idea is that if the public knows where a convicted sex offender lives, people have a better chance of protecting themselves and their children from these pedophiles. Ms. Madigan has put together a sex offender registration team that consists of victim advocates and leaders in law enforcement. This team specifically targets the problems associated with unregistered sex offenders and they update needed changes in the sex offender registry to ensure its accuracy and accessibility. Madigan stressed:

> Too often registration information is out of date, inaccurate, incomplete, or inaccessible. Many offenders supply phony addresses or photographs to avoid accurate registration. We have to fix our sex-offender registration system. If registration is going to work we must impose and enforce penalties for those who fail to comply. We must make sure that the offenders' names, addresses, and photos are accurate and timely, and that police make it a priority to maintain an accurate registry.

Her office has honored the strength and courage of survivors of sexual assault nationwide by annually designating the month of April as Sexual Assault Awareness Month.

Numerous resources have been dedicated to the prevention of sexual exploitation, including treatment in mental health and correctional facilities. The Department of Justice and Project Safe Childhood released the first national strategy for child exploitation prevention and interdiction. The strategy provides the first ever comprehensive threat assessment of the dangers facing children from child pornography and online enticement. This plan builds upon the department's accomplishments in combating child exploitation by establishing specific, aggressive goals and priorities and increasing cooperation and collaboration at all levels of government and the private sector. Then-Attorney General Alberto Gonzalez was hopeful that improved investigative tools along with stiffer penalties would keep the worst sex offenders in jail. He noted that Project Safe Childhood brought 8,464 cases against 8,637 defendants. These cases included prosecutions regarding

- Online enticement of children
- Interstate transportation of children
- Production, possession, and distribution of child pornography

Donna Rice Hughes, president of Enough Is Enough (an organization dedicated to combating online exploitation of children), welcomed the Department of Justice's new coordinated and expanded efforts to identify, arrest, and prosecute child predators and those involved in child pornography. Passing tough sexual predator laws is a concern for many lawmakers today. Many states are imposing special restrictions and sanctions on where sexual offenders can live. Iowa has taken a proactive approach in mandating a few laws against sexual offenders that prohibit anyone convicted of a sexual offense against a minor from living within 2,000 ft of a daycare center or school. Another Iowa bill requires DNA samples from all sex offenders and mandates life in prison for anyone convicted of a second sexual offense against a minor.

Although many people welcome tougher laws against sex offenders, a few critics are apprehensive about monitoring convicted sex offenders instead of finding out who is more likely to strike again and sexually exploit children. But few of the new laws have provisions for treatment. A 2002 survey of nearly 9,500 sex offenders found that those who underwent therapy were 40% less likely to reoffend than those who did not. Legislators and law enforcement personnel can only hope that the judicial system will mandate that sex offenders who repeatedly reoffend undergo mandatory therapy and treatment.

Civil Commitment

Under civil commitment, a person is deemed to be a danger to himself or herself or society or is unable to care for his or her basic needs. This is decided by a judge as the person is housed in a hospital or mental health facility. Graydon Comstock is a sex offender who was incarcerated for possessing child pornography. The state of South Carolina declared that Mr. Comstock was certified not fit to return to society and petitioned for civil commitment, just 6 days prior to his serving his 37-month federal prison term. Mr. Comstock, along with three other inmates who were given the same news and who were also soon to be released, filed a lawsuit to stop the government enforcing the petition for civil commitment. They felt that they had served their time for their offense and were not dangerous to society.

The federal government and the US Supreme Court can keep particular pedophiles, sexual predators, and sex offenders committed indefinitely if inmates have displayed behavior that indicates they would be "sexually dangerous" if they were to be released into society. Supreme Court Justice Stephen Breyer wrote in a 7–2 majority decision that the federal government, as custodian of its prisoners, has the constitutional power to act in order to protect society from the danger such prisoners may pose. Comstock and the three inmates were set to be released nearly 3 years ago, but government appeals have blocked their freedom.

Defenders of the laws may claim that notification is merely a way to provide information, and many worried people believe that the rights of people should take precedence over the rights of convicted sexual offenders. Public notification may have improved personal safety, but it has also created fear. Society will always have a strong interest in protecting its people and that is why many people feel that public disclosure of a sex offender's history far outweighs the sex offender's right to privacy.

Notification Laws: Do They Protect the Public or Invade Privacy?

Opponents of Notification Laws

Sex offender registration and notification laws have a profound impact on the lives of convicted sex offenders who are released back into society. A large number of these discharged sex offenders have a difficult time finding a place to live in the hopes of rebuilding their lives. Mandelstam and Mulford (2008) stated that 27 states and hundreds of municipalities have passed laws that would prohibit sex offenders from living near schools, parks, playgrounds, or daycare centers. They noted that residency restriction laws typically require that an offender live more than 1,000 ft from a school or other venue that may attract a large number of children; depending on the locality, the distance can vary from 500 to 2,500 ft.

The Eighth Amendment of the US Constitution bans cruel and unusual punishment. Many convicted sex offenders believe that registration and notification laws constitute cruel and unusual punishment because they subject the released sex offender to additional punishment. They contend that it is unfair and unconstitutional to add another layer of punishment that is indefinite in length. A handful of lawyers, judges, and civil liberties groups such as the American Civil Liberties Union (ACLU) truly oppose the continued challenges that sexual offenders face. Critics of sex offender registration and notification and legal authorities have raised concerns that freed sex offenders continue to be prosecuted after serving their time and paying their debt to society. They feel that released sex offenders should be allowed to reenter society without substantial restrictions and limitations on privacy or liberty.

Critics contend that notification laws infringe upon sex offenders' privacy by disseminating a sex offender's personal history and what he or she was arrested for. Additional matters are that notification laws violate an individual's constitutional rights and that a released sexual offender should share the same expectations of privacy as other people. Another fear is the possibility of physical harm or harassment that a released sex offender may endure once released from prison. Convicted sex offenders who do move into the community may be subjected to taunts, threats, and vandalism. Communities often use this information to prohibit entry or to try to remove the individuals from their surroundings.

Sandler et al. (2008) stated that a sex offender registry has its place as one tool among many, but that its worth should not be overemphasized:

> The face of danger is more likely to be in a family snapshot than in a mug shot on a sex offender registry. This is obvious because a large number of these offenses occur within the family. The determining factor in these crimes is usually not geography, but relationships. The vast majority of sex crimes are committed by someone not listed on a sex offender registry. The vast majority of registered sex offenders never commit another sex crime.

Sexual Registration and Notification Laws

The heartbreaking stories of Jacob Wetterling, age 11; Megan Kanka, age 7; and Adam Walsh, age 6 (see Chapter 10) made national news. Kanka and Walsh were abducted by men who had past histories of sexual offenses. It was notably these three cases that forced the enactment of federal laws that would help to prevent future sexual assaults against children. In 1994, Congress passed the Jacob Wetterling Act, which mandated the creation of state sex offender registries that would also be accessible to law enforcement agencies.

The US Congress has passed several laws that require states to monitor registered sex offenders: the Jacob Wetterling Crimes against Children Act, the Pam Lychner Sex Offender Tracking and Identification Act, and Megan's law. On March 5, 2003, the Supreme Court ruled that information about registered sex offenders may be posted on the Internet.

Sex Offender Registration

In 2009, the Department of Justice said that registered sex offenders are required to update their information annually within 5 working days of their birthday. Some sex offenders must update more often: Transients must update every 30 days and sexually violent predators every 90 days. The Sex Offender Tracking Program keeps track of the next required update and, if a registered sex offender is in violation of the update requirements, the Internet website will show the registrant as being in violation. When registrants change their residence address or become homeless (transient), they are required to update their registration information with a local agency within 5 days. The local police agency then forwards this information to the Department of Justice, which updates its registered sex offender database and Internet site on a daily basis.

Today, 50 states have enacted comparable laws intended to inform communities about the presence of released sexual offenders residing within the community. The law helps the public obtain specific information about registered sex offenders and it permits criminal justice system officials to inform the public about the most dangerous offenders in their area. Law enforcement often has a difficult task keeping track of all sex offenders that have been released from prison because so many of them are transient and travel from state to state. Statistics have shown that since Jessica's law passed in November of 2006, the number of transient sex offenders has increased across the country and the likelihood is that this number will continue to increase steadily at a quicker rate than ever before. A report by the California Sex Offender Management Board, which includes state and local law enforcement, prosecutors, and treatment experts, cited research linking homelessness and a higher risk of sexual reoffending. The report said that "residential instability leads to unstable employment and lower levels of social support. Unstable employment and lack of social support lead to emotional and mental instability. Emotional and mental instability breaks down the ability to conform and leads to a greater risk of committing another sex crime."

Law enforcement officials across the United States have a challenging task of keeping track of convicted sex offenders. Many released sex offenders become transient and drift from state to state because they have a difficult time finding a job and acquiring housing. Many tent cities that house released sex offenders have popped up in remote areas throughout the southern states. Many other factors, including no transportation, drug and alcohol addiction, and mental illness, may also prevent sex offenders from registering with local law enforcement.

Global Positioning System

A global positioning system (GPS) is an electronic tracking system used by criminal justice authorities in order to be responsive to sexual offenders after incarceration. As of this writing, 12 states now use GPS to track sexual offenders. For example, sex offenders who have been released in Iowa are required to wear electronic monitoring devices. Radford (2006) explained that many states have become proactive in their approach to monitoring sex offenders by tracking them using satellite technology and have also banned sex offenders from living in certain areas. Radford stated, "Every state has notification laws to alert communities about former sex offenders. Many states have banned sex offenders from living in certain areas, and are tracking them using satellite technology."

Geographic Information System

A geographic information system (GIS) is a computerized software program that interprets and visualizes data of convicted sex offenders in a particular area. This interactive program can monitor sex offenders and sexual abuse data and project future incidents through incident mapping. GIS will benefit law enforcement in visualizing data and in the use of strategic planning involving convicted sex offenders and their whereabouts.

Mandelstam and Mulford (2008) said that laws have been enacted in almost every state that prohibit or restrict where sex offenders may reside. Sexual offenders who must register have been known to give false information regarding where they live or find it easier to live on the streets. GIS could be considered instrumental for many communities, especially if they are considering enacting residency rules.

Studies show that GIS mapping can be a valuable tool for local officials, especially for jurisdictions that are contemplating the passage of residency laws. Officials can use the mapping data to determine whether affordable housing will be available in an approved area. Such analysis could demonstrate if a proposed law is feasible. If restricted zones have sufficient affordable housing, offenders may be less likely to go underground, thereby remaining accessible to community corrections officers. Currently, California, New Jersey, and Ohio use GIS to analyze the impact of current laws or to project the outcome of laws. It has been noted that these states have found that legal residential areas for sex offenders are severely limited.

e-Stop

When he was New York's attorney general, Andrew Cuomo proposed the Electronic Security and Targeting of Online Predators Act (e-stop). This legislation was passed to assist in creating laws that would prohibit and restrict certain convicted sex offenders from using various social networking sites such as Xanga, MySpace, and Facebook, among a number of others. It was felt that this would help protect the safety of children.

Under the e-stop agreement, Internet users under the age of 16 are able to set their accounts on private. This measure ensures that no one is able to gain information from a child's profile. This feature can also block anyone who is over 18 years old from contacting those under age 16, and people over 18 cannot add anyone who is under 16 as a friend in their network unless they have a last name or e-mail address.

New York's Division of Criminal Justice Services (DCJS) implemented a plan of action regarding e-stop. They sent out letters to over 25,000 convicted sex offenders listed in the sex offender registry to let them know of the change in the law and how it affected them. Under this law, sex offenders in New York are required to register all e-mail accounts used for the purpose of online chatting, instant messaging, or social networking. The New York State Division of Criminal Justice Services (NYSDCJS) is authorized to release state sex offender Internet identifiers. These identifiers include e-mail addresses and designations used for chat sites, instant messaging, social networking sites, certain online services, or other similar Internet communication. Essentially, this information may be used to prescreen or remove sex offenders from using the site's services and to notify law enforcement authorities and other government officials of potential violations of law and threats to public safety.

This law also requires that as a condition of probation or parole, mandatory restrictions be implemented on a sex offender's access to the Internet in cases where the offender's victim was a minor, the Internet was used to commit the offense, or the offender was designated a level 3 (highest level) offender. These offenders are banned from accessing social networking websites and pornographic materials, communicating with anyone for the purpose of promoting sexual relations with a minor, and communicating, in most circumstances, with anyone under the age of 18. Offenders will have 10 days to comply when they create a new e-mail account or new online profile. Failure to comply with this law is classified as a felony.

Hess (2008) stated, "If this law provides any protection, it is minimal at best. It is hard to imagine that any knowledgeable person could dispute the proposed law's ineffectiveness. E-mail addresses are easily created using anonymous information." A registered sex offender might want to publish the real facts online. Unfortunately, this legislation may make it impossible for him to do so. In our society, the right of free speech must be protected even for unpopular individuals. If not, we may all be denied the right to hear and speak the truth.

New York Senator John J. Flanagan noted that "the Internet is a great tool when used in the right way, and we must remain vigilant in our efforts to make sure New York laws remain as strong as possible to protect our residents. While parents need to remain active in their children use of the Internet, e-stop will provide some help and some piece of mind."

Legislators in Arizona have implemented a similar program that would make using the Internet difficult for sexual offenders. The state wants to take measures that force sex offenders to register any online alias or additional e-mail addresses that they have acquired.

Homeless Sex Offenders

The problem that many sex offenders face is finding a place to live after they have been released from prison. A vast majority of released sex offenders end up homeless, and a number of homeless shelters restrict their access to the facility because they are sex offenders. Because of the restrictions enacted from Jessica's law, which prohibits released sex offenders from living within 2,000 feet of a park or school, sex offenders find it challenging to restore their lives to normal. Transient sex offenders will move from state to state and fail to register with local authorities, making it difficult to keep track of them.

Profile of a Female Sex Offender

Traci is 47-year-old woman from California who was arrested for allegedly engaging in a sexual relationship with a male teen victim identified as a family friend. Traci, a mother of four, was released on $30,000 bail after being arrested on three felony counts of having sex with a minor. She will have to register every year as a sex offender. According to the police report on the case, Traci and the 17-year-old-boy, a student from a nearby high school, had an intensive relationship, sharing over 5,000 texts and 800 phone calls during a 6-month period.

According to the police report, the secret sexual relationship between them began to unravel when the boy's parents sent him to a special camp to receive therapy for marijuana use and other problems. While he was at the camp, his parents were able to gain access to the contents of his cell phone and computer. According to the report, Traci and the teenager had known each other for 5 years. He went to Traci's home to do homework with one of her sons and often slept over. He told police that he and Traci started having sex when she kissed him for the first time. The boy also received money from Traci to buy pot, booze, and cigarettes. He said he did not want to have sex with Traci, but did it for the free drugs. When police interviewed Traci, she downplayed what had happened at first, calling the boy one of her son's "sweet and innocent" friends. When police confronted her with evidence from the boy's BlackBerry phone and computer, she admitted having sex with him.

Profile of a Male Sex Offender

The Department of Homeland Security and police served Frank, a registered sex offender, with a search warrant after allegations that he used fraudulent information to obtain a census job. The government agency issued the warrant after an employee noticed his picture on a local sex offender registry and alerted authorities. Frank had served time in prison for inappropriate contact with children. He was also convicted for sexually assaulting a young girl in 1996 and had inappropriate contact with another child. Frank has been known to use 16 aliases and was not hired as a census worker after he failed the fingerprint and background check.

In My Opinion

Father Tony Pizzo

I had the opportunity to interview a Catholic priest from a large parish on the South side of Chicago. Father Pizzo has been in Catholic ministry for 27 years and is recognized for his integrity and truthfulness throughout the community. Regarding the subject of sexual predators, Father Pizzo believes that pedophile behavior within priestly ministry as well as in any other circumstance can never be tolerated. It is sinful and deviant behavior and no one is justified in taking advantage of anyone, much less a child for sexual gratification. Father Pizzo recognizes sexual predation as an illness, especially if the perpetrator's focus is geared toward an innocent vulnerable child or a person with disabilities. A child molester who cannot control him or herself has a sickness—not a weakness.

In the last several years many have alleged abuse by priests (and in some cases, religious sisters and brothers) with whom they were in contact. Some accusations of priestly sexual misconduct date back 20–50 years. Father Pizzo said that a time factor is considered in a criminal accusation because of the statute of limitations that may be operative in some states where the alleged abuse occurred. A case of previous sexual abuse that is brought up after many years may be problematic due to lack of full substantial evidence or any evidence at all outside of the alleged victim's testimony. Often in these types of cases, it is hearsay evidence or "he said, she said." Several priests that have been accused after such a long period of time are most likely deceased, retired, or out of ministry completely.

Father Pizzo noted that if a priest is exonerated of a sexual misconduct allegation he may return, with permission, to some type of ministry but will not return to the parish where the allegation originated.

If a priest or religious person abuses a child who is pre-pubescent and continues in this behavior, he is considered a pedophile. A priest who abuses any victim who is considered post-pubescent is not necessarily considered homosexual, but rather this behavior may be an indication that he suffers from a psychosexual disorder. It may be some kind of psychological and sexual arrest meaning that the level of sexual maturity has not developed normally.

The lack of action on the part of some Catholic bishops to remove a pedophile priest has caused much anguish and dissension. Several Catholics left the Church because of what has happened and because of the media focus. Father Pizzo considers a lack of response to a substantiated claim of sexual misconduct against a child to be potentially destructive on several levels. Many have accused Catholic bishops for not taking immediate and corrective action. Any negative publicity is always going to call into question the Church's credibility.

Father Pizzo however, emphasizes that the Church believes and preaches forgiveness and healing. Healing toward the abused is first and foremost. The emotional and psychological impacts on the victim are enormous. Forgiving the incident would be up to the victim with the help of professionals if he or she so chooses. However, many professionals would agree that positive steps toward healing would be for the perpetrator to seek forgiveness and the victim to move toward forgiving his or her abuser.

Sexual abuse is an enormous problem in our society today. Father Pizzo noted that sexual abuse within the same household is more prevalent than we think. He recalls victims of sexual abuse within their own family who have come forward and revealed this to him. There is tremendous shame and suffering and along with this comes the stigma of having been abused by a family member. Father Pizzo says that if he hears of abuse in the confessional he will immediately offer guidance, support, direction, and advice to seek professional help and to report it to the authorities. When asked what type of penance would he offer to someone who confesses abuse, he said that he would strongly encourage the person to see him outside of the seal of confession. If the individual refuses he would then consider offering a penance of seeking professional help immediately and/or turn him/herself in to law enforcement.

When asked about the pornography industry, Father Pizzo remarked that we need to be more aggressive as a society to put a stop to a business that exploits children. We need to arrest and convict anyone who intentionally destroys and devastates a child's life.

Definitions of Chapter Key Terms

Civil commitment: Under civil commitment, a person is deemed to be a danger to himself or herself or society or is unable to care for his or her basic needs. This is decided by a judge as the person is housed in a hospital or mental health facility.

e-Stop: Under the e-stop agreement, Internet users under the age of 16 will be able to set their account on private. This measure will ensure that no one will be able to gain information from a child's profile. This feature can also block anyone who is over 18 years old from contacting them, and people over 18 cannot add anyone who is under 16 as a friend in their network unless they have a last name or e-mail address.

Geographic information system (GIS): A computerized software program that interprets and visualizes data of convicted sex offenders in a particular area. This interactive program can monitor sex offenders and sexual abuse data and project future incidents through incident mapping. GIS will benefit law enforcement in visualizing data and the use of strategic planning involving convicted sex offenders and their whereabouts.

Global positioning system (GPS): An electronic tracking system used by criminal justice system authorities in order to be responsive to sexual offenders after incarceration. As of this writing, 12 states now use GPS to track sexual offenders.

References

Christian Science Monitor. (2004, February 17). Get serious about sex offender registration. Boston, MA: Christian Science Publishing.

Hess, C. D. (2008). e-Stop—Another placebo sex offender law (http://theparson.net/so/estop.htm).

Jenkins, J. P. (2010). Sexual predator law. Chicago, IL: Encyclopedia Britannica.

Mandelstam, J., and Mulford, C. (2008). Unintended consequences of sex offender residency laws. *Corrections Today* 70 (4): 104–105.

Radford, B. (2006). Predator panic: A closer look. *Skeptical Inquirer* 30 (5): 20–21, 69.

Sandler, J. C., Freeman, N.J., and Socia, K. M. (2008). Does a watched pot boil? A time-series analysis of New York state's sex offender registration and notification law. *Psychology, Public Policy, and Law* 14 (4): 284–302.

State of Illinois. (2006). A guide to sex offender registration and community notification in Illinois.

Specific and Significant Laws Regarding Sex Offenders   12

> We just started talking in a chat room; after about 10 minutes he started asking sexual questions, and if I have ever been in love. He was creepy.
>
> **Girl on the Internet**

> We talked on the Internet for months, I felt funny meeting him, and I did not tell my Mom. I made a big mistake; I knew I was in trouble when he had me alone.
>
> **Victim of a predator**

Walter Mondale Child Abuse and Treatment Act

This initial child protection system began in the early 1970s. The Mondale act was initiated to provide incentives for states to set up programs for child abuse research, identification, prosecution, and treatment. Federal funding was made available to match state spending, and this served as an incentive for states to create such programs.

Protection of Children against Sexual Exploitation Act 1977

This act made it illegal for anyone to circulate child pornography involving minors under the age of 16. Child pornography laws also include trading, creating, sending, owning, and promoting child pornography materials. The definition regarding child pornography varies in different states and also differs in various countries.

Child Abuse Victims Act of 1986

This act gave children who became victims of sexual exploitation the right to claim civil damages.

Victims of Child Abuse 1990

It came to the attention of Congress that there were increased reports of child abuse and child neglect in the juvenile and family court system. The government recognized that it had provided little assistance in meeting the considerable demands imposed on the court system. Congress soon authorized the Office of Juvenile Justice to establish children's advocacy centers throughout the country. These centers were created for various reasons:

- To improve case dispositions, investigations, and prosecution of child abuse cases
- To coordinate judicial and social service programs
- To strengthen court-appointed programs
- To encourage team decisions about managing young victims
- To prevent reoffending of abused children
- To provide necessary services to child victims and their families
- To offer child abuse training programs for judicial personnel and practitioners
- To ensure victims' protections and rights under federal law

Child Online Protection Act and the Children's Internet Protection Act

Both acts outlaw child pornography and also cover new media such as websites and other online forms of child pornography.

Sex Crimes against Children Prevention Act of 1995

- Directs the United States Sentencing Commission to amend the sentencing guidelines to increase the base offense level
- Directs the commission to submit a report to Congress concerning offenses involving child pornography and other sex offenses against children

Communication Decency Act (CDA) of 1996

This act makes it illegal for sexually explicit material of children to be shown on the Internet.

Telecommunications Act 1996

This act was created and amended to stop sexual predator communications in person, by telephone, or by mail that would entice minors less than 18 years of age into prostitution or any other sexual activity. The penalty for this offense ranges from a minimum sentence of 10 years to life imprisonment.

The Child Pornography Prevention Act (CPPA)

The act was designed to deal with lawmakers' struggle in dealing with issues with virtual child pornography and computer-generated imagery. The CPPA restricts child pornography in any medium and includes any images that appear be a minor child. Graham (2000) said,

> The CPPA is the latest adaptation of a 1977 federal statute known as the Protection of Children against Sexual Exploitation Act. In 1996, a portion of this act outlawed virtual child pornography or images that appear to be a minor engaging in sexually explicit conduct. Under the CPPA, the definition of child pornography includes not only images of actual sexual abuse of children but also computer-generated child pornography that does not use real children for its production.

In 2003, the CPPA also made it illegal to receive, transmit, or create child pornography that is composed using the computer.

The Child Online Protection Act (COPA) 1998

The Child Online Protection Act (COPA) stated that commercial websites would be required to limit access to any material deemed pornographic or harmful to minors. This act was intended to keep pornography away from children. The question that arose was who determines what is decent or indecent. In 2002, the Supreme Court overturned the verdict in *Ashcroft v. The Free Speech Coalition*. Justice Anthony Kennedy, writing for the majority, specified that "virtual pornography records no crime and creates no victims by its production."

Protection of Children from Sexual Predators Act of 1998

The Protection of Children from Sexual Predators Act of 1998 established new criminal offenses, amended existing statutes, and provided for enhanced penalties. The bill was signed and became effective on October 30, 1998. Three new offenses or definitions of offenses were created:

- Use of interstate facilities to transmit information about a minor, use of the mail or facility of interstate or foreign commerce to transmit information about a minor under the age of 16 for criminal sexual purposes. The facility of interstate or foreign commerce may be a computer. This statute is in response to a case from Illinois where an individual posted a 9-year-old girl's name and telephone number on the Internet indicating that she was available for sex. The individual initiating the transmission can be fined, imprisoned for up to 5 years, or both.
- Transfer of obscene materials to minors, use of the mails or a facility of interstate or foreign commerce to knowingly transmit, or attempt to transmit, obscene materials to minors under the age of 16. The individual transmitting the materials may be fined, imprisoned for 10 years, or both.
- Definition of criminal sexual activity to include the production of child pornography. Previously, several cases presented for federal prosecution could not be charged because the individual transported a minor or traveled to meet a minor to produce child pornography but not for sexual activity.

The Bureau of Justice Assistance (BJA) was directed to carry out the Sex Offender Management Assistance (SOMA) program to help eligible states comply with registration requirements. Prohibited federal funding to programs that gave federal prisoners access to the Internet without supervision was prohibited.

The Campus Sex Crimes Prevention Act of 2000

This act was passed as part of the Victims of Trafficking and Violence Protection Act. The Campus Sex Crimes Prevention Act

- Requires any person obligated to register in a state's sex offender registry to notify the institution of higher education at which the sex offender works or is a student of his or her status as a sex offender and to notify the same institution if there is any change in his or her enrollment or employment status
- Requires that the information collected as a result of this act be reported promptly to local law enforcement and entered promptly into the appropriate state record systems

- Amends the Higher Education Act of 1965 to require institutions obligated to disclose campus security policy and campus crime statistics also to provide notice of how information concerning registered sex offenders can be obtained

Prosecutorial Remedies and Other Tools to End the Exploitation of Children Today (PROTECT) Act of 2003

The PROTECT Act specifically implemented several amendments in connection with sex tourism and commercial sexual exploitation:

(a) Transportation with intent to engage in criminal sexual activity. A person who knowingly transports an individual who has not attained the age of 18 years in interstate or foreign commerce, or in any commonwealth, territory, or possession of the United States, with the intent that the individual engage in prostitution or in any sexual activity for which any person can be charged with a criminal offense, shall be fined under this title and imprisoned not less than 5 years and not more than 30 years.

(b) Travel with intent to engage in illicit sexual conduct. A person who travels in interstate commerce or travels into the United States, or a United States citizen or alien admitted for permanent residence in the United States who travels in foreign commerce, for the purpose of engaging in any illicit sexual conduct with another person shall be fined under this title or imprisoned not more than 30 years, or both.

(c) Engaging in illicit sexual conduct in foreign places. Any United States citizen or alien admitted for permanent residence who travels in foreign commerce and engages in any illicit sexual conduct with another person shall be fined under this title or imprisoned not more than 30 years, or both. [In the area of sex tourism, it is sufficient to show that a United States citizen or lawful permanent resident traveled abroad and engaged in any illicit sexual conduct with a minor, regardless of what his intentions may have been when he left the United States.]

(d) Ancillary offenses. Whosoever, for the purpose of commercial advantage or private financial gain, arranges, induces, procures, or facilitates the travel of a person knowing that such a person is traveling in interstate commerce or foreign commerce for the purpose of engaging in illicit sexual conduct shall be fined under this title, imprisoned not more than 30 years, or both. [The PROTECT Act also changed the sentencing scheme for traveling for a criminal sex act; the maximum sentence was upgraded to 30 years' imprisonment.] (https://awasartn.org/HUMAN_TRAFFICKING.html)

The act

- Required states to maintain a website containing registry information
- Required the Department of Justice to maintain a website with links to each state website
- Authorized appropriations to help defray state costs for compliance with new sex offender registration provisions
- Established a program to obtain criminal history background checks for volunteer organizations
- Authorized wiretapping and monitoring of other communications in all cases related to child abuse or kidnapping
- Offered stronger laws to combat child pornography and exploitation
- Increased penalties for sex offenses against children, including life imprisonment for repeat offenders
- Eliminated statutes of limitations for child abduction or child abuse
- Barred pretrial release of persons charged with specified offenses against or involving children
- Authorized fines and/or imprisonment for up to 30 years for US people or residents who engaged in illicit sexual conduct abroad, with or without the intent of engaging in such sexual misconduct
- Established the national "Amber Alert" network and "Code Adam" systems to recover abducted children
- Assigned a national Amber Alert coordinator

Children Safety and Violent Crime Reduction Act of 2005

Library of Congress Bill H.R. 4472 incorporates and implements the Children Safety and Violent Crime Reduction of 2005. This act specifically improves the sex offender registration and notification program in that it

- Ensures that sex offenders register and keep current where they reside, work, and attend school
- Requires quarterly verification, in-person verification, and regular notarized verification mailings
- Requires public access to state websites
- Creates the Dru Sjodin national sex offender public website to search for sex offender information in each community

Specific and Significant Laws Regarding Sex Offenders

- Expands terms to include juvenile sex offenders
- Requires states to notify one another when a sex offender moves from one state to another
- Expands sex offenses covered by registration and notification requirements to include military, tribal, foreign, and sex crimes and increases the duration of registration requirements to protect the public
- Expands community notification requirements to include active efforts to inform law enforcement agencies, schools, public housing, social service agencies, and volunteer organizations in areas where sex offenders reside, work, or attend school
- Creates a new criminal penalty of a maximum of 20 years' incarceration for sex offenders who refuse to comply with registration requirements
- Protects foster children from sexual abuse and exploitation

PROTECT Our Children Act of 2008

This act was established because of the lack of manpower and funding to catch Internet predators. A vast majority of child pornography leads will never be investigated because law enforcement is overwhelmed and underfunded. The PROTECT Our Children Act of 2008 requires the Department of Justice to develop and implement a national strategy child exploitation prevention and interdiction. This act was signed into law October 13, 2008 it

- Improves and increases funding for the Internet Crimes against Children Task Force
- Increases resources for regional computer forensic labs
- Makes other improvements to increase the ability of law enforcement agencies to investigate and prosecute child predators

Keep the Internet Devoid of Sexual Predators Act of 2008 (KIDS)

This law required convicted sex offenders to register e-mail addresses and user names on social networking sites. The Department of Justice will house this information in a secure database and permit certified social networking sites to securely contrast their subscriber lists against the sex offender database. Sexual predators use the Internet to find victims, and kids who use the Internet should not have to worry about whom they meet online and their parents should not have to worry either. This legislation will help to keep sexual predators off the social networking sites where teens are more likely to visit when they use the computer.

This bill was signed into law October 14, 2008, and directs the attorney general to

- Require sex offenders to provide to the National Sex Offender Registry all Internet identifiers (i.e., e-mail addresses and other designations used for self-identification or routing in Internet communication or posting) used by such offenders
- Specify requirements for keeping Internet identifier information current
- Exempt Internet identifiers provided by a sex offender from public disclosure
- Establish procedures to notify sex offenders of changes in requirements for providing Internet identifier information

The bill requires the attorney general to establish and maintain a secure system to allow social networking websites to compare information contained in the national sex offender registry with the Internet identifiers of users of their websites. It allows social networking websites to use such systems to conduct searches as frequently as the attorney general may allow. It authorizes the attorney general to deny, suspend, or terminate use of the system by a social networking website for misuse. It prohibits the attorney general and social networking websites from releasing to the public any list of the Internet identifiers of sex offenders.

Children's Internet Protection Act (CIPA)

In May of 2008, the Supreme Court upheld a 2003 law designed to limit the proliferation of child pornography on the Internet that specifically dealt with digital sexual imagery created on the Internet vis-à-vis the Children's Internet Protection Act (CIPA). This act mandated that schools and libraries receive technology subsidies from the federal government.

Effective Child Pornography Prosecution Act of 2008

This act provided for more effective prosecution of cases involving child pornography. This act would prohibit the broadcast of live images of child abuse. The bill was signed into law by President George W. Bush on October 8, 2008.

First Amendment Rights

The First Amendment to the US Constitution guarantees freedom of speech. The issue has arisen as to whether someone can be charged for exercising this right over the Internet. There are laws in place that make an adult communicating with a minor for sexual purposes over the Internet a crime punishable by law. An issue that most defense attorneys will argue is that their client did not realize that the person with whom he was communicating was a minor. Only a few rights pertaining to freedom of speech over the Internet are protected. If an adult knowingly uses the Internet to convince or entice a minor into sexual relations, the speech used to commit this act is not protected under the law.

Phillip R. Greaves, II, was sexually abused by an older woman when he was 7 years old. He wrote a book, *The Pedophile's Guide to Love and Pleasure* (2010). He wanted to address what he considers unfair portrayals of pedophiles in the media. Greaves believes that a person who is a true pedophile really cares for and loves children and would never hurt the children. He indicates that his book strives to make more juveniles feel safer in the presence of pedophiles. Greaves suggested that pedophiles should adhere to certain rules he proposes in his book. He thinks that his book would cause less hatred and confusion in understanding a pedophile. A substantial number of people criticized his book saying they thought it would initiate pedophilia, sexual predation, and a host of other sexual offenses. Greaves has stood by his self-published book and his First Amendment rights to free speech

Fourth Amendment Rights

Under the Fourth Amendment, search warrant requirements regarding online child enticement can only be issued with probable cause. The Fourth Amendment with regard to computer cases deals with an individual's reasonable expectation of privacy in electronic information stored within computers (or other electronic devices) under the individual's control. The important factor is the probability that exploitive images will be found in the place or residence to be searched. The warrant must be specific and must include everything inside and outside the computer. An individual may lose his Fourth Amendment protection when he relinquishes his control to a third party. An example of this is when a person has his computer repaired by a repair shop.

Eighth Amendment Rights

The Eight Amendment represents a person's right against cruel and unusual punishment. The laws in question are the registration and notification directives that mandate that a person convicted of a sexual crime must register as a sex offender with local law enforcement after release from prison. Many sex offenders feel their Eighth Amendment rights are violated after they have already served their sentence for committing a sexual crime. A substantial number of defenders of this law assert that the notification process is a method to provide information to communities that would prohibit sex offenders from carrying on a decent and normal life. One main objection concerns the ability to find and establish a decent place to live because many states restrict where a sex offender can reside and work. Sex offenders also feel that the notification process may prompt people in the community in which they intend to stay to harass and threaten them. These released offenders have reiterated that they have served their time in prison and that the notification laws are another layer of punishment that they must endure. Sex offenders feel that the notification process goes against their Eighth Amendment rights because of the additional pain and suffering from the notification laws that make discovering a new way of life nearly impossible because it

- Amends the federal criminal code to expand the jurisdictional basis for prosecutions of sexual exploitation of children, selling or buying of children, or child pornography crimes to include activities that use any means or facility of interstate or foreign commerce to complete such crimes
- Amends the federal criminal code to:
  - Include child pornography that contains a visual depiction of an actual minor engaging in sexually explicit conduct and the production of such pornography for importation into the United States as predicate crimes for money laundering prosecutions
  - Define the word "possess" with respect to crimes of child sexual exploitation and child pornography to include accessing by computer visual depictions of child pornography with the intent to view

Internet Dating Safety Act

In 2008, New Jersey enacted Bill S-1977, which is also known as the "Internet Dating Safety Act." This bill requires online websites to take on more responsibility in making their sites safe and foster safe practices for the consumer. These particular sites will be required to post clearly whether or not they provide online background checks of all participants. These websites will have to provide online safety tips about what clients need to be aware of.

Profile of a Female Sex Offender

Candice, a 31-year-old woman from Florida, has been arrested for multiple child sex offenses that stemmed from an investigation into her involvement with child porn. Her alleged involvement with child pornography was first investigated by the Department of Homeland Security and Immigration and Customs Enforcement, according to a sheriff's report. Officials with those organizations showed deputies images they believe showed the woman's involvement in producing pornographic pictures of her children. One photo captured the woman giving her 14-year-old son oral sex. Another showed her son and 9-year-old daughter, naked, sitting on a bed.

Profile of a Male Sex Offender

A 6-year veteran police officer in a northern Chicago suburb was found guilty of sexually abusing a 10-year-old girl in 2006. The officer's bond was revoked by a Lake County judge because the officer had been accused of molesting two preteen girls at a birthday slumber party. The jury deliberated for 6 hours and found him guilty of two counts of aggravated criminal sexual abuse. The officer, who had served in the Navy, was suspended from the police force.

In My Opinion

From an Illinois Assistant State's Attorney

A Cook County, Illinois, assistant state's attorney (ASA) who wished to remain anonymous said this regarding pedophiles: "Pedophiles are like drug addicts addicted to heroin; they are always looking to get more, and they are good at getting what they want." The ASA has worked in the felony review section for sex crimes and has interviewed over 500 victims and offenders in her career. She reviews many areas of a case: the testimony from the victim as well as the offender, physical evidence, previous criminal history of the offender, the offender's personal and family background, and if the offender has exhibited any patterns in the past. After this detailed investigation, the ASA takes all of this information into consideration and then determines if the offender should be arrested and charged with a felony.

Once a pedophile is classified as a sexually violent person, he is seen by an Illinois Department of Corrections psychologist. Under Illinois State Law 725 ILCS 205/15, under sexually violent persons commitment, a person is considered sexually violent if he or she has been convicted of a sexually violent offense;

has been found not guilty of a sexually violent offense by reason of insanity, mental disease, or mental defect; and

is dangerous to others because the person's mental disorder creates a substantial probability that he or she will engage in acts of sexual violence.

The psychologist employed by the state determines if the offender is a sexually violent person or has a mental disability that needs to be addressed. This review will also determine if the offender has pedophilia or paraphilia tendencies, definitive factors in the family background (including being a victim of abuse), and the likelihood that he will reoffend if given the chance. The sexual offender is given the option of refusing treatment (at which time he or she will be incarcerated) or to participate in a treatment program. If the respondent decides on treatment, he will be sent to the Illinois Department of Human Services Treatment & Detention Facility in Rushville, Illinois. This is not a punitive facility, but rather a rehabilitation site that houses 450 sex offenders statewide.

In 1998, Illinois passed the Sexually Violent Persons Commitment Act. The following four standards must be met for an individual to be committed under this act:

- The person must be within 90 days of release from an adult criminal sentence for a qualifying sexual offense.
- The person must have a justifiable DSM-IV diagnosis of mental disorder.
- The person must have a substantial probability of committing future acts of sexual violence because of his mental disorder.
- It must be proved, beyond a reasonable doubt, that the person's risk of future sexual violence is the result of his mental disorder.

The sex offender enters a five-phase program. The first stage is to admit what he did. Another stage is to create a safety plan that deals with managing the illness. This plan deals with lifestyle issues, such as drug use, which often affect the ability to reoffend. This volitional control of the disease often depends on the ability to regulate or manage sexual urges.

Respondents who are committed under the act are remanded to the custody of the state. Once admitted to this secure residential treatment facility, residents are provided with a full range of diagnostic treatment and rehabilitative services to address sexually violent and deviant behaviors. Treatment modalities include individual and group counseling, behavior modification, psychopharmacology, substance abuse counseling, psychosocial and psychoeducational programming, and therapeutic and recreational activities.

Clinical services at the facility are provided through a long-term service contract with Liberty Healthcare Corporation. Liberty employs over 30 experienced psychologists, social workers, mental health counselors, psychiatrists, substance abuse counselors, recreation therapists, and activity leaders. The state of Illinois employs a full complement of security and paraprofessional staff to secure the facility and ensure the safety of the facility's staff and residents. Residents who are discharged from the facility into the community are served by Liberty's *Community Conditional Release Program.* This community-based program employs aggressive case management, GPS monitoring, regular polygraph examinations, drug and alcohol screening, and ongoing outpatient assessment and treatment services.

The ASA remarked that sexual offending is an illness or a sickness that cannot be cured but only managed and controlled. She stated, "It is like a little video playing inside the sexual offender's head, abusing a child. They replay the same exploitative scene over and over in their mind. They eventually seek out other children, store those captivating memories of the latest victim, and replay them over and over again."

Definitions of Chapter Key Terms

DSM-IV: An acronym for the *Diagnostic and Statistical Manual of Mental Disorders,* fourth edition. This manual was last published by the American Psychiatric Association in 1994. It covers all mental health disorders for both children and adults, and it assists mental health professionals to understand their patients' illnesses better. The DSM-IV lists (1) known causes of these disorders, (2) statistics in terms of gender, (3) age at onset of the disorder, (4) prognosis and projections, and (5) research concerning the optimal treatment approaches.
First Amendment: Guarantees freedom of speech. The issue has arisen as to whether someone can be charged for exercising this right over the Internet.
Fourth Amendment: Search warrant requirements regarding online child enticement can only be issued with probable cause. The Fourth Amendment in regard to computer cases deals with an individual's reasonable expectation of privacy in electronic information stored within computers (or other electronic devices) under the individual's control.
Eighth Amendment: Protects a person from cruel and unusual punishment. Many sex offenders feel their Eighth Amendment rights are violated after they have already served their sentence for committing

a sexual crime. The laws that are in question are the registration and notification directives mandating that a person convicted of a sexual crime must register as a sex offender with local law enforcement after release from prison.

References

Graham, W. (2000). Uncovering and eliminating child pornography rings on the Internet. *Michigan State University Law Review* 2 (457): 458–484.

Greaves, P. (2010). *The pedophile's guide to love and pleasure: A child-lover's code of conduct.* Self-published.

Internet Safety and Education   13

> I was wrong; I was his teacher and took advantage of him at school and in my home. I still think of him, but it cost me my profession. I knew there was a chance of getting caught, but I let my emotions get the best of me.
>
> **Convicted teacher**

> It was easy for me as a Boy Scout leader; I got away with a lot before I got caught. All of the parents trusted me. My wife has since divorced me.
>
> **Convicted boy scout leader**

Authoritative Parents

Some experts feel that that the best defense parents can have is to be more authoritative and not necessarily have a relaxed attitude when it comes to the Internet. Parents should help their children develop their own critical thinking by explaining the true intentions of sexual predators.

Behavior

Many sexual predators count on a child being lonely, shy, and reserved. This type of child is easier prey with less likelihood of the child talking about sexual encounters or overtures encountered. Often, this type of child may not have many friends or may not be well liked in school and sees the Internet as an opportunity to become popular and make new friends. Parents should recognize a change in a child's behavior such as secretiveness, inappropriate sexual knowledge, or mention of unknown adults, or if the child is having nightmares or a difficult time sleeping.

Behavior outside the Home

Parents worry about what their child is doing when he or she is away from the house. Experts believe that how children act at home is how they are most likely to act on the Internet. If teens are promiscuous and adventurous normally and often defy their parents, they will do the same on the Web.

Computer in a Common Area

It is good to have a computer in a bedroom, but not one that has Internet capabilities. Keeping a computer that is tied into the Internet in a common area may assist in controlling secretive behavior or promiscuous or unwanted websites appearing on the computer screen. Most mothers do not consider their children's bedrooms safe. The chances of teens being mischievous on the Internet increase when they are alone or no one is near the computer. That is why it is imperative that a computer be kept in an open area if possible. Recent studies show:

- Four out of ten parents allow their children to use the computer in their bedrooms or private areas in the house.
- Five out of ten moms worry about their child's safety online, especially being unsupervised in a bedroom.

Computer Lingo

A substantial number of teens conceal their Internet conversations from their parents by using acronyms (Internet lingo) that their parents do not understand. Recent studies indicate four out of ten teens use code words to conceal their Internet conversation.

A few examples of some of the more popular acronyms are as follows:

A/S/L: Age, sex, location.
ASLMH: Age, sex, location, music, hobbies
A3: Anytime, anyplace, anywhere
BIL: Boss is listening
D&M: Deep and meaningful
DIKU: Do I know you?
F2F: Face to face
LMIRL: Let's meet in real life
IPN: I'm posting naked
IWSN: I want sex now
KOC: Kiss on cheek
KOL: Kiss on lips
KPC: Keeping parents clueless
MoF: Male or female
NP: Nosey parents
NIFOC: Naked in front of computer
OLL: Online love
P911: My parents are coming
PA: Parent alert
PAL: Parents are listening
PANB: Parents are nearby
PAW or PRW: Parents are watching
PCM: Please call me
PIR: Parents in room
PM: Private message
POMS: Parents over my shoulder
POS: Parents over shoulder
SoG: Straight or gay
SSC: Super, sexy, cute
TDTM: Talk dirty to me
TOY: Thinking of you
WTGP: Want to go private
8: Oral sex
9: Parent is watching
53X: Sex
99: Parent is no longer watching
143 or 831: I love you
1174: Nude club

Educated and Computer-Savvy Parents

Informed parents mean safer kids online. Regardless of law enforcement's ability to detect and arrest child sexual predators using the Internet, the most effective protection against child victimization is an involved and educated parent. Children and adolescents are often naïve and unaware of the dangers of the Internet. Experts claim that it is very important for parents and educators to gain knowledge about the computer and become more computer savvy.

Many parents are not familiar with the detailed operation or intricacies of a computer but their children are often well aware of these things. The reality is that many teens have an extensive technological knowledge of the computer and can often hide or clear their questionable activities online.

Most parents do not want to look foolish in front of their children when it comes to computer literacy and teens are less likely blatantly to access harmful material on the Internet if their parents can check what they are doing. An article written by Alan Cohen in *PC Magazine* in 2006 stated, "The Internet may have broadened our view of the world and made our professional lives easier, but it has certainly complicated parenting. One particular challenge is that most kids know a lot more about the Internet than do their parents, and they use the knowledge gap to win more time and less supervision online." Parents are encouraged to report any inappropriate sexual behavior that has been discovered or revealed to the law enforcement section that handles these cases.

- Seven out of ten teens know how to hide what they do online from their parents.
- Five out of ten moms do not always know what their child is doing on the Internet or online.
- Three out of ten kids clear the browser history when they have finished using the computer.

Law Enforcement on Internet Safety

Law enforcement officials at the federal level have developed strategies that will help restrict offenders from victimizing children online. According to the FBI-Parent Guide to Internet Safety, in 2008, Pennsylvania State Representative John Taylor endorsed legislation that would update registration laws to restrict a convicted sex offender's use of the Internet and other high-tech devices. Taylor emphasized that "the Internet has given sexual predators an insidious new way to stalk victims. These criminal have learned how to link up with other offenders and create online communities dedicated to preying on kids who see the Internet as a safe place to make new friends."

According to the Federal Bureau of Investigation, a special unit called the Innocent Images National Initiative (IINI) was formed to stop sexual predators from victimizing children and teens on the Internet. Of the 56 FBI field offices, 28 had undercover agents working in this IINI operation. These undercover operations include law enforcement officials posing as teens to identify predators who are trying to meet underage children and teens online. Since 1995, this initiative has led to more than 10,000 investigated cases and more than 3,000 convictions.

Limit Time on the Computer

It may be important for a parent or guardian to limit children to kid-friendly Internet service providers. The more time a teen spends in a chat room, the greater the odds he or she will be approached by a stranger.

Meeting a Predator in Real Life

A substantial number of parents have no idea of the threats that exist regarding the potential dangers of online sexual predation and the possibility of meeting a sexual offender in real life. Many children and teens rely on their friends to get advice about suspicious or unusual behavior they encounter on the Internet. Internet-based interaction via chat rooms, instant messaging (IM'ing), and e-mails often keeps a sexual offender in constant communication with the potential victim and substantially increases chances of meeting him or her at a discreet location. Parents should explain to their child the true meaning of friends and friendship and explain how provocative online profiles may encourage a stranger to want to meet them. The ultimate goal for a sexual predator is to have a face-to-face meeting after school, at the mall, in the child's home, in a park, or at party. Teaching children and adolescents that it is unsafe to meet a stranger in real life is vital, especially if the child has encountered that stranger online.

Open Communication

Parents or caregivers who have open communication and who do not judge their child are less likely to have the child develop a secretive online relationship. It is important to realize that most children can become a victim without meeting the sexual predator in person. The biggest complaint teens have is the lack of understanding a parent may have regarding newfound relationships over the Internet. Parents have to be good listeners and not criticize their children even when they have made a mistake or done something wrong, especially on the Internet. They should not overreact or get angry at the teen. It is important that the teen can come to the parent with any problem without the parent getting angry or upset or using threats that would include taking privileges away or not using the computer.

A difficult situation is having open communication with sons or daughters, especially when they become teenagers or older. Older children are exploring new areas of their life, especially of the virtual world of the Internet, and they rarely seek approval from their parents regarding friends or strangers with whom they converse. This open communication may detect and uncover signs of what a child is doing online. It is important to establish an atmosphere in which any questions can be asked and answered without shame, humiliation, fear, or judgment. Everyone in the family should speak up if something or someone's behavior does not seem right or appropriate.

Dr. Lauren Barrow of Kaplan University (personal communication) said, "The child might not be the one engaged in the at-risk behavior. Parents need to remind their children that they are ALL involved in the protection of one another. I call it 'deputizing' the younger children to watch out for one another." Mike Sullivan, deputy chief in the Illinois attorney general's office articulates that it is important for parents to teach their children to trust them. The best defense is for a child to learn how to say, "I'll have to check with my parents." That will stop a predator in his tracks. Sullivan added, "Remember the strongest weapon an online predator has against your child is secrecy. The strongest weapon a parent has against online predators is communication. Take the time to talk to your children." Teaching your child how to behave responsibly and carefully online, as you would teach him or her to behave in the real world, is the first step to keeping the child safe.

Parents

Be a concerned parent and spend time with your children online. Review what is on your child's computer. Be inquisitive about the chat rooms visited, instant messaging, and e-mail. It would be a good idea for parents to visit their child's most frequented websites.

Predators on the Internet: Hiding Their Identity

Pedophiles and sexual predators make it their mission to interact with children on the Internet. Predators can conceal their identities, even pretending to be another child or a person of the opposite sex. Adults are not likely to notice a stranger prowling online as they might notice a stranger near a school playground or park. The Internet allows sexual predators to hide their true identity, often lying about their age and where they live. Many sexual offenders use made-up or anonymous screen names and false identities. Parents should warn their children that the individuals they meet online may not necessarily be who they say they are and that sexual predators may use sexually suggestive conversation to entice their intended victim. It is also important to let children know they should not respond to anything inappropriate sent online. This especially applies to any material that may be of a sexual nature even if it is in a joking manner. Unfortunately, most children are curious and may respond; that is why parental interaction is imperative.

Sexual Predator as a Friend

Internet predators will often portray themselves as a big brother or person who listens or someone who is there for moral support and truly cares. They tend to be the parenting and concerned adult type who encourages the child to be with their friends, do their homework, and do their chores. The sexual predator is often delighted to step into this new role as friend and confidant. It will not take long for the predator to win the child over by listening to what he or she needs, and the child will be quick to point out that family or parents just do not understand what he or she is going through.

Safe Childhood Program

According to the US Department of Justice (2008), the Safe Childhood program was created in 2006 with the intention of helping to combat the use of technology, such as the Internet, in the sexual exploitation of children. This program initiative involved a partnership between federal, state, and local law enforcement agencies and child advocacy organizations. It investigates and prosecutes sexual predators who have victimized or have attempted to victimize children on the Internet.

Secrets and Secret Relationships

"The number one thing I would tell parents is that a sexual predator's strongest weapon online is secrecy," said Sullivan of the Illinois attorney general's office. "And a parent's strongest weapon against sexual predators is communication." The sexual predator's message is, "This is our secret. You can trust me. You don't tell anyone. I won't tell anyone." An important message that must be discussed and agreed upon is that there should not be any secrets within the family, no matter what was done or said. Parents must always be open and objective, no matter how difficult that may be. Often a secret online relationship will prompt children and teenagers to use the Internet at a friend's house or library instead of at home where their parents might catch them. Two out of ten teens have created a private or secret e-mail address or social networking profile to hide what they do online from their parents (Sullivan, 2008).

A Child's Self-Confidence

A parent should speak about self-confidence to his or her child. This is often an excellent way to help guard against sexual predators who try to encounter teens with low self-esteem.

Sexual Advances on the Internet

Sexual advances over the Internet are at epidemic proportions in our society and we need to stop exploiting our children and start prosecuting sexual offenders and pornographers. Many sexual predators will often post a sexual message just to see what a child's reaction will be and to test the limits of the Internet conversation. Adolescents have a tendency to gravitate to sexual material. Will the child respond to the predator's sexual advances? Will the child tell someone? The sexual predator is banking on some type of response from the child. If the child questions or balks at his sexual remark, it is likely the sexual predator will respond that it was a mistake and that he was just kidding or just playing around. Parents need to remind their children that no one should speak to them in a sexual manner. It is imperative that a parent know immediately from the child if this ever occurs and especially keep these lines of communication open:

- Six out of ten children have received links to pornographic websites.
- Four out of ten girls have sent their picture or their physical description to someone they do not know.
- One out of four teens believes it is safe to post a picture online.
- Four out of ten teenage girls have been sexually pressured in a chat room; one out of ten has told her parents about it.

Sharing e-Mail Accounts

Parents should share e-mail accounts with their children. This would enable a parent to see all correspondence coming into their home computer as well as correspondence that is sent out. Many criminal justice system officials suggest that parents should scrutinize a child's e-mail, be aware of the Internet location their child is visiting, and

- check the child's e-mail
- check the e-mail addresses that the child is using
- not place the child's e-mail address in any directory

Six out of ten teens have sent an e-mail or instant message to a stranger.

Sharing Personal Information

The Department of Justice, in cooperation with the National Center for Missing and Exploited Children, has published public service announcements warning teenagers about the dangers of sharing personal information online and has also donated resources designed to teach parents how to keep their kids safe from Internet predators. The "think before you post" campaign was a public service announcement that stressed to teenagers (mainly teenage girls) that anyone could see anything posted online: family, friends, and even not-so-friendly people. They should give their e-mail address or start a buddy list only to people who they know and trust.

Children should never give out their name, home phone number, cell phone number, parent's or guardian's name, school name or address, or home address to anyone online—even if they feel they know the person. Teaching a child how to behave responsibly and carefully online, as you would teach them to behave in the real world, is the first step to keeping them safe.

Children are evasive in their Internet actions to avoid arousing their parents' suspicions and supervision. Kids will always want to break the rules and stretch the boundaries and parents have to give them their space and privacy. Recent studies show:

- Six out of ten teens have given out personal information online to someone they did not know.
- One out of five teens has told people on the Internet his or real name.
- One out of five teens believed it was safe to put his or her address on the Internet.

Internet Safety and Education

Strangers on the Internet

One common denominator that parents have instilled in their children from when they were younger is never to speak with strangers. Many teens forget that logic when they are on the Internet because they feel that nothing will ever happen to them. Every parent believes that it will not be his or her child who responds to a sexual question from someone on the Internet. That unknown person is just waiting to take a foothold in the child's life. Will the parent be able to hold back his or her anger and frustration in this type of situation? A safe suggestion for parents is to ask their children to tell them if they encounter anything online that they consider strange, frightening, or inappropriate (including anyone, stranger or friend, asking for photos of them with little or no clothes on). Many mothers fear the behavior and communication their children have with strangers on the Internet. Six out of ten teens believe that it is safe to meet a stranger with whom they have been chatting online.

Websites: Reporting

The National Center for Missing and Exploited Children (NCMEC) acknowledged that hundreds of websites condone sexual promiscuity with children. NCMEC was instrumental in developing an informative website in 1998 called CyberTipline.com. This site is a helpful public resource for protecting children online and it can be done anonymously. It was created so that parents and caregivers could report a myriad of sexual offenses against children such as the possession, manufacture, and distribution of child pornography. In response to CyberTipline.com, the NCMEC has received tens of thousands of leads from parents, law enforcement authorities, teachers, and other concerned individuals who want to protect their children from the dangers of the Internet and sexual predators.

What Kids Do Online

There are a number of suggestions and recommendations that a parent or guardian can initiate that would help deter a child from dangerous Internet activity. Many parents face another online challenge trying to keep track of what their children do and with whom they interact:

- Seven out of ten sixth graders use the Internet, and nine out of ten seventh graders use the Internet.

- Nine out ten teenage girls chat online without their parents being aware of it.
- Seven out of ten girls do things online that they do not want revealed to their parents.

Firewalls, Antivirus Software, and Privacy Filters

A 2004 study by Dombrowski et al. acknowledged that the following technological and protective considerations can prevent online solicitation:

- Installing a firewall on a computer will provide a barrier between the computer and the Internet that prevents third parties from controlling the computer.
- Monitoring the browser history on your home computer shows stored communication and information of online use.
- Privacy filtration, such as Netscape Nanny 5.0, helps block personal information from transmission over the Internet. This software also provides tools for blocking intrusive pop-up ads that may be pornographic and allows for time limit controls of Internet use. Many companies sell software programs to help monitor, filter, and block inappropriate material so that a child cannot access or receive any unwanted solicitation. Filtering software is the best way to protect children from Internet predators who lurk in chat rooms because it filters and/or blocks undesirable web content. Some popular programs are SpectorPro, Cyber Sentinel, and IamBigBrother. Computer technology has advanced so far that a few select software programs will regularly notify a parent or adult about any potential infringement that may occur.
- Chat logging records save the plain text communications on the hard drive. Monitored online conversations can ensure that only appropriate content is being seen.
- Spam blocker and antivirus software or site advisor can be installed as primary precautions.

Six out of ten parents do not have monitoring software on their computers.

Safe Internet Sites

A few recommended Internet sites that are safe, controlled, and protected include:

Internet Safety and Education

- BeNetSafe.com
- GetNetWise.org
- ISafe.org
- NetSmartzKids.org
- NetSmartz.org
- SafeKids.com
- WiredSafety.org

BeNetSafe.com

BeNet Safe.com is a paid-subscription website for concerned parents comprising technology veterans. They believe the Internet is a transformational power and feel it is their job to implement safeguards that protect children through checks and balances. The company believes the job of parents is to trust but also verify the online environment their children are entering.

BeNetSafe automatically monitors a child's online activities, including social networking sites like MySpace, Xanga, and Friendster, and then reports any potentially dangerous or reckless behavior back to the parent. One advantage of BeNetSafe is that it is discreet and the child will not know that the parent is aware of his or her online activity. This service will also notify the parent of any other potential "red flag" items such as references to drugs, alcohol, sex, etc. Parents will be notified of their child providing information online, especially if the child gives a phone number, e-mail address, home address, or school information, or that the child may be linked to dangerous or illegal activity.

GetNetWise.org

GetNetWise.org is a project of the Internet Education Foundation and the Center of Democracy and Technology (including their advisors and corporate sponsors) that provides children with useful and helpful information to be safe on the Internet. The site wants to ensure that Internet users have a safe, constructive, educational, and entertaining online experience. The entire team feels that Internet users should make informed decisions about user's and their families' use of the Internet. GetNetWise.org. has a *spotlight* section that is devoted to the latest issues and concerns facing Internet users. This segment illustrates helpful safety tutorials. One example noted from this section is how to use privacy settings of social networking sites and how to activate safe search features. GetNetWise has a safety-by-age segment (http://kids.getnetwise.org/safetyguide/age/):

> Ages 7 to 10. During this period, children begin looking outside the family for social validation and information. This is when peer pressure begins to

become an issue for many kids. It's also a time when kids are looking for more independence from parents...During these years, children should be encouraged to do a bit more exploring on their own, but that doesn't mean that the parents shouldn't be close at hand. Just as you wouldn't send children at this age to a movie by themselves, it's important to be with them—or at least nearby—when they explore the Net. For this age group, consider putting the computer in a kitchen area, family room, den, or other areas where the child has access to mom or dad while using the computer. That way, [he or she] can be "independent" but not alone. Also, consider using a filtering program or restricting [your child] to sites that you locate via a child-safe search engine. Another option for this age group is a child-friendly browser.

When your child is at this stage you need to be so concerned not so much about what [he or she] is doing online, but [rather] how much time [he or she] is spending online. Be sure that [the child's] time on the computer and the Internet doesn't take away from all...other activities. Kids need variety, and it's not a good idea for them to be spending all of their time on any single activity, even reading books. One way to deal with this might be through the use of a software time-limiting tool. It's even important to be sure that they are varying what they do online. Encourage them to explore a variety of websites, not just one or two of their favorites....

Ages 10–12. During this pre-teen period, many kids want to experience more independence....This is also an age when you have to be concerned not just about what kids see and do on the Internet, but how long they are online.... Set limits on how often and how long kids can be online...At about age 12 children begin to hone their abstract reasoning skills. With these enhanced skills, they begin to form more of their own values and begin to take on the values of their peers....It's important at this age to begin to emphasize the concept of credibility. Kids need to understand that not everything they see on the Internet is true or valuable, just as not all advice they get from their peers is valuable....

Ages 12–14. This is the time when many kids become very social and when they are most likely to be interested in online chat. Go over the basic privacy rules with your kids to be sure they understand to never give out information about themselves or to get together with anyone they meet online without first checking with their parents. Also, emphasize the importance of never exchanging photographs with people they don't know. At this age they need to understand clearly the fact that people on the Internet may not be who they appear to be.

This is also an age where many children start expressing interest in sexual matters. It is natural for them to be curious about the opposite (or even same) sex and it is not unheard of for them to want to look at photos and explore sexual subjects. During this early exploratory period, it is especially important for kids to know that their parents are around and aware of what they are doing. You may not need to be in the same room as your kids the entire time they're on the Net, but they do need to know that you and other family members can walk in and out of the room at any time, and will ask them about what they are doing online.

Don't be alarmed if a child at this age is interested in exploring sexual material. How you manage this, of course, depends on your own view of such material. It's important to be aware that some of the materials they might find on the Internet are different—and more explicit—than some of the magazines that may have been around when you were that age. If kids search hard enough, they can probably find websites and newsgroups that explore sexual fantasies that they…might find disturbing or even frightening. This is probably the strongest argument for Internet filters, but it's also an argument for close parental involvement…creating a climate of trust and openness between parents and children.

Children at this age are likely to be interested in games that they can download from the Internet to play either online or offline. Some of these games may have content that parents feel is inappropriate, so it's important to be aware of what your kids are doing on the computer, even when they're not connected to the Internet. Monitoring software may help you [become more aware of this behavior].

Ages 14–17. Your teen is beginning to mature physically, emotionally, and intellectually and is anxious to experience increasing independence from parents.…Teens are complicated in that they demand both independence and guidance at the same time. Teens are also more likely to engage in risky behavior both online and offline.…There is always the possibility that [your child] will meet someone online that makes him feel good and makes him want to strike up an in-person relationship. It is extremely important that teens understand that people they meet online are not necessarily who they seem to be.… Although it's sometimes difficult to indoctrinate teens with safety information, they can often understand the need to be on guard against those who might exploit them. Teens need to understand that to be in control of themselves means being vigilant, and on the alert for people who might hurt them.

The greatest danger is that a teen will get together offline with someone she meets online.…Set reasonable expectations. If your teen confides in you about something scary or inappropriate that he encountered online, your first response should not be to take away his Internet privileges. Try to be supportive and work with your teen to help prevent this from happening in the future [along with reporting this inappropriate Internet activity to local law enforcement].

i-SAFE

i-SAFE is a nonprofit organization that is dedicated in its efforts to empower and educate the youth of America to take control of their online experiences safely and responsibly. Founded in 1998, i-SAFE Inc. is the leader in Internet safety education. i-SAFE is available in all 50 states; Washington, DC; and Department of Defense schools located across the world. According to its website (http://www.isafe.org/channels/?ch=ai),

The goal of i-SAFE is to educate students on how to avoid dangerous, inappropriate, or unlawful online behavior. i-SAFE accomplishes this through dynamic K–12 curriculum and community outreach programs to parents, law enforcement, and community leaders. it is "the only Internet safety foundation to combine these elements."

Since its inception, i-SAFE has revolutionized the way the world looks at Internet safety education. In this day and age everyone knows students can explore the marvels of the world and travel to the most intelligent realms of our galaxy on the Internet....Concerned people now realize awareness and true safety online is not found in software filters—it is found in education and community support. Educated people realize true education and community support is found within i-SAFE.

i-SAFE has worked with law enforcement and teachers to provide a cybersafe environment for every community.

NetSmartzKids.org

This website specializes in Internet safety for young children. It does not link into any outside Internet sources. This site is very safe for children and features activities, games, and videos that reinforce Internet safety concepts.

NetSmartz.org

NetSmartz.org offers real-life scenarios of teens that encountered dangers online and success stories from teens that avoided the dangers of sexual offenders. NetSmartz is a free website that recommends that children, teens, and parents be aware of the dangers of the Internet. Often these workshops provide children with extended safety awareness and self-confidence that will assist them whenever they go online. NetSmartzKids.org is a safe website designed specifically for young children. These websites are beneficial and safe because they do not link to any outside sources. NetSmartz offers multimedia Internet safety presentations that are customized for specific audiences, especially younger children, teens, parents, and communities. The NetSmartz website offers the latest statistics, online resources, videos, and expert tips to educate, engage, and empower children and adults to be safer online.

A study by Malena Brookshire and Christine Maulhardt (2005) of George Washington University evaluated the effectiveness of the NetSmartz program and the National Center for Missing and Exploited Children. The study was designed to determine students' existing Internet behaviors and their conceptions of safe Internet behavior. The data obtained from surveying Maine students between the ages of 9 and 14 proved that involvement in the NetSmartz program resulted in more responsible online behavior by children.

Internet Safety and Education

SafeKids.com

SafeKids.com is a website that contains information about the dangers of children using the Internet. It provides rules for children using the Internet, and advice and tips relating to child security and the web. This site also mentions cell phone safety, cyberbullying, location sharing, and password and safety tips.

WiredSafety.org

WiredSafety is headed by Parry Aftab, an international cyberspace privacy and security lawyer and children's advocate. Other volunteers find and review family-friendly websites, filter software products, and Internet services. WiredSafety is proud of its reputation as the one-stop shop for all cyberspace safety, privacy, security, and help needs.

WiredSafety is a 501(c) (3) program and the largest online safety, education, and help group in the world. Its members are a cyberneighborhood watch organization and operate worldwide in cyberspace through more than 9,000 volunteers. (WiredSafety is run entirely by volunteers.) Four major areas of WiredSafety include

- Help for online victims of cybercrime and harassment
- Assistance to law enforcement worldwide on preventing and investigating cybercrimes
- Education
- Providing information on all aspects of online safety, privacy, and security

WiredSafety is also affiliated with www.wiredcops.org, which is an organization comprising specially trained volunteers that patrol the Internet looking for child pornography, child molesters, and cyberstalkers. It also offers a wide variety of educational and help services to the Internet community, such as programs on

- Cyberstalking, missing kids, harassment, and other cybercrimes
- Child pornography, e-mail safety, sexual predators, Internet instruction, and cyberlaws

Conclusion

My Thoughts on Sexual Predation

Although counseling and therapy have educated and helped many sexual offenders, most sexual offenders believe they still would not be totally rehabilitated upon their return to society. Sexual predators live and work in all social, economic, and educational levels of the spectrum. Growing up in a dysfunctional family is often the norm for most sexual offenders. A majority of sexual offenders come from families who also had encounters with the law and behavioral problems that include alcoholism, drug addiction, mental illness, medical issues, and self-abuse. Studies have indicated that an overwhelming number of sexual predators have felt empathy for their victims but it was not until counseling that they were able to realize the extent of the damage that they had caused.

The Internet

The Internet introduces a new venue that allows sexual predators to fantasize and masturbate over child pornography. A sexual predator will use the Internet as a main thoroughfare to attract victims. The Internet does not necessarily contribute to their deviant behavior; however, the advent of this technology has made it easier for sexual offenders to seek out their victims. Many sexual offenders have the mind-set that looking at, collecting, buying, selling, and distributing child pornography on the Internet is not hurting anyone, but it is truly quite the opposite. Mike Sullivan, deputy chief in the Illinois Attorney General's office (personal communication) said, "The realization is that these kids have suffered tremendously, Child pornography is the actual crime scene pictures of a sexual assault as it is occurring." It defies society's moral and ethical standards.

No family is immune to the possibility that their child could be exploited and harassed on the Internet. The danger to children has increased because the Internet provides predators anonymity. Whether the victimization occurs in person or over the Internet, the process is still the same, and the predators use the information to target the child. These young, naive adolescents are likely to engage in conversation that is interesting and exciting; the predator may initiate an online friendship with the child, engage in conversation that is interesting, share hobbies and interests, and eventually exchange gifts and pictures.

The online predator will spend a lot of time befriending and grooming the child. The predator relies on trust, which eventually allows sexual predators to attain their ultimate goal: to sexually exploit the innocent child without getting caught. A few factors make some children more vulnerable to predators than others. Older children tend to be at greater risk to predators because they use the computer unsupervised and are more likely to engage in chat rooms and other vicarious online discussions. Some victims participate in chat rooms, trade e-mail messages, and send pictures of themselves online. Sexual predators are continuously searching for troubled or rebellious teens who are seeking a release from parental authority because they can be vulnerable. The risk of victimization is even greater for those teens who are dealing with emotional issues regarding their sexual identity.

Parent Awareness

Parents, as well as the public, need to be educated on what is needed to protect children and to be reminded just how serious this problem of online predators has become in our society. Parents can track their children's computer activity and monitor the websites they have been viewing. Parents must be vigilant in their explanation regarding their child's computer dialogue—especially posting online. They should reiterate to their children that anyone can view what they write and see pictures they send. Children may not realize that pictures posted online will be there forever because there is no way to delete them permanently. It is vital not only that parents are educated, but also that their children are educated. Parents need to be made aware of what types of incidents they should report and to whom.

Keeping communication open between the parent and the child is extremely important, especially regarding the websites that are often visited by the child or suggested by unknown individuals. Many children are receiving unwanted pornographic material over the Internet and they have been solicited for sex by people they meet online. From their homes, sexual predators can gain access to a number of victims in a short amount of time.

Parents need to listen to their "sixth sense" when it comes to their children. Relying on "gut feeling" is the first warning sign that something may be wrong with your child. What is different about his or her behavior? Be an inquisitive and nosy parent. Instruct your children never to meet a stranger who they have met online in person. Predators can be very convincing in their approach of being sincere, trustworthy, and truthful. Many coworkers, immediate family, and friends of the sexual predator are amazed when they discover his secret life.

Computer Technology

Unfortunately, given the broad spectrum of computer technology, it is nearly impossible to identify specific individuals who attempt to use the Internet for sexual purposes after their conviction. There are many ways in which a convicted sex offender can obtain the tools necessary to access the Internet, including using a fake name and social security number to purchase services from an Internet provider. The continued use of sting operations by law enforcement agencies, updating and changing of laws through legislation, and further advancement of computer technology for the protection of children are often the best defenses. Tools (e.g., firewalls, antispyware software, and antivirus software) are also available to deal with private sector issues in an attempt to safeguard computers and children from predators.

Law Enforcement

Many law enforcement officials have implemented strategies that combat online child exploitation and abuse. The strategies are designed to curb

Internet exploitation by working with the community and making the public aware of the dangers of sexual predation. Awareness and prevention must be the main focus for parents and teens each and every day.

I have found that most sexual predators integrate what I call the 10-Ps of the predatory process when they form a relationship with a child. This is a 10-step progression in the sexual predator's quest to groom and maintain a connection with the child he intends to pursue and exploit.

Definitions of Chapter Key Terms

Access: User's ability to view the data collected about him or her and to challenge its accuracy and completeness.

Antivirus software: Detects and removes computer viruses.

Blacklisting software: A form of filtering that blocks only sites specified as harmful.

Blocking software: Computer programs that block access to websites or other services available on the Internet.

Chat: A feature offered by many online services or websites that allows participants to "chat" by typing messages that are displayed almost instantly on the screens of other participants who are using the chat room. Chatting is one of the most popular uses of the Internet. Generally, the participants remain anonymous, using nicknames or pseudonyms to identify themselves.

Communication: An effective way of sending messages, thoughts, opinions, or information.

Consent: Explicit permission given to a website by a visitor to handle personal information in specified ways.

Cyberspace: Various information resources available through computer networks and the Internet, as well as to communities that have developed through their common use of such resources, and to the culture developing in such electronically connected communities. May also be used to distinguish the physical world from the digital or computer-based world.

e-Mail (electronic mail): A service that allows people to send messages with pictures and sounds from their computers to any other computer in the world. An e-mail account and the recipient's address are needed to send a message.

Encryption: A means of making data unreadable to everyone except the recipient of a message.

File-sharing programs: Programs that allow many different users to access the same file at the same time.

Filtering software: Different methods that screen out unwanted Internet content including whitelisting, blacklisting, monitoring activity, keyword recognition, or blocking specific options (e-mail or instant messages).

Instant messaging (IM or IM'ing): A service that allows people to send and see the messages almost instantly. This is real-time private communication that allows the user to transmit video as well as text from the computer.

Firewall: A security software program that helps to prevent unwanted and unauthorized access such as informational material, spam, viruses, etc., from the Internet.

Mouse trappings: A commonly used technique by pornography sites where a user gets "locked" into a website. While surfing the Internet, it is possible to click onto a website where multiple undesirable websites will be open. When this happens, a person cannot close or back out of the sites and thus must close the web browser completely.

Multimedia: A combination of different types of programs that allows a person to see graphics, animation, and text.

Online jargon: Hybrid language of acronyms or abbreviations to communicate online. This is another name for cyberslang, hi-tech lingo, or hybrid shorthand.

Online relationships: These often begin with two people who have never met before but have begun a friendship online. This online couple will often assess their feelings and emotions through verbal and physical indicators. A person's honesty is often questioned in this type of relationship because it is easy to deceive someone online.

Online safety: Being aware of any inappropriate communication or behavior over the Internet that could further lead to a crime.

Posting: Sending a message to a discussion group or other public message area on the Internet. The message is called a "post."

Privacy policy: The policy that a company or organization operating a website uses for handling the personal information collected about visitors to the site.

Solicitation: To approach a person often with the intention of satisfying a sexual desire.

Software: Written programs, procedures, or rules and associated documentation pertaining to the operation of a computer system.

Website: A collection of "pages" or files linked together and available on the World Wide Web. Websites are provided by companies, organizations, and individuals.

Whitelisting: A form of filtering that only allows connections to a preapproved list of sites that are considered useful and appropriate for children.

References

Brookshire, M., and Maulhardt, C. (2005). Evaluation of the effectiveness of the NetSmartz program: A study of Maine public schools.

Cohen, A. (2006). Do you know where your kids are clicking? *PC Magazine* 25 (12): 88–96.

Dombrowski, S. C., LeMasney, J. W., Ahia, C. E., and Dickson, S. (2004). Protecting children from online sexual predators: Technological, psychoeducational and legal considerations. *Professional Psychology: Research and Practice* 35 (1): 65–73.

FBI-Parent Guide to Internet Safety (No date). www.FBI.GOV/Stats-Service/Publications/ParentGuide.

Sullivan, M. (2008). Online predators: A parents' guide for the virtual playground. Xulan Press.

Definitions of Terms

Access: User's ability to view the data collected about him or her and to challenge its accuracy and completeness.

Adaptation: Adjusting to one's environment. Most sexual predators adapt to the environment of the victim they seek out.

Address: A series of letters and numbers that identify a location. On the Internet, typing in an address lets a person send or receive information from a specific source.

Age of consent: This term varies depending on the state and the jurisdiction. The age of consent is often the age a person is considered or thought of as capable of consenting or acquiescing to sexual acts. Most states in the United States have their own age of consent, all agreeing that 16 years of age up to 18 years of age should be considered the age of consent.

Approach strategies: A calculated and systematic plan that sexual predators use to get to know and entice their victim.

Antivirus software: Detects and removes computer viruses.

Attachment: A file that has been added to an e-mail.

Blacklisting software: A form of filtering that blocks only sites specified as harmful.

Blocking software: Computer programs that block access to websites or other services available on the Internet.

Blog: Short for web log; a web log is usually classified as a personal or noncommercial website that uses a dated log format (usually with the most recent at the top of the page) and contains links to other websites along with commentary about those websites. A web log is updated frequently and sometimes groups links by specific subjects, such as politics, news, pop culture, or computers.

Bookmark: A way to access a favorite website quickly.

Browser: A program that allows users to view web pages.

Bulletin board service (BBS): A place where people can post messages on a particular topic.

Cappers: Another term for a sophisticated and well-organized group of young online sexual predators who are attempting to seduce teenage girls using their webcams. These men will secretly record females whom they persuade to disrobe partially or fully in front of the camera. They entice these young girls by saying that they could be models or actresses.

CD-ROM: Contact disk, read only memory.

Character: A person's moral and ethical actions. Sexual predators will often show this side of their personality when they are out in the public.

Chat: A feature offered by many online services or websites that allows participants to "chat" by typing messages that are displayed almost instantly on the screens of other participants who are using the chat room. Chatting is one of the most popular uses of the Internet. Generally, the participants remain anonymous, using nicknames or pseudonyms to identify themselves.

Chat room: An interactive forum on the Internet where a person can engage in real-time discussions with other participants. The chat room is where the chat is taking place and where common interests are often discussed. A person can freely broadcast messages in this venue.

Chemical castration: Injection of an antiandrogen drug that will reduce the male's testosterone level and eventually reduce his sex drive. This is most commonly accomplished by injection of Depo-Provera, a derivative of progesterone that significantly reduces the testosterone level, sexual fantasies, and arousal. It also believed to reduce the recidivism rates in sex offenders.

Child abuse: Mistreatment that includes sexual abuse, physical abuse, emotional abuse, and neglect.

Child erotica: Displays a child in a photograph or video in a sexually suggestive manner.

Child molester: A person who commits some form of sexual act with a child.

Child pornography: Not just a picture of a naked child, it involves the lewd exposure of the child's genitals, sexual exploitation including rape of a child, explicit sexual activities including simulated or replicated or genuine sexual activities including masturbation of a child with the intention of sexual arousal and gratification. Child pornography also reveals images of minors who are engaged in sexual acts. In child pornography you will never see the offender's face. The difference between child pornography and pornography is that the former is sexually explicit photographs or video that depicts a person under the age of 18 involved in sexually graphic conduct, such as sexual intercourse, masturbation, and sexual cruelty.

Child sexual abuse: Mistreatment of children in a sexual context with an adult who is predominantly sexually attracted to children.

Civil commitment: Under civil commitment, a person is deemed to be a danger to himself or herself or society or is unable to care for his or

Definitions of Terms

her basic needs. This is decided by a judge as the person is housed in a hospital or mental health facility.

Coercion: To put pressure on or persuade someone to do something against his or her will. This is seen in many families that have experienced incest with a family member.

Communication: An effective way of sending messages, thoughts, opinions, or information.

Consent: Explicit permission given to a website by a visitor to handle personal information in specified ways.

Copulation: To engage in sexual intercourse.

Crime prevention: Various means of effectively prohibiting or stopping an offender from committing a serious offense, especially sexual misconduct.

Cyberbullying: Sending or posting harmful or cruel text or images using the Internet or other digital communication devices.

Cybersex: The exchanging of explicit sexual messages, activity, discussion, display, or information via the Internet. This is the counterpart of a telephone sex line that typically takes place in an online chat room.

Cyberspace: Various information resources available through computer networks and the Internet, as well as to communities that have developed through their common use of such resources, and to the culture developing in such electronically connected communities. May also be used to distinguish the physical world from the digital or computer-based world.

Cyberstalking/harassment: The online enticement of children; rude or threatening messages, slanderous information, or repeated and/or unwanted messages.

Cycle of violence: Often thought of as repetitive acts of physical violence against a submissive person through intimidation and forced sexual encounters. These recurring acts of violence accompany elevated emotions and acts of reprisal and revenge.

Cyproterone: A synthetic steroid that suppresses testosterone in the body; it is available in Canada and Europe.

Deception: Misleading fabrication with the intention or act of deceiving someone. The act of being crafty, often giving the false impression of being a good person. Most, if not all, sexual predators have mastered the art of this behavior.

Denial: Denying that the accusations, allegations, or complaints against oneself are true. Most sexual offenders refuse to admit the truth or the reality of their actions taking place. They often deny or repudiate that a problem even exists.

Depo-Leupron: A man-made hormone that reduces the amount of testosterone and also decreases the sex drive in adult males.

Depo-Provera: A man-made hormone that reduces the amount of testosterone and also decreases the sex drive in adult males.

Desire: An inclination or preference to covet things or a person. Sex offenders often have this feeling that accompanies an unsatisfied condition.

Discussion group: A group of people who exchange information about a common topic

DSM-IV: An acronym for the *Diagnostic and Statistical Manual of Mental Disorders,* fourth edition. This manual was last published by the American Psychiatric Association in 1994. It covers all mental health disorders for both children and adults, and it assists mental health professionals to understand their patients' illnesses better. The *DSM-IV* lists (1) known causes of these disorders, (2) statistics in terms of gender, (3) age at onset of the disorder, (4) prognosis and projections, and (5) research concerning the optimal treatment approaches.

Dyadic abuse: Most common type of sexual abuse that involves one victim and one offender.

Eighth Amendment: Protects a person from cruel and unusual punishment. Many sex offenders feel their Eighth Amendment rights are violated after they have already served their sentence for committing a sexual crime. The laws that are in question are the registration and notification directives mandating that a person convicted of a sexual crime must register as a sex offender with local law enforcement after release from prison.

e-Mail (electronic mail): A service that allows people to send messages with pictures and sounds from their computer to any other computer in the world. An e-mail account and the recipient's e-mail address are needed to send a message.

Emoticons: Animated faces that a person can send in an e-mail when chatting with another person online or when using instant messaging (IM). Emoticons are a way to show feelings to someone online.

Emotional abuse: To manipulate a person psychologically in a harsh manner that will cause persistent anxiety.

Emotional blackmail: The pressure of using penetrating threats by way of a victim's sensitive and delicate state of mind or circumstances.

Encryption: A means of making data unreadable to everyone except the recipient of a message.

Enticement: To seduce or lure a person into a desired behavior.

Entrapment: Luring or enticing a person into committing a crime and then prosecuting him or her for it.

Ephebophile (ephebophilia): A pedophile who is interested or desires males from 12 to 16 years of age, often considered under the legal age of consent. These types of pedophiles are often more interested in children who are post-puberty.

Definitions of Terms

e-Stop: Allows social networking websites to identify sexual predators and prevent them from harming again. Under the e-stop agreement, Internet users under the age of 16 will be able to set their account on private. This measure will ensure that no one will be able to gain information from a child's profile. This feature can also block anyone who is over 18 years old from contacting them, and people over 18 cannot add anyone who is under 16 as a friend in their network unless they have a last name or e-mail address.

Exhibitionism: A behavior that involves the exposure of one's genital area to another person.

Exploitation: Taking unfair advantage of an unknowing child or individual, often by coercing him or her into doing something immoral, wrong, or harmful.

Fantasies: Forming mental images, visions, or aspirations using imagination or conceptualization. This is most often associated with sexual predators, pedophiles, and sex offenders in their conquest of realizing what has replayed often in their mind.

Fascination: The capacity or influence of being passionately interested in someone or something. Most sexual predators have a fascination with sexually abusing their victim.

Fetishes: Often, an attraction of a sexual nature toward one particular inanimate object. An individual may fantasize about and/or masturbate to this object.

File-sharing programs: Programs that allow many different users to access the same file at the same time.

Filtering software: Different methods that screen out unwanted Internet content including whitelisting, blacklisting, monitoring activity, keyword recognition, or blocking specific options (e-mail or instant messages).

Firewall: A security software program that helps to prevent unwanted and unauthorized access such as informational material, spam, viruses, etc., from the Internet.

First Amendment: "Congress shall make no law respecting an establishment of religion, or prohibiting the free exercise thereof; or abridging the freedom of speech, or of the press; or the right of the people peaceably to assemble, and to petition the government for a redress of grievances." Guarantees freedom of speech. The issue has arisen as to whether someone can be charged for exercising this right over the Internet.

Flaming: Sending out deliberate confrontational messages to others on the Internet.

Fondling: Touching, caressing, or stroking breasts and genitalia to provoke arousal and sexual stimulation.

Fourth Amendment: Search warrant requirements regarding online child enticement can only be issued with probable cause. The Fourth Amendment in regard to computer cases deals with an individual's reasonable expectation of privacy in electronic information stored within computers (or other electronic devices) under the individual's control.

Frotteurism: Rubbing genitalia against a child.

Geographic information system (GIS): A computerized software program that interprets and visualizes data of convicted sex offenders in a particular area. This interactive program can monitor sex offenders and sexual abuse data and project future incidents through incident mapping. GIS will benefit law enforcement in visualizing data and the use of strategic planning involving convicted sex offenders and their whereabouts.

Global positioning system (GPS): A service that transmits, via satellites, information regarding positioning and navigation.

Grooming: The gradual erosion of sexual boundaries through plotting and calculated moves after gaining trust from the victim. This is the first step of the process that sexual predators use in their quest to sexually abuse their victims. This type of grooming often involves developing the child's sexual awareness and may take days, weeks, months, or, in some cases, years.

Group therapy: Sexual offenders are able to speak in a relaxed environment and share the same issues and problems.

Guilt: Remorse caused by feeling responsible for, embarrassment about, regret for, shame about, and culpability for being the victim in a sexual crime.

Hacker: A popular term for someone who accesses computer information either illegally or legally.

Hard copy: This is the printed/paper copy of a file from a computer.

Hebephile (hebephilia): Pedophiles who are attracted to or engage in any sexual conduct with young pubescent females who are often between the ages of 12 and 16 and considered under the age of legal consent. These types of individuals are known to have relationships with their victims, and they have a tendency to be opportunistic when engaging in their sexual exploits.

History: A list of websites that people have visited using a particular computer.

Homepage: A web page that a browser displays when it starts up or the main page of any website.

Hyperlinks: An image or a portion of text that, once clicked, allows electronic connections. These connections access other Internet materials such as images, sounds, animations, videos, or other web pages.

Definitions of Terms

Incest: Unacceptable and inappropriate sexual activity between one family member and another family member or relative. The most common cases of incest involve father and daughter (sometimes referred to as intrafamilial child sexual abuse) and stepfather and stepdaughter relationships. This type of crime is often underreported due to the unwillingness of the child to cause dissension in the family and the secrecy, and privacy of the crime. The victim often experiences low self-esteem, unhealthy future sexual activity, contempt for other women, and emotional problems. This type of crime is considered taboo in most societies.

Infantophilia: A pedophile who is interested in a child younger than 5 years old.

Instant messaging (IM or IM'ing): A service that allows people to send and get messages almost instantly. This is real-time communication that is private and allows the user to transfer video as well as text from one computer to another computer.

Internet: A global system of interconnected computer networks that facilitate data translation and information via telephone lines, fiber optic cables, and satellite links. It is often referred to as the "Net."

Internet protocol (IP) address: A numerical label that uniquely identifies a node on the Internet and is assigned to any device participating in a computer network.

Internet relay chat (IRC): A system that enables people to join online in live discussions to engage in real-time conversation. Instant relay chat is a virtual conference where people from all over the world can meet and talk.

Internet service provider (ISP): A company that provides Internet access to customers.

Isolation: To alienate a person or keep a person alone or concealed.

Isolation strategies: A careful set of plans devised by the sexual offender or predator to get the victim alone in an attempt to have sex.

Manipulation: A sexual predator skillfully controls the situation with the intent of taking advantage of his or her intended victim.

Martymaculia: Considered paraphilia, this involves the sexual attraction of having others watch the performance of a sexual act.

Masturbation: Stimulation or manipulation of one's genitals.

Molestation: The act of imperiling or subjecting a person to unsolicited and inappropriate sexual advances.

Monitoring software: Software products that allow parents to monitor or track the websites or e-mail messages that a child visits or reads.

Mouse trappings: A commonly used technique by pornography sites where a user gets "locked" into a website. While surfing the Internet, it is possible to click on a website where multiple undesirable websites then open. When this happens a person cannot close or back out of the sites and must close the web browser completely.

Multimedia: A combination of different types of programs that allow a person to see graphics, animation, and text.

Navigate: Moving from page to page or website to website when online; also called browsing or surfing.

Netiquette: A term for courtesy, honesty, and polite behavior that should be practiced on the Internet.

Network: Created when computers are connected; allows people to share information. The Internet is an example of a large network.

Newsgroups: Subject-specific virtual message boards or discussion groups on the Internet. Participants in a newsgroup conduct discussions by posting messages for others to read and respond to. User groups are similar to a community bulletin board where a person can post and read messages.

Online: Having access or being connected to the Internet or a computer network.

Online grooming: Using the Internet to manipulate and develop trust of a minor as a first step in gaining information a predator may use eventually to meet the intended victim. This type of grooming often involves developing the child's sexual awareness and may take days, weeks, months, and, in some cases, years to manipulate the minor. The final triumph is for the predator to be able to sexually manipulate the victim when that meeting occurs.

Online jargon: Hybrid language of acronyms or abbreviations to communicate online. This is another name for cyber slang, hi-tech lingo, or hybrid shorthand.

Online relationships: These often begin with two people who have never met before but have begun a friendship online. This online couple will often assess their feelings and emotions through verbal and physical indicators. A person's honesty is often questioned in this type of relationship because it is easy to deceive someone online.

Online safety: Being aware of any inappropriate communication or behavior over the Internet that could further lead to a crime.

Paraphilia: Adult and adolescent pedophiles who enjoy abnormal or unusual sexual activity. Children who were often themselves victims now have become the offenders.

Password: The secret word a person uses when signing on to the Internet or an online service that helps to confirm that person's identity.

Pattern of behavior: Routine or regular behavior. The sexual predator has two different and succinct patterns of behavior. One is how he acts during his daily routine or how the public perceives that person to be (e.g., caring dad, businessperson, friend). The other is how he

Definitions of Terms

acts in the surroundings of his victim (e.g., conniving, calculating, manipulating).

Pedophile (pedophilia): A sexual preference for children (boys or girls or both), usually of prepubertal or early pubertal age. A child younger than 11 is in the age group most often associated with pedophiliac behavior. This sexual attraction is often characterized by lust for or infatuation with a child that leads to a variety of sexual acts that include molestation and intercourse, often against the child's will. Pedophiles will try to develop a relationship with a child and will often seek out shy, withdrawn children or a child who may be handicapped because they are least likely to reveal or tell on the offender. Pedophiles will enhance the child's self-esteem, especially if the child is from a troubled home.

Persuasion: Coaxing interaction often used by the sexual offender through reasoning, rationalization, and assurance that the nature of the sexual encounter is normal, acceptable, and appropriate.

Pharming: An online scam that attacks the browser's address bar. A person may type in what appears to be a valid website address and be unknowingly redirected to an illegitimate site that steals personal information.

Phishing: An online scam that uses e-mail to "fish" for the user's private information by imitating legitimate companies. People are often lured into sharing user names, passwords, account information, or credit card numbers. The phishing e-mail contains a link to an illegitimate site.

Post: An electronic message on a newsgroup or bulletin board.

Posting: Sending a message to a discussion group or other public message area on the Internet. The message is called a "post."

Predatory behavior: Obsession or passion often targeting an innocent victim to satisfy the predator's needs.

Predisposed: To put a person at risk or to make a person vulnerable by a position held.

Prepubescent: A child who has not reached puberty.

Privacy policy: The policy that a company or organization operating a website uses for handling the personal information collected about visitors to the site.

Profile: Exhibits diverse characteristics about a person's lifestyle and an account of the series of events making up a person's life.

Pubescent: The age at which a young person reaches puberty or the age when sex glands become functional.

Recidivism: Reoffending or committing the same type of crime again.

Search engine: A program that searches for information on the World Wide Web by looking for specific keywords and returns a list of information found on that topic.

Secrecy: Custom or practice of keeping or maintaining privacy. A sexual predator depends on secrecy and concealment, especially if he is sexually involved with a young, innocent victim.

Seduction: Often associated with enticing a victim from veracious or virtuous behavior to commit a sexual act. Sex offenders will charm their victim for sexual favors or sexual intercourse.

Self-gratification: Manual contact other than sexual intercourse with the intent of satisfying one's own desires or sexual pleasure.

Sex offender: Any person, more likely a male than female, who is convicted of a sex crime almost exclusively against a child. These crimes range from rape (sexual assault) to sexual harassment to child molestation to distributing and producing child pornography.

Sexual abuse: Unwanted sexual activity that is forced upon an individual or child through threats, intimidation, or coercion. This is another term for sexual assault.

Sexual abuse of a child: The mistreatment of children in a sexual manner, by sexually touching, fondling, or penetrating the child. Sexual assault or illegal sexual contact with a victim who is incapable of giving consent or by a person with authority.

Sexual addiction: An obsession with sex that includes continuous thoughts of sex and sexual predispositions. This type of individual has unusually intense sex drive tendencies.

Sexual assault: The illegal sexual contact or unwanted sexual act against a person's will that frequently involves force. This type of statutory offense is often inflicted upon someone who may be incapable of giving consent because of age (child) or mental or physical incapacity. It may also be considered conduct of a sexual or indecent nature accompanied by actual or threatened physical force that induces anxiety, shame, humiliation, and mental and psychological problems. Many states have replaced the common term "rape" with the term "sexual assault."

Sexual exploitation: Taking advantage of or manipulating a person sexually.

Sexual perversion: A condition in which a person's sexual arousal and gratification depend on a fantasy theme of an unusual situation or object that becomes the principal focus of sexual behavior (another term for paraphilia).

Sexual predator: Often describes a person with an obsession and passion to target an innocent victim sexually to satisfy his or her needs for sexual gratification.

Sexually transmitted disease (STD): There are eight forms of this disease or infection that rely on sexual transmission to survive and endure. The common forms of this condition can be caused by bacteria, viruses, or parasites. The eight noteworthy conditions are chlamydia (bacteria), gonorrhea (bacteria), trichomoniasis (parasite), HIV (virus), genital herpes (virus), genital warts (virus), hepatitis symptoms (virus), and syphilis (bacteria). A few sexually transmitted diseases are often asymptomatic (show no signs or symptoms).

Sexually violent person: Someone who has been convicted of a sexually violent offense, adjudicated delinquent for a sexually violent offense, or found not guilty of a sexually violent offense by reason of insanity and who is dangerous because he or she suffers from a mental disorder that makes it substantially probable that the person will engage in acts of sexual violence.

Social networking sites: Mostly web-based services that provide an outlet for people to interact; a collection of various ways for users to interact. A few examples are by chat, e-mails, and sharing pictures and videos. Social networking has revolutionized the ways that members of society communicate and share information with one another. Millions of people use numerous social networking websites every day.

Sodomy: An unnatural form of sexual intercourse often associated with anal intercourse.

Solicitation: To approach a person often with the intention of satisfying a sexual desire.

Software: Written programs, procedures, or rules and associated documentation pertaining to the operation of a computer system.

Spam: Unwanted and unsolicited e-mail from an unknown person, company, or source.

Spamming: Mass mailings often sent as instant messages to users that often feature explicit sexual pornography sites.

Streaming (media): The exchange of video clips, sound, or other types of media over the Internet.

Surfing the web: Searching for information via the Internet.

Surgical castration (orchiectomy): Removal of the male's testes. This procedure will make the male sterile and ultimately affect, decrease, and inhibit his sexual desire.

Teleiophile (teleiophilia): A pedophile who prefers mature or older companions between 16 and 19 years of age.

Threat: The intentional act of inflicting harm, pain, or injury; instigating panic or fright.

Traveler: A term generally used by law enforcement agencies to refer to an online sexual predator who travels (often across state lines) to meet victims that were first met on the Internet.

Triptorelin: A synthetic drug that overstimulates the body's own production of certain hormones, causing the production of these hormones to shut down temporarily.

Trust: Often associated with the victim believing in the honesty, righteousness, and sincerity of the sex offender.

Verbal abuse: Often associated with a pattern of behavior. A person uses crude and coercive remarks that are meant to hurt, criticize, or cause an individual emotional pain.

Virtual child pornography: A relatively new phenomenon depicting minors engaging in illicit sexual acts, even though no children are used. This type of pornography is produced by generating images that are enhanced by computer and digital technology.

Virus: A computer program that can destroy files. Viruses can be sent via e-mail or through other file-sharing programs.

Webcam: A camera, often on top of a computer, that is used to transfer live video on the Internet.

Website: A collection of "pages" or files linked together and available on the World Wide Web. Websites are provided by companies, organizations, and individuals.

Whitelisting: A form of filtering that only allows connections to a preapproved list of sites that are considered useful and appropriate for children.

World Wide Web (web): A vast network of electronic files and a collection of Internet sites that serve an extensive user community over the Internet.

Contacts

Anton, M., Cook County Sheriff's Police Department, Criminal Intelligence Special Investigations, 1401 Maybrook Drive, Maywood, IL, 60153.
Barrow, L., PhD, Kaplan University.
Basalay, E., PsyD, postdoctorate fellow, Chicago, IL.
Boston Globe Newspapers. feedback@boston.com, (617) 929-7900; Fax: (617) 929-7975; Boston.com, 135 Morrissey Boulevard, Boston, MA, 02125, Attention Privacy Manager.
Carter, M., director of sex offender management, Office of Justice, US Department of Justice.
Cole, C., PhD, Rosenberg Clinic, 1103 25th Street, Galveston, TX, 77550.
Collins, R., retired police detective, Chicago Police Department Sex Crimes Unit.
Coyne, D., clinical law professor at Kent Law School, Kent State University, Kent, OH.
Dimeo, M., Chicago Police Department Youth Investigations Unit, 1240 S. Damen Avenue, Chicago, IL, 60608.
Dorris, B., outreach director, Survivors Network of Those Abused by Priests (SNAP), PO Box 6416, Chicago, IL, 60680-6416.
Dru Sjodin website: Drusvoice.com
Flanagan, J., New York State Senator District Office, 260 Middle Country Road, Suite 203, Smithtown, NY, 11787, (631) 361-2154.
Hanger, E., Virginia State Senator, PO Box 2, Mt. Solon, VA, 22843-0002, (540) 885-6898.
Hart, K. National Child Abuse Defense & Resource Center, PO Box 638, Holland, OH, 43528, (419) 865-0513.
Hoffman, J., Illinois State Representative, PO Box 134, Collinsville, IL, 62234.
Human Rights Watch. No Easy Answers, 350 Fifth Avenue, New York, NY, 10018.
Hunter, M. Family and marriage counseling and clinical psychology, 357 Kellogg Boulevard East, St. Paul, MN, 55101.
Illinois State Police, Internet Crimes Unit, Public Information Office, (217) 782-6637, www.ISP.State.il.us
Jacob Wetterling Foundation, Jacob Wetterling Resource Center, 2314 University Avenue West, Suite 105, St. Paul, MN, 55114, (651) 714-4673.
Jackman, D. Detective, Louisville Police, Metro Police Department Headquarters, 633 W. Jefferson Street, Louisville KY, 40402.
KINSA Foundation, 145 King Street West, Toronto, Ontario, Canada, M5H 1J8, info@kinsa.net
Kruk, A. Detective in the special investigations unit, Chicago Police Department, 1240 S. Damen, Chicago, IL, (312) 492-3810.
McSpadden, M. Judge, Harris County Criminal Justice Center 1201 Franklin, Houston, TX, 77002.

Megan Nicole Kanka Foundation, Inc., PO Box 9956, Trenton, NJ, 08650 (609) 890-2201; Fax: (609) 890-2541.

National Academy of Sciences. (2003). *NetSafeKids, a Resource for Parents,* Internet, 500 Fifth Street NW, Washington, DC.

National Association of Secondary School Principals (NASSP). 1904 Association Drive, Reston, VA, 20191-1537.

National Center for Missing and Exploited Children. (2008). US Department of Justice, the Office of Juvenile Delinquency Prevention, and the Office of Justice Programs. Not-for-profit clearinghouse of information for missing and exploited children, Washington, DC.

National Children's Advocacy Center, 210 Pratt Avenue, Huntsville, AL, 35801.

National Children's Alliance, 516 C Street, NE, Washington, DC, 20002.

Office of Justice Programs, Office of Sex Offender Sentencing, Monitoring, Apprehending, Registering and Tracking (SMART), www.ojp.usdoj.gov

Perverted Justice. admin@perverted-justice.com

Rice Hughes, D. ProtectKids.com, 746 Walker Road, Box 116, Great Falls, VA, 22066.

Ruffoni, T. Cook County Sheriff's Police Department, Criminal Intelligence Special Investigations, 1401 Maybrook Drive, Maywood, IL, 60153.

Schmallenger, F. Distinguished professor emeritus at the University of North Carolina at Pembroke.

Schwartz, M. Masters and Johnson Clinic, 800 Holland Road, Ballwin, MO, 63021, (636) 256-7512.

Stack, A. Cook County Sheriff's Police Department, Criminal Intelligence Special Investigations, 1401 Maybrook Drive, Maywood, IL, 60153.

Taylor, J. 4725 Richmond Street, Philadelphia, PA, 19137, (215) 744-2600; Fax: (215) 744-2605; www.legis.state.pa.us/cfdocs/legis/home/member

US Department of Justice, Child Exploitation and Obscenity Section.

US Department of Justice, United States Attorney's Manual (USAM) Criminal Resource Manual 645. 1997. 950 Pennsylvania Avenue, NW, Washington, DC. 20530-0001.

Index

A

Abbott, Greg, 123
ABCs, Internet safety, *xxvii*
ability and knowledge hierarchy, 9
access, 230
"accidental exposure," 135
accusations, not taking seriously, 2, *see also* False accusations
ACLU, *see* American Civil Liberties Union
acronyms, 214
acting out, 2–3
Adams and Fay studies, 19
Adam Walsh Child Protection Act, 174–175
Adam Walsh Child Protection and Safety Act (2006), 175
adaptation, 28
addiction symptoms, Internet, 114–115
address, 128
affection, predators offering, 4
AFIS, *see* Automated Fingerprint System database
Aftab, Perry, 227
age
 of consent, 28
 as deterrent, 47
 difference, punishment based on, 31
 GetNetWise safety segment, 223–225
 preferences, 51, 53
 rate of success, based on victim's, 10
alcohol, 47, 63
Amber Alert system, 149
American Civil Liberties Union (ACLU)
 chemical castration, 155
 opponents of notification laws, 190
 surgical castration, 160
America's Most Wanted, 125
America's Most Wanted: America Fights Back, 174
animals, 2, 16

"An Investigation of Online Sexual Predation of Minors by Convicted Male Offenders," *xxv*
"An Ongoing Study of Group Treatment for Men Involved in Problematic Internet-Enabled Sexual Behavior," 114
anonymity, 111, 228
antisocial cognitions, 55
antivirus software, 222, 230
Anton, Michael, 137–139
approach strategies, 28
April (month), 187
Archives of Pediatrics and Adolescent Medicine, 127
Arcus studies, 32
ASA, *see* Assistant state's attorney (ASA)
Ashcroft v. Free Speech Coalition, 99, 201
assault, elusive concept, 8
assistant state's attorney (ASA), 209–211
"at-risk youth," 126
attachment, 6, 128
attention, 4
authoritative parents, 213
authority, position of, 78–80, 139
Automated Fingerprint System (AFIS) database, 144
awareness, ABCs, Internet safety, *xxvii*
Azaola, Elena, 46–47

B

Bailey, Michael, 159
Barrow, Laura, 8–10, 217
Basalay, Erin, 86
BBS, *see* Bulletin board service
behaviors
 changes, long-term prognosis, 28
 changes in children, 213
 offline *vs.* online, 213
 outside the home, 213

progression of, 15–21
  sexual addiction, 64–65
Beiber, Justin, 9
belief, social bond theory, 6
Bell studies, 91
Benedict XVI (Pope), 59
BeNetSafe website, 223
Benuto and Zupanick studies, 63
Berlin, Fred, 158, 162
Berliner and Conte, 14
Biden, J.R. "Joe," 178
Bill S-1977 (Internet Dating Safety Act), 208
Birmingham, Rev. Joseph, 61–62
BishopAccountability website, 72
BJA, *see* Bureau of Justice Assistance
blacklisting software, 230
blackmail, emotional, 22–24
Blair studies, 104
blame, *see also* Guilt; Minimization of behavior
  blaming victims, 16, 20, 28
  deception, 20
  lack of control, 5
  victims' self-blame, 2
Blanchard, Seto, Cantor and, studies, 90
blog, 128
bookmark, 129
Boston Globe, 60
boundaries, destroying through drugs and alcohol, 47
Bourke and Hernandez studies, 91–92
Bowker, 111
Boy Scout leaders, 26–27, 46, 213, *see also* Camp counselors; Position of authority
Brach, Helen, 104
Bradford and Pawlak studies, 156, 157–158
Bradley studies, 122
Breyer, Stephen, 189
Brookshire, Malena, 226
browser and browser history, 129, 215, 222
bulletin board service (BBS), 129
Bureau of Justice Assistance (BJA), 202
Bush, George W., 174, 177, 206
Butler, Steven Allen, 159
Buttell and Carney studies, 161

C

California Sex Offender Management Board, 191
Cambodia, 68
Campagna and Martin studies, 17
camp counselors, 7–8, *see also* Boy Scout leaders; Position of authority
Campus Sex Crimes Prevention Act (2000), 202–203
Cantor, and Blanchard, Seto, studies, 90
cappers, 122, 129
Carich, Kassel, and Stone studies, 154
Carnes and Wilson studies, 63
Carney, Buttell and, studies, 161
Carter, Madeline M., 177
castration
  chemical, 156–158
  cyproterone, 157–158
  Decapeptyl-Cr, 158
  Depo-Leupron, 157
  Depo-Provera, 156–157
  fundamentals, 155–156
  surgical, 158–160
  triptorelin, 158
catastrophic exhibitionism, 56
Catholic Church, 59–62, 72, 195, *see also* Position of authority; Priests; Survivors Network of Those Abused by Priests (SNAP)
causes, sexual violence, 2–3
CDC, *see* Centers for Disease Control (CDC) and Prevention
CD-ROM, 129
cellphones, hiding conversations, *1*
Center for Sex Offender Management, *see also* Department of Justice
  female teachers, publicized cases, 79
  one-size-fits-all approach, 177–178
  recidivism, 154
Center of Democracy and Technology, 223
Centers for Disease Control (CDC) and Prevention, 43
character, 29
characteristics, female sexual offenders, 76–77
characteristics, sexual predators
  Barrow, Laura, 8–10
  causes of sexual violence, 2–3
  characteristics and patterns, 3–4
  cognitive behavioral theories, 4–5
  female sexual offender profile, 6–7
  fundamentals, *xxvii*, 1–2
  key terms, 10–11
  male sexual offender profile, 7–8
  social bond theory, 6

Index

chat rooms
  defined, 129, 230
  fundamentals, 115–116
  limiting time on computer, 216
  logging records, 222
  parental concern, 217
chemical castration, 164–165, *see also* Surgical castration
child abuse, *see also* Incest
  defined, 47
  female victim's perspective, 32–35
  fundamentals, *xxviii*, 31–32
  male victim's perspective, 35–38
  terms, 38
  traits of female victims, 35
  traits of male victims, 38
Child Abuse Prevention and Treatment Act, 183
Child Abuse Victims Act (1986), 199
child erotica, 107
Child Exploitation and Obscenity Section (DoJ), 67
child molester, 72
Child Online Protection Act, 200
Child Online Protection Act (COPA; 1998), 201
child pornography
  Child Pornography and Protection Act (1996), 98–101
  Child Protection Act (1984), 97–98
  Child Protection and Obscenity Enforcement Act (1988), 98
  Child Sexual Abuse Act (1986), 98
  Communications Decency Act (1996), 98
  Coyne, Daniel T., 103–107
  defined, 107, 139
  Durr, Floyd, 106
  erotica, 90
  female sex offender profile, 101–102
  Ferber v. New York, 96–98
  fundamentals, *xxviii*, 89–90
  key terms, 107–108
  law enforcement, 91–95
  laws, 95–101
  Lieberman, Brad, 106–107
  male sex offender profile, 103
  Miller v. California, 96
  Osborne v. Ohio, 98
  seven laws, 95
  Sexual Exploitation of Children Act (1977), 96
  Stanley v. Georgia, 95–96
  victimization, 91
  virtual child pornography, 98–101
Child Pornography and Prevention Act (1996), 99
Child Pornography and Protection Act (1996), 98–101
Child Pornography Prevention Act (CPPA), 99, 201
Child Protection Act (1984), 96–98
Child Protection and Obscenity Enforcement Act (1988), 98
children
  characteristics and patterns, 3–4
  not coming forward, grooming, 21–22
  viewed as sex objects, 4–5
Children's Advocacy Center (Chicago), 142
Children Safety and Violent Crimes Reduction Act (2005), 204–205
Children's Internet Protection Act, 200
Children's Internet Protection Act (CIPA), 123–124, 206
Child Sex Offender Registration Act, 186, *see also* Habitual Child Sex Offender Act; Sex Offender Registration Act
child-sex tourism, 67–69
child sexual abuse, 47
Child Sexual Abuse Act (1986), 98
child's self-confidence, 219
Christian Science Monitor, 187
civil commitment, 188–189, 197
Clifford studies, 90, 100
Clinton, Bill, 168, 173
"cluster" victims, 10
Code Adam, 174
CODIS (Combined DNA Index System), 144–145
coercion, 47
cognitive behavioral theories, 4–5
Cohen, Alan, 113, 215
Cole, Collier, 157
Collier, Anne, 23, 125–128
Collins, Bob, 142–143
Combined DNA Index System (CODIS), 144–145
coming forward
  boys reluctance, 46
  incest, 43
  refusal to, grooming, 21–22
commitment, social bond theory, 6

communication
  ABCs, Internet safety, *xxvii*
  defined, 230
  Internet, 216–217
  strongest weapon against predators, 219, 229
Communication Decency Act (1996), 200
Communications Decency Act (1996), 98
Community Conditional Release Program, 211
compliance, prepubescent children, 10
compulsive sexual behavior, 63
Computer Crimes Unit, Bergen County Prosecutor's Office, 134
computers
  in common area, 214
  evidence, 147–148
  limiting time on, 216
  lingo, 214
  savvy parents, 215
  schools, 122–124
  technology, 229
Comstock, Graydon, 189
confidence, 1, 164
confusion, 164
Connect Safely, 23, 125
consensual adult incest, 43
consent, 230
control, 4–5
conversations, sexual nature, 58
Cooper, Mansson, and Daneback studies, 115
Cooper studies, 121
coping strategy, *see* Emotional dysregulation
copulation, 47
Couey, John, 170
courtship analogy, 19
Coyne, Daniel T., 103–107
CPPA, *see* Child Pornography Prevention Act (CPPA)
Crimes Against Children Program (FBI), 67, 94
Crimes Against Children Research Center, 10, 126–127
crime scene processing, 141
Crisanto studies, 116
Cuomo, Andrew, 192
curiosity, 80–81
cyberbullying, 126–127, 129
Cyber Crimes Program, 93
cyberharassment, 126–127, 129

Cyberology Consultants, 135
Cyber Sentinel, 222
cybersex, 121–122, 129
cyberspace, 129, 230
cyberstalking/cyberharassment, 126–127, 129
CyberTipline website, 8, 221
cycle of violence, 47
Cyproterone, 165
Czech Republic, 159

D

Dandescu and Wolfe studies, 17
Daneback, Cooper, Mansson and, studies, 115
Dateline NBC, 148
Dateline (NBC), *xxix*, 148
Davis studies, 123
DCFS, *see* Department of Children and Family Services
DCJS, *see* Division of Criminal Justice Services (New York)
DeBecker, Gavin, 1, 3, 4
deception
  defined, 29
  grooming, 16, 20–21
  using, 1
deer hunting analogy, 9
Deleting Online Predators Act (2006), 123
denial, 29
Denmark, 159
Department of Children and Family Services (DCFS), 72, 77, 141, 142
Department of Defense schools, 225
Department of Justice, *see* US Department of Justice
Depo-Leupron, 165
Depo-Provera, 165
deputizing children, 217
desensitizing child, drugs and alcohol, 47
desire, 17–18, 29
deviant fantasies, 17
Diagnostic and Statistical Manual of Mental Disorders, *see* DSM-IV
"digital is forever," 10
dimensions, human behavior, 2–3
DiMeo, Mark, 139–142
"dirty old man in a raincoat" stereotype, 57
disabilities, 52
disbelief, false accusations, 164
discussion groups, 129

Index

display, chat room conversation, 109
distance, relaxing because of, 139
distorted sexual scripts, 54
Division of Criminal Justice Services (FBI), 147
Division of Criminal Justice Services (New York), 193
DNA evidence, 143–145
DNA testing, 141, 143–145, 188
Doermann studies, 52
Dokecki, Paul, 59
Dombrowski studies, 115, 117, 222
Donofrio, Andrew, 134–136
Dorris, Barbara, 71–72
double life, grooming, 15–16
drugs, desensitizing child, 47
Dru Sjodin website, 204, *see also* Sjodin, Dru
Dru's law, 177–178
DSM-IV (*Diagnostic and Statistical Manual of Mental Disorders,* fourth edition), 104, 211
Dubois, Amber, 179
Dugard, Jaycee Lee, 44, 180
Durr, Floyd, 106
dyadic abuse, 48
dysfunctional family life, 3, 67

E

ECPAT, *see* End Child Prostitution, Child Pornography, and the Trafficking of Children
educated parents, 215
Effective Child Pornography Prosecution Act (2008), 206
EGuardian program, 123
Eighth Amendment
    chemical castration, 155
    defined, 211
    opponents of notification laws, 189–190
    rights, 207–208
    surgical castration, 159
electronic mail, *see* e-mail (electronic mail)
Electronic Security and Targeting of Online Predators Act, *see* e-Stop
e-mail (electronic mail)
    defined, 129, 230
    parental concern, 217
    sharing, 220
emoticons, 129
emotional abuse, 87
emotional blackmail, 22–24, 29
emotional connection, 76
emotional dysregulation, 55
emotions, engaging to manipulate, 2
encryption, 230
End Child Prostitution, Child Pornography, and the Trafficking of Children (ECPAT), 68
English studies, 20, 161
Enough is Enough, 188
enticement, 129
entitlement, 5
entrapment and entrapment defense, 145–147, 151
ephebophile and ephebophilia, 72–73
ephebophilia, 56
erotica, child pornography, 90
erotic conversations, 58
Essex studies, 100
e-Stop, 192–194
e-Stop (Electronic Security and Targeting of Online Predators Act)
    defined, 151, 197
    fundamentals, 192–194
evidence of abuse, 22, 23, 32, 41–42
excuses, 5, 80
exhibitionism, 56, 73
exploitation, 53, 151
eyewitnesses, 142

F

Facebook
    Deleting Online Predators Act, 123
    e-Stop, 193
    fundamentals, 117–118
    MySpace comparison, 118
    popularity, 117
    teen online behavior, 111
factual impossibility, 149
Fallon, L.F., Jr., 57, 58
Falseabuse website, 164
false accusations, 163–164, 181–183, *see also* Accusations, not taking seriously
false confessions, 142
false information, registration, 181, 187, 192
family members
    deputizing children, 217
    female sexual offenders, 81
fantasies
    defined, 29
    excuses, reinforcement, 5

feeding desire, 4
   grooming, 16–17
   human behavior dimension, 3
fascination, 17–18, 29
Fay, Adams and, studies, 19
FBI, *see* Federal Bureau of Investigation
fear, *see also* Threats
   false accusations, 164
   victims feeling, 2
Federal Bureau of Investigation (FBI),
      see also Division of Criminal
      Justice Services; Innocent Images
      National Initiative; Regional
      Computer Forensics Lab
   Crimes Against Children Program, 67, 94
   Cyber Crimes Program, 93
   FBI-Parent Guide to Internet Safety, 215
   newsgroups and media information, 117
female sexual offenders
   abusing family members and relatives, 81
   Basalay, Erin, 86
   characteristics, 76–77
   curiosity, 80–81
   fundamentals, *xxviii*, 75–76
   holding a position of authority, 78–80
   key terms, 87
   major components in abuse, 81–82
   male partner domination, 78
   mothers who abuse their children, 77–78
   profiles, 85
   recidivism, 83–84
   risk factors, 82
   risk taking, 80–81
   traits of, 76
   treatment, 84–85
female sexual offenders, profiles by name
   Char, 101–102
   Debbie, 149–150
   Lisa, 85
   Mandy, 44–45
   Melinda, 179–180
   Nancy (foster parent), 6–7
   Nancy (teacher), 69
   Sylvia, 24–25
   Theresa, 162–163
   Traci, 194–195
   Wendy, 124
female victims, traits of abuse, 35
Ferber v. New York, 96–98
fetishes, 57–58, 73

Fichtner, Grossman, Martis and, studies, 155
file-sharing programs, 230
filtering software, 231
FindLaw website, 155
fingerprints, 144–145
Finkelhor, Mitchell, and Wolak studies, 112, 116
Finkelhor, Williams and, studies, 40, 41
Finkelhor, Wolak, Mitchell and, studies, 92
Finkelhor studies, 32, 127–128
firewalls, 222, 231
First Amendment
   ban on possession of child pornography, 98
   defined, 107, 211
   entrapment defense, 147
   Ferber v. New York, 97
   Miller v. California, 96
   rights, 207
   Roth v. United States, 96
   Stanley v. Georgia, 95
fisherman analogy, 18
Fitzpatrick, Michael G., 123
flaming, 129
Flanagan, John J., 193
"flashing," 56
Flora studies, 35, 38
fondling, 48
fooling parents, 18
fooling professionals, 20
forensic interview, 140–141
Fort Worth Star-Telegram, 123
foster homes and parents, 7, 164
Fourteenth Amendment, 95, 155
Fourth Amendment, 147–148, 207, 211
Fox television stations, 118
Freeman, and Socia, Sandler, studies, 187
Freeman, Sandler and, studies, 75, 83
Freeman-Longo studies, 154
Fremin, Keith, 159
Frey, David, 113
Frey, R., studies, 56
friendships
   developing, 2, 21, 218, 228
   grooming as part of, 9
Friendster, 123, 223
frotteurism, 57, 73

G

Gardner, John Albert, III, 179

Garrido, Phillip, 44
Geoghan, John, 61
geographic information system (GIS), 192, 197
Germany, 159
GetNetWise website, 223–225
getting help, false accusations, 164
GIS, *see* Geographic information system
global positioning system (GPS)
    defined, 151, 197
    fundamentals, 192
    sexually violent persons, 105
Globe Spotlight Team, 61
glossary, 233–244
Gonzalez, Alberto, 188
Google, 117
Gordon studies, 159
GPS, *see* Global positioning system
Graham studies, 201
Gramm, W.P. "Phil," 178
Greaves, Phillip R., II, 207
Gregoire and Jungers studies, 60
grooming
    characteristics and patterns, 3
    children not coming forward, 21–22
    committing offense, 138
    deception, 20–21
    defined, 29
    desire, 17–18
    double life, 15–16
    emotional blackmail, 22–24
    fantasies, 16–17
    fascination, 17–18
    female sex offender profile, 24–25
    fundamentals, *xxvii–xxviii*, 9, 13–15, 228
    guilt, 22–24
    isolation strategies, 19
    key terms, 28–30
    Leach, Maryanne, 27–28
    male sex offender profile, 26–27
    manipulation, 18
    masturbation, 16–17
    memorabilia collection, 46
    motivation, 17–18
    parental/predator abuse, 22–24
    persuasion, 20
    progression of behavior, 15–21
    secrecy, 15–16
    seduction, 18–19
    self, acceptable behavior, 86
    10-Ps, *xxvi–xxvii*, 230

Grooming Law 720 IlCS 5/11-25, 138
Grossman, Martis, and Fichtner studies, 155
group therapy, 162, 165
Guardian newspaper, 91
guilt, *see also* Blame
    defined, 29
    grooming, 22–24
    victims feeling, 2
gut feelings, 4, 229

H

Habitual Child Sex Offender Act, 186, 187, *see also* Child Sex Offender Registration Act
Hackensack, New Jersey, 134
hacker, 129
hands-off paraphilia, *see* Exhibitionism
Hanger, Emmet, Jr., 160
Hanger Bill, 160
Hansen, Chris, *xxv*, 148
Hansen, Kenneth, 104
harassment, 126–127
hard copy, 129
"harmful to minors, 124
Harris, Ryan, 106
Hart, Kimberly, 181–183
Harvey, Del, 149
hebephile and hebephila, 55, 73
Heller studies, 160
helplessness, 2
Hernandez, Bourke and, studies, 91–92
Hess studies, 193
hiding identities, 217–218
hierarchy, ability and knowledge, 9
Higher Education Act (1965), 202
Hirschi, Travis, 6
history, 130
Hoffman, Jay, 43
homeless man, false accusations, 181–182
homeless sex offenders, 194
homepage, 130
"How to Recognize Grooming," 23
HRW, *see* Human Rights Watch
Hudson, Donald C., 159
Hughes, Donna Rice, 53, 188
Hughes, R., studies, 10
human behavior, dimensions, 2–3
Human Rights Watch (HRW), 168
Hunter, Mic, 79
hyperlinks, 130

I

IamBigBrother program, 222
ICU, *see* Internet Crimes Unit
identities, online, 10
Identity website, 123
IESB, *see* Internet Enabled and Sexual Behaviors (IESBs)
ignoring child's outcries/revelations, 21–22
Illinois
    Department of Corrections psychologists, 209
    Department of Human Services, 107
    Department of Human Services Treatment & Detention Facility, 210
    incest criminal code, 43
    State Law 725 ILCS 205-15, 209
Illinois State Police
    "Guide to Sex Offender Registration and Community Notification in Illinois," 187
    Internet Crimes Unit, 133–134
imagination, feeding desire, 4
IM or IM'ing, *see* Instant messaging
impossibility defense, 149
impulsiveness
    antisocial cognitions, 55
    characteristics and patterns, 3
    human behavior dimension, 3
inanimate objects, 2
incarceration, *xxix*, 153–154
incest
    defined, 48
    familial progression, 47
    fundamentals, *xxviii*, 38–43
    types of incestuous fathers, 40–41
infantophilia, 55, 73
In My Opinion
    assistant state's attorney, 209–211
    Azaola, Elena, 46–47
    Barrow, Laura, 8–10
    Basalay, Erin, 86
    Collier, Anne, 125–128
    Coyne, Daniel T., 103–105
    Dorris, Babara, 71–72
    Hart, Kimberly, 181–183
    Leach, Maryanne, 27–28
    Pizzo, Father Tony, 195–196
    Rufo, Ron, 227–230
    Schmalleger, Frank, 150–151
    Sullivan, Mike, 163–164

Innocent Images National Initiative (IINI), *see also* Federal Bureau of Investigation
    child pornography, 93–94
    fundamentals, 134
    law enforcement on the Internet, 216
instant messaging (IM or IM'ing)
    chat rooms, 116
    defined, 130, 231
    Internet, 115–116
    parental concern, 217
Internet
    addiction symptoms, 114–115
    antivirus software, 222
    authoritative parents, 213
    behavior changes in children, 213
    behavior outside the home, 213
    BeNetSafe website, 223
    "best practices" discussions, 10
    cappers, 122
    chat rooms, 115–116
    child's self-confidence, 219
    Collier, Anne, 125–128
    communication, 216–217
    computer in common area, 214
    computer lingo, 214
    computer-savvy parents, 215
    computer technology, 229
    cybersex, 121–122
    defined, 130
    display, chat room conversation, 109
    educated parents, 215
    e-mail accounts sharing, 220
    Facebook, 117–118
    failure to legislate, 8
    female sex offender profile, 124
    firewalls, 222
    frequenting sites that children visit, 9
    friendship, 218
    fundamentals, 109–111
    GetNetWise website, 223–225
    hiding identities, 217–218
    identities, gathering information, 10
    instant messaging, 115–116
    Internet Enabled and Sexual Behaviors, 115
    i-Safe, 225–226
    key terms, 128–131, 230–231
    law enforcement, safety, 215–216, 229–230
    limiting time on computer, 216
    male sex offender profile, 124–125

Index

media information, 117
meeting a predator in real life, 216
most searched-for topic, 109
MySpace, 118–119
NetSmartzKids website, 226
NetSmartz website, 226
new policies and procedures, *xxvi*
newsgroups, 117
online behavior, 111
online child enticement, 111
parent awareness, 229
parent concern, 217
perceptions of safety, 112–114
personal information, sharing, 220
popular websites, 117–120
privacy filters, 222
reporting websites, 221
risks, 112
Safe Childhood Program, 218
SafeKids website, 227
safe sites, 222–227
safety and education, *xxix–xxx*, 213–231
schools, 122–124
secrets and secret relationships, 218–219
security on social websites, 120
sex offenders sharing information, 53–54
sexting, 121
sex tourism trade, 68–69
sexual advances, online, 219
sexual predators, *xxviii*, 109–111
social networking sites, 117–120
statistics, online behavior, 221–222
strangers on the Internet, 221
time, amount logged on, 9
triple A theory, 114
using friends house or library, 219
vices, availability, *xxv*
webcams, 120–121
WiredSafety website, 227
Internet Crimes against Children (ICAC) Task Force program, 94, 126
Internet Crimes Unit (ICU), 133–134
Internet Dating Safety Act, 208
Internet Education Foundation, 223
Internet Enabled and Sexual Behaviors (IESBs), 115
Internet protocol (IP) address, 130
Internet relay chat (IRC), 130
"Internet Sex Crimes against Minors: The Response of Law Enforcement," 92

Internet Watch Foundation, 100
interstate sex trafficking, 67, *see also* Travelers
interviews with alleged offender, 142
intimacy/social skills deficit, 54
intrafamilial child sex abuse, 140, *see also* Incest
intuition, 4
involvement, social bond theory, 6
IP, *see* Internet protocol address
IRC, *see* Internet relay chat
i-Safe, 123, 225–226
isolation
    defined, 29, 87
    grooming, 19
    incest, 39
    Stockholm syndrome, 44

J

Jackman, Dan, 116
Jacobson v. United States, 146
Jacob Wetterling Act, 167–168
Jacob Wetterling Crimes against Children Act, 173, 190
Jacob Wetterling Crimes against Children and Sexually Violent Offender Registration Act, 173
Jacob Wetterling Improvements Act (1997), 169
Jayne, Silas, 104
Jenkins studies, 185
Jessica's law, 170, 191, 194
John Jay College of Criminal Justice, 59
Johns Hopkins University, 158, 162
Johnston, Shawn, 158
joking about sex, 218
Jungers, Gregoire and, studies, 60
"Justice for All" group, 178
justification, *see* Blame

K

Kanka, Megan, 171–173, 190
Kassel, and Stone, Carich, studies, 154
Keep the Internet Devoide of Sexual Predators Act (KIDS; 2008), 205–206
Kelly, Chris, 118
Kennedy, Anthony, 201
key terms
    characteristics, sexual predators, 10–11

child abuse and incest, 47–48
child pornography, 107–108
female sexual offenders, 87
grooming, 28–30
incarceration, recidivism, and
 rehabilitation, 164–165
Internet, 128–131
Internet safety and education, 230–231
law enforcement, on the Internet, 151
laws regarding sex offenders, 211–212
pedophile and pedophilia, 72–74
registration and notification laws, 197
Kids Internet Safety Association (KINSA), 113
King, Chelsea, 179
knowledge and ability hierarchy, 9
Kruk, Alan, 136–137

L

landmark legistration, tragedies behind
 Dubois, Amber, 179
 Kanka, Megan, 171–173
 King, Chelsea, 179
 Lunsford, Jessica, 170
 Lychner, Pam, 178–179
 Sjodin, Dru, 176–178
 Walsh, Adam, 174–176
 Wetterling, Jacob, 167–169
Law, Bernard, 62
law enforcement, child pornography, 91–95
law enforcement, on the Internet
 Anton, Michael, 137–139
 CODIS, 144–145
 Collins, Bob, 142–143
 computer evidence, 147–148
 Dateline NBC, 148
 DiMeo, Mark, 139–142
 DNA evidence, 143–145
 Donofrio, Andrew, 135–136
 entrapment defense, 145–147
 female sex offender profile, 149–150
 Fourth Amendment, 147–148
 fundamentals, *xxviii–xxix*, 133–134
 key terms, 151
 Kruk, Alan, 136–137
 legal impossibility defense, 149
 male sex offender profile, 150
 Perverted Justice, 148–149
 police reports, 145
 Schmalleger, Frank, 150–151
 wiretapping, 149

law enforcement, safety, 215–216, 229–230
laws, and government policies, *xxix*
laws, child pornography, 95–101
laws, specific and significant
 Campus Sex Crimes Prevention Act, 202–203
 Child Abuse Victims Act, 199
 Child Online Protection Act, 200–201
 Child Pornography Prevention Act, 201
 Children Safety and Violent Crimes Reduction Act, 204–205
 Children's Internet Protection Act, 200, 206
 Communication Decency Act, 200
 Effective Child Pornography Prosecution Act, 206
 Eighth Amendment rights, 207–208
 First Amendment rights, 207
 Fourth Amendment rights, 207
 fundamentals, *xxix*, 167
 Internet Dating Safety Act, 208
 Keep the Internet Devoide of Sexual Predators Act, 205–206
 Prosecutorial Remedies and Other Tools to End the Exploitation of Children Today Act, 203–204
 Protection of Children against Sexual Exploitation Act, 199
 Protection of Children from Sexual Predators Act, 201–202
 PROTECT Our Children Act, 205
 Sex Crimes against Children Prevention Act, 200
 Telecommunications Act, 201
 Victims of Child Abuse, 200
 Walter Mondale Child Abuse and Treatment Act, 199
Leach, Maryanne, 27–28
learning disabilities, 52
legal cases
 Ashcroft v. Free Speech Coalition, 99, 201
 Ferber v. New York, 96
 Jacobson v. United States, 146
 Mathews v. United States, 146
 Roth v. United States, 96
 Stanley v. Georgia, 98
legal impossibility defense, 149
legal ramifications, incest, 43
legislation, *see also specific legislation*
 enacted after Megan's law, 170
 failure, online behavior, 8, 10
Lewis and Miller studies, 116

Index

Liberty Healthcare Corporation, 211
library, using computer at, 219
Library of Congress Bill H.R. 4472, 204
Lieberman, Brad, 106–107
limiting time on computer, 216
logins, 9, *see also* Screen names
low-risk strategies, 3
low self-esteem, *see* Self-esteem
Lundsford, Jessica, 170
Lychner, Pam, 178–179

M

Madigan, Lisa, 1, 187
major components in abuse, 81–82
male partner domination, 78
male predators, *xxv*
male sexual offenders, profiles by name
    Al, 26–27
    Bradley, Earl, 85
    Curtis, 163
    Grant, 150
    Internet, 124–125
    Jon, 70–71
    Michael, 7–8
    Paul, 103
    Phillip, 180–181
    police officer, 194
    Rich, 45–46
male victims
    seen as lucky, 79, 83
    traits of abuse, 38
Mandelstam and Mulford studies, 189, 192
manipulation
    defined, 29
    grooming, 18
    incest, 39
    using, 1
    vs. coercion, 53
Mansson, and Daneback, Cooper, studies, 115
Marshall (Justice), 95
Martin, Campagna and, studies, 17
Martis, and Fichtner, Grossman, studies, 155
martymaculia, 57, 73
Massachusetts Department of Corrections, 157
Masters and Johnson Clinic, 58
masturbation
    defined, 29
    grooming, 16–17

human behavior dimension, 3
    voyeurism, 59
Mathews v. United States, 146
Maulhardt, Christine, 226
McGrain, Ramsland and, studies, 79
McSpadden, Michael T., 159
media information, 117
medical examination, 141, 144
meeting a predator in real life, 216
Megan Nicole Kanka Foundation, 172
Megan's law
    fundamentals, 172–173
    legislation enacted after, 170
    prior to passage, 186
    sexual registration and notification laws, 190–191
memorabilia collection, 46
Men Don't Leave, 79
mental health assessment, 27
mental health treatment, 161–162
Middleton studies, 54
mild exhibitionism, 56
Miller, Lewis and, studies, 116
Miller test, 96, 97
Miller v. California, 96
minimization of behavior, 28, *see also* Blame
Miranda rights, 134
Mitchell, and Finkelhor, Wolak, studies, 92
Mitchell, and Wolak, Finkelhor, studies, 112, 116
moderate exhibitionism, 56
molestation, 48
monitoring child's behavior, 21–22, 222
monitoring software, 136
Montgomery, Dave, 122–123
Morse, Jeffrey, 159
most searched-for topic, 109
mothers who abuse their children, 77–78, *see also* Female sexual offenders
motivation, 1–2, 17–18
mouse trappings, 107, 231
Mulford, Mandelstam and, studies, 189, 192
multimedia, 107, 231
multiple dysfunctional deficits/mechanisms, 55
multiple victims, baiting, 111
Murdoch, Rupert, 118
MySpace
    BeNetSafe website, 223
    Deleting Online Predators Act, 123
    e-Stop, 193

fundamentals, 118–119
teen online behavior, 111
My Tutor, 79

N

Nangle, Father Tom, *xxv*
National Academy of Sciences, 149
National Association of Secondary School Principals (NASSP), 122
National Catholic Reporter, 59
National Center for Missing and Exploited Children (NCMEC)
    CyberTipline website, 221
    dual offenders, 101
    interstate sex trafficking, 67
    NetSmartz program evaluation, 226
    registered sex offenders, 186
    sharing personal information, 220
    Walsh, John, 174
National Center on Child Abuse, 40
National Children's Advocacy Centers, 39
National Commission on the Future of DNA Evidence, 143
National Crime Prevention Council, *xxvi*
National Institute for the Study of Prevention and Treatment of Sexual Trauma, 162
National Sex Offender Registry (NSOR), 179, 206
navigate, 130
NBC *Dateline, xxix,* 148
NCMEC, *see* National Center for Missing and Exploited Children
NetFamilyNews, 23
netiquette, 130
Netscape Nanny 5.0, 222
NetSmartz, 134
NetSmartzKids website, 226
NetSmartz website, 226
network, 130
neurobiological development, 27–28
New Jersey, 134, 208
newsgroups, 117, 130
New York State Division of Criminal Justice Services (NYSDCJS), 193
Nichols, Edward, 163
Nichols Consulting, 163
Nigam, Hemanshu, 119
"No Easy Answers: Sex Offenders Laws in the United States, 168
nonphysical violence, 2

normal fantasies, 17
NSOR, *see* National Sex Offender Registry
NYSDCJS, *see* New York State Division of Criminal Justice Services (NYSDCJS)

O

Office of Sex Offender Sentencing, Monitoring, Apprehending, Registering, and Tracking (SMART Office), 175–176
Office of the Juvenile Justice and Delinquency Protection (OJJDP), 94
OJJDP, *see* Office of the Juvenile Justice and Delinquency Protection
older brothers, incest as power, 42
Olson, Loreen, 14
Omnibus Crime Bill (1994), 169
online issues, *see also* Internet
    behavior, 111
    child enticement, 111
    defined, 130
    grooming, 29, 130
    jargon, 231
    relationships, 231
    safety, 231
Online Safety & Technology Working Group, 127
online sexual activities (OSA), 121, *see also specific activity*
open-ended questions, 142
Operation Innocence Lost, 67
opinions
    assistant state's attorney, 209–211
    Azaola, Elena, 46–47
    Barrow, Laura, 8–10
    Basalay, Erin, 86
    Collier, Anne, 125–128
    Coyne, Daniel T., 103–105
    Dorris, Babara, 71–72
    Hart, Kimberly, 181–183
    Leach, Maryanne, 27–28
    Pizzo, Father Tony, 195–196
    Rufo, Ron, 227–230
    Schmalleger, Frank, 150–151
    Sullivan, Mike, 163–164
opponents, registration and notification laws, 189–190
opportunistic, 46
orchiectomy, *see* Surgical castration

Index

Orzack, Hecht, 114
Osborne v. Ohio, 98

P

Pam Lychner Sex Offender Tracking and Identification Act
    sexual registration and notification laws, 190
Paquin, Ronald H., 61–62
paraphilia
    defined, 73
    human behavior dimension, 3
    pedophile and pedophilia, 51–52
parents
    abuse, grooming, 22–24
    amount of time children are logged on to Internet, 9
    authoritative, 213
    awareness, 229
    being fooled through manipulation, 18
    beliefs about their children, 113–114
    communication, 23
    concern, 217
    educated, 215
    e-mail accounts, sharing, 220
    Internet safety, *xxvii*
    lack of education, 136
password, 131
patience, predation process, *xxvi*
pattern of behavior, 29
Pawlak, Bradford and, studies, 156, 157–158
PC Magazine, 113, 215
PCR, *see* Polymerase chain reaction
pedophile and pedophilia
    behaviors, sexual addiction, 64–65
    Birmingham, Joseph, 61–62
    Catholic Church, 59–62
    child-sex tourism, 67–69
    defined, 73
    Dorris, Barbara, 71–72
    ephebophilia, 56
    exhibitionism, 56
    female sex offender profile, 69
    fetishes, 57–58
    frotteurism, 57
    fundamentals, *xxviii*, 51
    Geoghan, John, 61
    hebephilia, 55
    infantophilia, 55
    interstate sex trafficking, 67
    key terms, 72–74
    male sex offender profile, 70–71
    martymaculia, 57
    Paquin, Ronald H., 61–62
    paraphilia, 51–52
    prostituted children, 67
    sex rings, 65–66
    sexual addiction, 63–64
    sexual perversion, 52–59
    Shanley, Paul R., 61–62
    solo sex rings, 66
    Survivors Network of Those Abused by Priests, 61
    syndicated sex rings, 66
    teleiophilia, 56
    transition sex rings, 66
    victims with disabilities, 52
    voyeurism, 58–59
    vs. sexual predators, 120
"peeping Tom," 58
perceptions of Internet safety, 112–114
personal information, sharing, 220
persuasion
    defined, 30
    grooming, 20
    incest, 40
    predation process, *xxvi*
    using, 1
persuasion predators, 3
perversion, 52–59
Perverted Justice, *xxix*, 148–149
pets, 2, 16
pharming, 131
phishing, 131
physical force, 32
physical violence, 2
Pizzo, Father Tony, 195–196
plan, predation process, *xxvi*
pleasure, *xxvi–xxvii*
"plumber rapist," 106
police reports, 145
polygraphs, 141
polymerase chain reaction (PCR), 143
position of authority, 78–80, 139, 180, *see also* Boy Scout leaders; Catholic Church
posts and posting, 131, 231
posttraumatic stress disorder, 44
power, *xxvii*, 28
power predators, 3
praise, *xxvi*
predation process, *xxvi–xxvii*, 230

predators
    abuse, grooming, 22–24
    meeting in real life, 216
Predators, Pedophiles, Rapists, and Other Sex Offenders: Who They Are and How They Operate, 20
predatory behavior, 48
preferences
    predation process, *xxvi*
    tendency toward, 46
prepubescent, 73
prepubescent children, 10
priests, 46, *see also* Catholic Church; Survivors Network of Those Abused by Priests
privacy
    filters, 222
    issues, 189–194
    policy, 231
    predation process, *xxvi*
proactive behavior, *xxvii*
proficiency, *xxvi*
profiles, 131, *see also* Female sexual offender profiles; Male sexual offender profiles
progression of behavior, 15–21
Prosecutorial Remedies and Other Tools to End the Exploitation of Children Today (PROTECT) Act (2003), 203–204
prostituted children, 67
Protect Act (2003), 149
"Protecting Children from Online Sexual Predators," 117
Protection of Children against Sexual Exploitation Act (1977), 199
Protection of Children from Sexual Predators Act (1998), 201–202
ProtectKids website, 53
PROTECT Our Children Act (2008), 205
Prozac, 157
puberty, *xxvi*
pubescent, 73
"pure pedophile behavior," 55

R

Radford studies, 170, 192
Ramsland and McGrain studies, 79
rape kit, 144
RCFL, *see* Regional Computer Forensics Lab

Reagan, Ronald, 97
rearrest, 84
recanting statements, 141
recidivism
    defined, 165
    female sexual offenders, 83–84
    fundamentals, *xxix*, 154–155
Regional Computer Forensics Lab (RCFL), 137, *see also* Federal Bureau of Investigation
registered sex offenders, 186–188
registration, 191, *see also specific law*
    belief that it works, 142
    false information provided, 181, 187
rehabilitation, *xxix,* 153, 155–163, *see also* Treatment
relationships, *see also* Social bond theory
    establishing with children, 9
    healthy bonds, 27
    incest offenders, 42
    secret, 218–219
    sex offenders, with parents, 52
    sex offenders in adult, 54
relatives, female sexual offenders, 81
remorse, 3, 28
reporting websites, 221
research, false accusations, 164
restrictions placed on offenders, 28
risk factors, 82
risks
    Internet, 112
    of rejection, 54
    taking, female sexual offenders, 80–81
ritualistic offenders, 3
Roberson, Cliff, *xvii–xviii*
Roberts, Jeffery, 2, 16
Roberts, T., studies, 59
Robinson's Woods, 104
Rodriguez, Alfonso, Jr., 176–178
Rosenberg Clinic, 157
Roth v. United States, 96
Ruffoni, Tiffany, 137, 139
Rufo, Ron
    "An Investigation of Online Sexual Predation of Minors by Convicted Male Offenders," *xxv*
    child's outcries/revelations ignored, 21
    correlation, masturbation and sexual fantasies, 16
    distinct attraction, specific age group, 1, 53
    dysfunctional family background, 3

Index

professional background, *xxiii*
sense of entitlement, 18
sexual predation, 227–230
types of sexual offenders, 3
vulnerable victims, 18

S

Safe Childhood Program, 218
SafeKids website, 227
safe sites, 222–227
Salter, Anna, 1, 2, 17–18, 20
Sandler, Freeman, and Socia studies, 187
Sandler and Freeman studies, 75, 83
Sandler studies, 190
Saradjian, Jacqui, 75, 77
Schmalleger, Frank, 150–151
Schmallenger, Frank, 6, 150–151
Schneider, Weiss and, studies, 121
Schober studies, 157
schools, 122–124
Schuessler case, 104
Schwartz, Barbara, 157
Schwartz, Mark, 58
Schwarzenegger, Arnold, 179
screen names, *see also* Logins
    display, chat room conversation, 109
    grooming, 138
    predators, 218
    sexually suggestive, 116, 185
searched-for topics, Internet, 109
search engine, 131
secrecy
    counting on, 23
    defined, 30
    e-mail addresses, 219
    grooming, 15–16
    incest, 39
    Internet, 218–219
    predator's strongest weapon, 218
    using, 1
secret life, discovery, 4
security on social websites, 120
seduction, 18–19, 30
self-esteem, low
    cybersex, 112
    human behavior dimension, 3
    incest, 39
    male victims, 41
    masturbation, 16–17
    parent/caregiver relationships, 27
    in potential target, 21

self-gratification, 48
Sentinel Tech, 119
Seto, Cantor, and Blanchard studies, 90
seven laws, child pornography, 95
severe exhibitionism, 56
Sex Addicts Anonymous, 64
Sex Crimes against Children Prevention Act (1995), 200
sex objects, children viewed as, 4–5
Sex Offender Management Assistance Program (SOMA), 175, 202
Sex Offender Registration Act, 186, *see also* Child Sex Offender Registration Act
Sex Offender Registration and Notification Act (SORNA), 175–176
Sex Offenders Registration Act, 138
Sex Offender Tracking Program, 191
sex rings, 65–66
sexting, 121
sex trade business, *see* Child-sex tourism
sexual abuse, 11
sexual addiction, 63–65, 73
sexual advances, online, 219
sexual assault, 48
Sexual Assault Awareness Month, 187
sexual conversations, 58
Sexual Disorder Clinic, 158
Sexual Exploitation of Children Act (1977), 96
sexual identity, confusion, 228
sexually transmitted disease (STD), 48
Sexually Violent Persons Commitment Act, 103–105, 186, 210
sexually violent person (SVP), 74, 105
sexual offenders, 10
sexual offenders, registration and notification laws
    civil commitment, 188–189
    earlier issues, 185–186
    e-Stop, 192–194
    false information, 187, 192
    female sex offender profile, 194–195
    fundamentals, *xxix*, 185, 190–191
    geographic information systems, 192
    global positioning systems, 192
    homeless sex offenders, 194
    male sex offender profile, 194
    opponents, 189–190
    Pizzo, Father Tony, 195–196
    privacy issues, 189–194

registered sex offenders, 186–188
registration, 191
sexual offenders *vs.* predators, 151
sexual perversion, 52–59, 73
sexual predators
    defined, 11, 131
    vs. offenders, 151
    vs. pedophiles, 11
Sexual Recovery Institute, 109
sexual violence, 2–3, 43–44
Shanley, Rev. Paul R., 61–62
shark analogy, 4
Shestokas studies, 145
shock, false accusations, 164
sibling incest, 81
Siegart model, *see* Ward and Siegart pathway model
signs
    of abuse, 22, 23, 32, 41–42
    children, online predators, 213
"sixth sense," 229
Sjodin, Dru, 176–178, *see also* Dru Sjodin website
SMART Office, *see also* Office of Sex Offender Sentencing, Monitoring, Apprehending, Registering, and Tracking
SNAP, *see* Survivors Network of Those Abused by Priests (SNAP)
Socia, Sandler, Freeman and, studies, 187
social bond theory, 6
social networking sites
    defined, 131
    fundamentals, 117–120
    goals, 118
    grooming, 23
    secret profile, 219
social skills deficit, 54
social websites, 120
sodomy, 48
software, 231
solicitation, 231
solo sex rings, 66
SORNA, *see* Sex Offender Registration and Notification Act
South American countries, 68
Southeast Asian countries, 68
spam and spamming, 131, 222
SpectorPro, 222
spotlight section, GetNetWise website, 223
Stack, Anthony, 137, 139
Stanley v. Georgia, 95–96, 98

statistics
    Catholic Church, 59
    chat rooms, 116
    incest, 40
    Internet safety perceptions, 112–113
    interstate sex trafficking, 67
    male predators, *xxv*, 1
    number of registered sex offenders, 133
    online behavior, 221–222
    risks of the Internet, 112
    social indicators, 127–128
STD, *see* Sexually transmitted disease
stepfamilies, 42–43, 47
Stockholm syndrome, 44
Stone, Carich, Kassel and, studies, 154
strangers on the Internet, 221
streaming (media), 131
"street priest," 62
Strickland, Susan, 82–83
Sullivan, Mike, 163–164, 217–219, 228
Summer of '42, 79
surfing the web, 131, *see also* Internet
surgical castration (orchiectomy), 165, *see also* Chemical castration
surveillance agents, 105
Survivors Network of Those Abused by Priests (SNAP), 61, 71–72
Sutherland, Edwin, 6
SVP, *see* Sexually violent person
Swift, Taylor, 9
syndicated sex rings, 66

T

taking advantage of situations, 3
"talking dirty," 121
Taylor, John, 215
teacher-student/lover classification, 79–80
Telecommunications Act (1996), 201
teleiophile and teleiophilia, 56, 74
telephone sex, 58
10-Ps, predation process, *xxvi–xxvii*, 230
tent cities, 191
Thailand, 68
The Gift of Fear, 1
The Pedophile's Guide to Love and Pleasure, 207
threats
    defined, 48
    lack of cooperation, 2
    secrecy and double life, 16
    uncooperative victims, 18

Index

time, amount on Internet, 9
Timmendequa, Jesse, 171
To Catch a Predator, xxv, 139, 148
tools for grooming, 15
traits
    female sexual offenders, 76
    female victim abuse, 35
    male victim abuse, 38
transition sex rings, 66
travelers, 134, 136–138, 151, *see also* Interstate sex trafficking
treatment
    female sexual offenders, 84–85
    necessary reality, 28
    programs, 160–162
triangulation, relationships, 9
triple A theory, 114
Triptorelin, 165
trust
    abuse from someone trusted, 2
    breaking down, 20
    building, 1, 228
    children, lack of realization of act, 4
    defined, 30
    future ability, 52
    incest, 39–40
    physical force, 32
20th Century Fox, 118

U

underreporting, 39
uniform code of military justice (UCMJ), 169–170, 175
University of New Hampshire, 10
US Bureau of Justice statistics, 154
US Department of Justice, *see also* Center for Sex Offender Management; Office of Sex Offender Sentencing, Monitoring, Apprehending, Registering, and Tracking
    abduction by nonfamily members, 174
    Child Exploitation and Obscenity Section, 67
    Child Pornography and Prevention Act, 99
    child pornography transactions, 100
    Crimes Against Children Research Center, 126
    inmates, sexual offenses, 126
    national strategy, child exploitation prevention and interdiction, 188
    pornography/physical molestation difference, 94
    predator prevalence, 134
    Protect Our Children Act, 205
    Safe Childhood Program, 218
    sex rings, 65
    sharing personal information, 220
    solo sex rings, 66
US Department of Justice Criminal Resource Manual, 146
US Sentencing Commission, 117

V

Valente studies, 39, 41, 52
verbal abuse, 87
verbiage, police reports, 145
victimization
    child pornography, 91
    online, 126–127
Victims of Child Abuse (1990), 200
Victims of Trafficking and Violence Protection Act, 202
Violence Against Women, 16
virtual child pornography, 98–101, 107–108
"virtual Sears catalog," 110
virus, 131
volunteering, 51, 139
Von Erck, Xavier, 149
voyeurism, 58–59

W

"wall of shame," 137
Wal-Mart, 174
Walsh, Adam, 174–176, 190
Walsh, John, 174
Walter Mondale Child Abuse and Treatment Act, 199
Ward and Siegart pathway model, 54
Washington Monthly, 162
web, *see* World Wide Web
webcams, 120–121, 131
websites
    BishopAccountability, 72
    Club Penguin, 9
    Connect Safely, 23, 125
    CyberTipline, 8
    CyberTipline website, 221
    defined, 231
    Dru Sjodin, 204

Facebook, 111, 117–118
Falseabuse, 164
FindLaw, 155
Google, 117
Identity, 123
Internet, 117–120
Jacob Wetterling Crimes against Children and Sexually Violent Offender Registration Act, 173
Nickelodean, 9
popular, 117–120
PROTECT Act sentencing scheme, 204
ProtectKids, 53
University of New Hampshire, 10
video sites, 9
Webkinz, 9
YouTube, 117
Weiss, Robert, 109
Weiss and Schneider studies, 121
Wells studies, 92
Western Europe countries, 68
West's Encyclopedia of American Law, 145–146
Wetterling, Jacob, 167–169, 190
whitelisting, 231
Whitman, Christine, 172
Williams and Finkelhor studies, 40, 41
Wilson, Carnes and, studies, 63
Winfrey, Oprah, *xxv*, 182
Winston Law Firm, 107
WiredSafety website, 227
wiretapping, 149
Wolak, Finkelhor, Mitchell and, studies, 112, 116
Wolak, Mitchell, and Finkelhor studies, 92
Wolak studies, 110, 116
Wolfe, Dandescu and, studies, 17
Women Who Sexually Abuse Children, 75
World Wide Web (web), 131, *see also* Internet; Websites

X

Xanga, 123, 193, 223

Y

YouTube, 117

Z

Zupanick, Benuto and, studies, 63